Harvey N. Hearl

THE COMPLETE
COOK BOOK FOR MEN

THE
complete

HARPER

AND

BROTHERS

PUBLISHERS

NEW

YORK

cook book
FOR MEN

BY FREDERIC A. BIRMINGHAM

THE COMPLETE COOK BOOK FOR MEN
Copyright © 1961 by Frederic A. Birmingham
PRINTED IN THE UNITED STATES OF AMERICA

KL

Library of Congress catalog card number: 61–12225

TO

*JANE
UNPLAIN*

CONTENTS

with Beer . . . Serve a Swiss Fondue Bourguignonne . . .
All You Knead to Know: Baking the Staff . . . The Lobster Plot . . . A Down-East Clambake . . . Roast a Suckling Pig

Implements . . . Grills . . . Fuels . . . Heat: Its Care and
Treatment . . . Meats and Vegetables for Outdoor Cook-
ing . . . Barbecue Sauces . . . Bonanza Barbecue Recipes
. . . Kebabs . . . Game Cookery . . . On the Trail

Salads . . . Salad Dressings . . . Sauces . . . Variations on
a Vegetable Theme . . . Last Resorts: Giving Them Their
Just Desserts

How to Use Your Blender

Celebrities' Favorites . . . Hot Sandwiches . . . Small-scale
Sandwiches . . . Foreign-Flavored Sandwiches

A Word About Champagne . . . Wine in Cooking . . .
Cocktails . . . Punches . . . Cocktail Tidbits . . . Food for
Large Groups . . . Envoi

ACKNOWLEDGMENTS

A special loving cup should be cast in gold and suitably engraved to my ally, Lillian Schaaf Tucker, who has made so many suggestions incorporated in this book.

There is a curious circumstance to this. Lillian is the highly decorative and talented wife of a well-known sportsman whose career and avocations take them to all parts of the masculine world. Charles Tucker is equally famous on the European ski slopes and (after a brilliant career as a college backfield star) as one of the top football field judges in this country. That is both enviable and fortunate, for as a result Lillian—a graduate of a number of *haute cuisine* academies and an accomplished hostess—has cultivated the art, virtually extinct among women today, of appealing to men in their own terms in the realm of food.

Many is the recipe Lillian has wheedled with infinite charm from some celebrity or famous athlete both here and abroad, which I have in turn, without any charm whatsoever, wheedled from the Tuckers. I acknowledge a great debt to Lillian's male-oriented cuisine (a Freudian phrase which means that she cooks as well as Charlie Chan), which has harmonized so happily, now and again, with the general overtones of this book.

I also thank my lucky stars to have such a collaborator as Bill Brown, the artist whose sketches enhance these pages. His witty drawings hint at the delightful companion that Bill is, and his capturing of the mood of this book is as happy an accomplishment as I have ever encountered.

I am indebted as well to the gentlemen of Chapter 7—chefs and proprietors of some of the greatest hotels, restaurants, and inns in the world—who so freely and generously took time out from their own crucial cares to share their secrets of cookery with you and with me. May their tables flourish!

There were times in preparing our recipes and other advice when it was helpful to the reader to offer information obtained directly from authoritative sources, and at other times to specify brand names of certain food products for the sake of accuracy in preparing a certain recipe or in isolating a special flavor. These passages were not intended to imply that any others not mentioned were downgraded: the two covers of this volume could not contain all the worthies who would be mentioned if our purpose were to assay them. To any omitted my true apologies: to the following, who were so co-operative in so many ways, my warmest thanks—

American Dairy Association; American Meat Institute; Armour & Company; Campbell Soups; Christian Brothers; Coffee Brewing Institute; College Inn Products; Department of Sea and Shore Fisheries, State of Maine, and the Maine Development Commission; General Foods; Hormel Foods; Moët & Chandon Champagnes; National Coffee Association; Oster Manufacturing Company; Lea & Perrins, Inc.; Lipton Soups; Meat Trade Institute; S & W Brands; S. A. Schonbrun; Seabrook Farms; Waring Products Corporation; and Taylor Wine Company.

I am boundlessly grateful to Miss Demi Marciano, my assistant in the preparation of the manuscript, for a devotion and dispatch in the handling of a diabolically confusing original which bordered on the angelic. She has clearly earned her wings.

And I am again in thrall to my wife, Frances, who prepares so many of our home meals herself, for my complete usurpation of the kitchen domain for a very trying period (both literally and figuratively) and for not, under extreme provocation, ever trying to improve the broth.

F.A.B.

THE COMPLETE
COOK BOOK FOR MEN

THOUGHTS WHILE HONING
A CARVING KNIFE

My favorite recipe above all, of course, is the one for Hungarian Omelet.

It begins:

"First steal six eggs . . ."

etc.

But not far behind it in my affections is the recipe for "a soup that may be used at any gentleman's table." I found it in the first cookbook I ever owned, an eighteenth-century volume entitled *Mackenzie's Ten Thousand Recipes.* In addition to advices on how to make "Red Coral Branches for the Embellishment of Grottoes," or "To Remedy the Effects of Dram Drinking," Mackenzie came up with this "Recipe for the Gentleman's Table," and dubbed it "Charitable Soup." You may judge for yourself how sturdy a gentleman's table would have to be to hold such a confection:

> Take the liquor of meat boiled the day before, with the bones of leg and shin of beef; add to the liquor as much as will make 130 quarts, also the meat of 140 pounds of leg

and shin of beef, also 2 Ox-heads all cut in pieces; add two bunches of carrots, 4 bunches of turnips, 2 bunches of leeks, ½ peck of onions, 1 bunch of celery, ½ pound of pepper and some salt. Boil it for six hours.

More ancient in its grandeur than even Mackenzie's fancies is *The Compleat Angler* by Izaak Walton. That blessed author, born in 1593, has been revered ever since for his memento to the English countryside and the joys of the fisherman. But in the mild furor over his philosophy and his ways with the piscine world, his original recipes have been forgotten. Therefore, as our first working recipe for *The Complete Cookbook for Men* we quote as follows:

Take a Carp (alive if possible), scour him, and rub him clean with water and salt, but scale him not, then open him, and put him with his bloud and his liver (which you must save when you open him) into a small pot or kettle; then take sweet Margerome, Thyme, and Parsley, of each half a handful, a sprig of Rosemary, and another of Savoury, bind them into two or three small bundles, and put them to your Carp, with four or five whole Onyons, twenty pickled Oysters, and three Anchovies. Then pur upon your Carp as much claret wine as will onely cover him; and season your claret well with salt, Cloves, and Mace, and the rinds of Oranges and Lemmons, cover your pot and set it on a quick fire, till it be sufficiently boiled; then take out the Carp and lay it with the broth into the dish, and pur upon it a quarter of a pound of fresh butter melted and beaten, with half a dozen spoonfuls of the broth, the yolks of two or three eggs, and some of the herbs shred, garnish your dish with Lemmons and so serve it up.

And, as Izaak remarks, this is a "dish of meat as shall make him worth all your labor; and though it is not without some trouble and charges, yet it will recompence both."

And so, if at times it strikes you that this *Complete Cookbook* may also visit certain trouble and charges upon you, yet do you await the recompense before carping at the writer.

This book is written in obvious answer to a need.

There has never really been a cookbook before that men could use.

True, there have been cookbooks for women—probably millions of them—and the majority excellent. Except that a man cannot use them. It is like looking for something in his wife's closet—he cannot see the forest for the shoe trees. He stands aghast at all this multiplicity.

Nor will it do to pretend that he is a woman, and thus try to accommodate to these worthy female cookbooks.

The simple basic fact is that a man is not a woman.

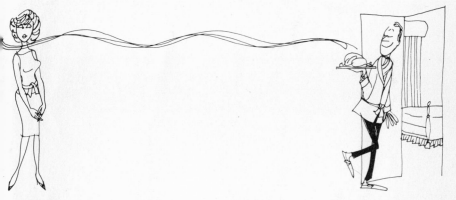

When he cooks he is not a housewife in trousers. He is not larking away at what is essentially a woman's task. He is actually asserting his claim to an art which is his masculine birthright.

Women, of course, cannot understand this. One of the major disasters of our civilization—the tendency to accept women simply as men in disguise—is due to them. When they met in Seneca Falls, New York, in the last century, and adopted those monstrous bifurcated garments known as bloomers to prove they could do anything as well as men, they set a pattern that has introduced painful bewilderments into patterns of education, business, and marriage.

So, to achieve triumph in our own kitchens, we must do more than reverse the feminine trend in cooking. We must abandon it. We must strike out anew. We must recognize that cooking is a man's prerogative and not a whim. New trails beckon. Let us go.

We start at the beginning.

A man's attitude toward cooking is special, to begin with.

A woman regards dinner as something she prepares after cleaning the house, and before she washes the dishes. A woman, therefore, cooks from a position of weakness. She must please a maximum of palates in a minimum of time. She must look to the morrow and the budget. There should be leftovers both in the kitchen and in the bank. As a result, she is expedient. Her roasts are timidly flavored; her favorite dishes are bland.

A man starts with none of these disadvantages.

To begin with, cooking is a task nicely attuned to his natural abilities. It is a blend of mathematics, timing, imagination, and manual skill.

The essential fact is that cooking is an art which also requires great physical co-ordination. Women make poor pianists because in the ultimate sense the instrument is a percussive mechanism, beyond their physical powers over an extended period. And painting, once you come to think of it, has the same muscular requirements. Like a dentist, who is actually only an architect working under limited conditions of space, the painter is merely reproducing the outside world in a two-dimensional form created by manual labor. And sometimes the physical side of painting approaches the athletic. Who but a man possessed of demonic strength and persistence could have stretched out supine upon a scaffolding for endless months while painting his glories on the ceiling of the Sistine Chapel?

Thus, man is equipped for cooking both by his mental and physical aptitudes.

But he has not always been given this latitude.

It would be ungracious not to recognize the excellence of certain cookbooks for men which have preceded this one. But they all fall into one of three schools, and if you have ever fallen in even one school, you will instantly divine that this is an unhappy situation.

The curriculum of the first school—the hair-on-the-chest academy —is based on the reasoning that most men do nothing but rub pipes on the sides of their noses to bring out the grain (in the pipes, silly). In the cookery line the textbook starts with hamburger and goes on to such feats as broiling whale steak or bear flanks over a bonfire that would be adequate for a regiment of starving Visigoths, or the thirsty mob which sipped old Mackenzie's Charitable Soup. Such massive retaliations we leave to Paul Bunyan and his ilk.

The second school might be called Seduction-in-the-Kitchen. When the various men's magazines suddenly realized that their cartoons had put the come-up-and-see-my-etchings gambit into discard as a prelude to amorous adventures they promptly embraced the idea that a male cooks only as a prelude to sexual conquest. I would hate to have to tot up the rental of all the candelabra and fine silver, reflected in champagne buckets and gleaming goblets, which have furnished the atmosphere in thousands of layouts created to illustrate this wishful theme. I never had any objection to this playful dream,

although strictly as cause-and-effect it never really came off very well. Kissing a girl whose lips taste like lobster newburg, or trying to get her into bed after a dinner of roast duck à l'orange, when what she really wants to do is to take a nice long walk, always struck me as a grievous and needlessly expensive error in strategy. Something not too cerebral on the hi-fi, with drinks served on the floor for better listening, inevitably works out far more romantically than the candlelight-and-wine routine.

The third, or lifted pinkie school, makes a bit more sense. It pictures man as a gourmet, a character in a high pancake hat, bounded on four sides by copper pots and pans, with his eyebrows lifted in mild surmise, as he samples a sauce piquante.

That is O.K. as far as it goes. But that is not far enough. That is concluding that a man cooks only as a hobby.

We see it otherwise.

He cooks as a hobby, yes—upon occasion.

But he also may cook because he is hungry. He may cook to entertain his friends. He may cook to feed unexpected guests. He may cook because he no longer can afford (or find) servants to do it for him, because he is a bachelor, because his wife is away, or because he prefers to.

Thus man turns to his cookery inspired by survival, conviviality, and virtuosity.

And each requires a different level of cookery.

Within these three categories we shall approach our task, and many are the delicious variants thereof. And always we shall eschew (a happy word in a cookbook) the flossy when something simpler will do.

There is nothing mysterious about cooking. Essentially, it consists of exposing such proteins as meat and eggs to heat until they are edible, or similarly abusing cellular growths such as vegetables until their fighting spirit is sufficiently reduced to be overcome by our inadequate gastric mechanisms. Such oversimplification does not keep us, however, from realizing that good cooking can make a pleasure out of a necessity. Our taste buds always work: so why shouldn't we?

Our approach has been entirely masculine—the first of its kind, we believe, regardless of the titles of the tomes preceding us.

This is a prejudiced book, gentlemen: prejudiced, that is, in your favor.

1. The recipes in this book have all been selected for men, tested by them. The dishes are guaranteed to appeal to any man in the business of preparation.

2. Flour sifting and eggbeating and the like have been held to a minimum. At no point will you be required to pull a straw from the broom you use to clean out under the garbage pails and stick it into a cake—a practice which causes not only cakes but hopes to fall.

We have taken into consideration that a man does not have all day to fool around in a kitchen, and if he does he usually doesn't want to.

Some salads, sauces, and desserts have been included, but kept to a necessary minimum. Those included are the ones we wouldn't want you to miss. Ditto on soups.

We have not sullied your confidence by instructing you as to how to make a Brown Betty or an Apple Pandowdy. We can't picture you humming your way around the kitchen, either, preparing hot cereals, putting up jams or jellies, cutting out cookies, or making sherbet.

The best way to keep a cake from falling, according to our figuring, is to go out and buy one that didn't. We assume that you'll want to follow suit when you feel like downing pastries, ice cream, or other fancy kitchen bits. Once in a while you may have a real yen for fresh carrots or peas, but the point is that frozen vegetables today are so good that the little bit they fall below the fresh variety is a small price to pay for the escape from the drudgery of shelling, draining, etc.

3. Not that this book will be entirely primitive in scope, however. Its arrangement, in brief, is this:

Start with the fundamentals of cooking. Speed and simplicity. How to make great dishes out of canned and frozen foods.

Then we move along to the next grade: all sorts of delicious stunts with eggs, casseroles, soups, stews, and one-dish miracles that you can whip up in a hurry.

Next step up: basic dishes for entertaining. This takes you through the preparation of roasts, chops, steaks, fowl, and the standards of the dinner table.

By this time, you've learned a number of tricks of the skillet. You're ready for explorations into more complex—but often more rewarding—foreign dishes. And finally, gourmet adventures on the grand scale, unforgettable feasts we have long cherished in our file of recipes, or the unique specialties contributed to this collection by the chefs in the most celebrated restaurants, hotels, and clubs in the world.

4. We haven't stressed side orders. There's a section on "go-togethers" but mostly you know what you want as side dishes and don't have to be told. If the main dish is as good—and plentiful—as you want it, the side dishes are not important, anyway.

We haven't made up any breakfasts, brunches, or dinner menus either, on the theory that a man often enjoys eating against the convention: that is (a thing no woman would dream of), he often would like a steak for breakfast, pancakes for lunch, or a good fish stew for a midnight snack.

He picks his "meals," therefore, by the *dish.*

So we have arranged the book largely as a collection of dishes—graded according to the time needed and complexity of preparation.

Here is the whole gamut. It should not require exceptional hardihood to follow any of the recipes in this book, and many of them you're going to find delightfully and absurdly simple.

There will be times, however, when you must call upon the artist growing within you, for absolute perfection. Then, you must rely—as so many fine actors do—upon The Method. You must put yourself in the place of a steak or a double lamb chop. You are on the griddle. Are you black on the outside and like a cold beet on the inside? Surgery will never help. One cut to look inside will spoil the whole job. You must think. Feel. Contemplate past successes and failures. Judge, and then take swift action, like a man. Every effort must be better than the last.

If you are ever downcast, reflect upon the nobility of that hero of the skillet who shall be our patron saint. It is written and a matter of record that when this martyr was roasted alive for his beliefs his tormentors jeered at him while he still breathed, hoping to draw from him some cry of weakness. But he conquered in the end. Turning a cold and scornful eye on his enemies, he calmly quoth: "Turn me over. That side is done."

There was a man indeed.

Happily, you have no need for such fortitude; only be patient and wait until your various skills have the chance to co-ordinate. Then, suddenly, like a sweet 250-yard drive straight down the fairway— one you hit without giving it a thought—all your effort and cogitation will come together in one seemingly easy and exhilarating success. Except that, in cooking, unlike golf, once you've got it, you'll never lose it. You'll just go on and on, getting better all the time.

Gentlemen—man the ranges!

2

CHAPTER

what's cooking

OR, HOW YOU CAN SUCCEED IN THE KITCHEN WITHOUT REALLY FRYING

Once upon a time, I appeared on a TV homemaker's program, and elected to mix a salad, in tandem with my hostess. The salad called for a fair amount of brandy in it (the recipe is given later on in this book, and the salad tastes great, even under lights) and since the lady was both a very genteel and a very sporting sort, she proceeded to lay on with the brandy as we tossed things about, and we had a fine sense of well being as we ate the *pièce de résistance,* smiling into the camera with unctuous self-congratulation.

At this point, with things running a little faster than anticipated, the lady remembered a conversation we had hastily whispered just before we went on camera. She had asked what was the most unusual dish I ever had cooked, and I had replied, baked porcupine. Now, with minutes to go, and our salad already gone, she reached desperately backward in her mind, and then unfortunately asked about that porcupine. How had I killed it? I had clubbed it to

10

death. Gamely—she went on: how was it prepared? Eviscerated but not skinned; washed, and rolled in mud. In absolute horror, she pursued her inexorable fate. What next? A fire built around it, and when thoroughly baked to the outside consistency of a ceramic, cracked open on a rock, and eaten like a melon.

With visions of bemusing her entire housewifely audience, the lady made a brave stab at rallying her program. Was there anything special I had to say about this somewhat unusual dish, something which set it apart from the more conventional? Yes, I mumbled, my mind betraying me: free toothpicks.

We are not committed in a cookbook for men to housewifely hints on tastifying leftovers or debating the relative merits of a needle-and-thread and a stapling machine when enclosing a turkey around its stuffing. Nor do we care greatly how to remove gravy and food stains: if you get your clothes dirty, send them to the cleaners.

Therefore, we are not going to be encyclopedic about such things as the names of all the herbs in the world, or append a comprehensive glossary of cooking terms. However, there are certain inescapable facts of life à la cuisine which must be scrutinized before you set out for the grail. Undoubtedly, if you are already established, you'll have most or many of the utensils I'll mention as necessaries, and know some of the other fundamentals. However, a quick once-over won't hurt.

Don't let these lists and descriptions scare you. The problem was whether to put them in here—so you know right away that here is your reference shelf—or to shove them to the back of the book before getting on to more colorful data. We decided to leave them here, with the thought that you'll give them the once-over, take a rain check on such operations as stocking an herb shelf or carving a roast leg of lamb, but be pleased to have them under the roof, so to speak, for later perusal.

First, a word on table settings. If you already have your ménage set up, you'll skip this. But if you're just equipping your first apartment, unless you're well heeled enough to go in for sets of fine china and hallmarked silver, play it simple and cheap. The 10-cent stores have remarkably attractive china and glassware. Look for unusual shapes in cups and glasses, stressing carrying power. Don't buy a whole set of the same color or pattern. Stick to white as a basic, and relieve this with odd pieces in side-dishware, cups, etc., so that there is some eye relief as your meal progresses.

Spend your money on good carving knives—you'll want three or four in various sizes for your kitchen operations and one good carving set on the more decorative side—and on a good set of steak knives for the table. Pick out from the following lists what seems

to you to be the most basic, but try to fill out the line-up as soon as possible, for the lists are already basic. After that shoot for your electric appliances.

Since the appliances are so much a part of the fun of cooking, and definitely masculine in concept, let's decide which you ought to have, and which are luxuries to keep in mind.

A man can live without these electric gadgets but he can't be happy without them:

A good toaster
A large coffee percolator (or other coffeemaker)

A small coffeemaker

A blender

An ice crusher, which adjusts to different sizes and turns out
different grades

A broiler, for hors d'oeuvres and hot dishes outdoors, or for
when you don't want to use the oven

And then, when you get around to it, you will enjoy:

A meat grinder

A frying pan

A hot tray

A smaller broiler for snacks and supplementary cooking (if
you bought a sizable one the first time)

A larger broiler if you've discovered in practice that your first
one was too small.

A warning word about electric broilers: examine them carefully
before you buy, to make sure that the heat gradients offer a wide
range. You'll want a low heat very often to keep plates of snacks
hot without burning them, and you'll also want a scorching top heat
to approximate outdoor flame. The same goes for electric frying
pans. They also need a wide range to carry you from scrambling
eggs or grilling cheese sandwiches all the way to pan broiling. The
real secret, alas, is generally in the price, if the label is dependable.
The higher-priced gadgets have more coils, higher resistance in
them to develop heat, and are more intricately wired for graduated
control.

Another point to look for in advance is simplicity. If there are
too many trays and racks, too many windows and inaccessible
crannies, you'll be sorry indeed when you have to clean the contraption for the umpteenth time. There is no escape from dirt and
grease in cooking—even warming up a cheese-covered cracker leaves
a residue of oils on your broiler—so look for designs with broad
metal surfaces, and a minimum of knobs and odd-shaped inner
appointments.

When all's said and done, your electric broiler and frying pan
can't do everything your regular oven and pan will do, and in most
cases a great deal less. But they're handy and they're movable.
Don't let the word "broiler" go to your head. Harbor no visions of

steaks running red or great double lamb chops emerging from your little two-by-four. It will do casseroles quite well; it is particularly effective for melting frozen foods and bubbling newburgs and the like into perfection. It is incomparable for warming up blueberry muffins so that they taste as if you're in a country kitchen; and it will do English muffins hotter and crispier than any toaster ever could.

It's also great for doing small fowl, cuts of chickens, etc. But it just can't work up enough searing heat to do steaks, chops, liver, etc. for you. That takes, at least in the order of my own preference —charcoal, outdoors; an iron frying pan almost as hot as fire itself for pan broiling; and finally, as a concession, the stove broiler. I broil over charcoal all winter, just outside my kitchen door on the terrace, even if I have to dress like an Eskimo and put the grill in the snow. It's a good excuse for a couple of hookers of Scotch as you get things going.

Probably at the end of the line in terms of economics, but don't rest until you get one, is an electric knife sharpener. If you haven't examined one, banish any thoughts you may have that it resembles in any way those nests-of-hard-metal-wheels through which you're invited to draw your knives and skin off curls of fine steel, which often wind up in your food. The electric grinder: a couple of abrasive wheels revolve in there; you put your knife lightly in a slit and draw it across the whirring wheel just like any professional. It beats hand honing by a mile, and if you feed your good steel in there with a light hand, your knives will last as long this way as any other, and you'll have the pleasure of a set constantly ready and sharp for use. And don't think that handling a sharp carving knife over a bird or a roast isn't one of the great pleasures of this life. You owe it to yourself. Get that sharpener.

UTENSILS

Garlic hand press
Fruit hand press (for squeezing lemons and limes)
Large salad bowl, fork, and spoon
Pepper mill
Large salt shaker
Cutting board
Poultry shears

2 long-handled meat forks
2 spatulas—1 square, 1 rectangular
Eggbeater
Meat cleaver or pounder
Wire whisk
Measuring spoons (set)
Measuring cup
Double boiler
2-cup pan—for melting butter, making sauces
2 large iron skillets
1 small iron skillet
Set of regular frying pans
Dutch oven
Casseroles
   1 three-quart capacity for usual cookery, 4 to 6 servings
   1 low, with cover
   1 especially deep, for bulky foods
   1 set individual dishes
   1 bean pot
Short and long steel skewers
Wooden toothpicks—for skewering tidbits
1 baster (syringe type)
Timing clock
4 asbestos mats
Potholders (padded mitts)
Colander
Funnel
Meat grinder
Coffee grinder
Cheese grater
Vegetable grater
Roasting pan, large enough for turkey or goose, with removable
   draining pan or rack
Baking sheet
12-quart pot or kettle—for boiling spaghetti, lobsters, etc.
3-quart pan—deep, for sizable boiling
1-quart pan—flat
Corkscrew
Can opener

Bottle opener
Set of bottle caps
Oven thermometer
Chafing dish
Tea strainer, small
Carving knives
Cocktail shaker
Paring knife
Vegetable parer
2 wooden mixing spoons
1 large soup ladle
Bacon frying pan, with curved top and draining canals
Strainer for lifting poached eggs
Steak tongs

HERBS AND SUCH

Here is an area where every writer of a cookbook is wont to pull out all the stops and run on for pages, describing scores of plants you may never hear about again, much less need to cook with. These require special herb closets and cabinets, and if they're not too extensive, we say get yourself one because they're mighty decorative.

But, a main point to keep in mind is that you must always buy herbs in small quantities because they tend to deteriorate in your kitchen once they are opened; kitchen humidity, which runs pretty high as a rule, doesn't help.

And—call them *H*erbs, like your friend Herb. There is a great debate on this, but the "in" way is to use the "h" the way the British do. After all, they started all this garden culture. They opine that dropping any kind of an "h" is a Cockney habit and undesirable. Americans do generally drop the "h," for practically the same status reason. But do you use it boldly and confidently, and you'll never suffer from the uncertainties which beset your friends. It's the only way, under the circumstances, to be 'appy.

Herbs should be used very moderately. They were once used to hide the fact that meat was spoiled or on the way. We don't have to do that any more, but we also recognize that they can tastify many a dish without obscuring its basic flavor, if used sparingly. About ¼ of a teaspoon of dried herbs will do for a dish serving four.

These are the spices and herbs you're going to be using more than the others. You may want to graduate to others, but this is a practical starting bin:

Allspice: A Jamaica pepper, resembling, as its name implies, cloves, cinnamon, and nutmeg. Multi-purpose.

Basil: Resembles cloves. For soups, meats, stews.

Bay: The old laurel of victory. With meats, roasts, soups.

Caraway seeds: With soft cheeses, fish.

Cayenne pepper: Strong with soup, casseroles, etc.

Celery seed: With salads, soups.

Cinnamon: The bark of the tree, with hot rum and whiskey drinks, tea, toast, and fruits.

Cloves: With baked ham, of course, also with hot rum and whiskey drinks, tea.

Curry powder: For many dishes—lamb, chicken, etc.—relying on this distinctive flavor.

Dill: With seafood.

Garlic salt or powder: With meats, salads.

Ginger: With baked dishes.

Ground mustard: You know about this one—but take it easy.

Mace: With meat gravies and sauces, also fish sauces.

Onion seasoning: For the haunting flavor.

Orégano: With tomatoes, salads, scrambled eggs.

Paprika: With salads, dressing, garlic bread.

Peppercorns: Use your own mill on table.

Rosemary: With chicken, fish.

Tabasco: With oysters, soups, Bloody Marys.

Thyme: On your hands, with fish chowders, stuffing for fowl.

Lea & Perrins Worcestershire sauce.

COMING TO TERMS WITH COOKING

Here are a number of terms you will run up against. Some are very familiar, but you still may not know precisely what they mean. At the risk of insult, then, we'll include some of the more obvious ones:

Antipasto: Assorted appetizers—cold cuts, fish, vegetables.

Aspic: Clear jelly, used to fancy up certain dishes.

Au gratin: Means "with crust" as in many casseroles.

Baste: To brush, spoon, or squirt liquid over a food.

Batter: Any mixture of flour, eggs, milk, etc., for pancakes, cakes, coatings, etc.

Bisque: A cream soup.

Bouillon: Clear soup.

Braise: To brown in a little fat, then slowly cook in covered pan with little liquid.

Capers: Buds of the caper bush, used in sauces.

Chutney: Sweet-sour relish, usually served with curries.

Croutons: Small cubes of toasted or fried bread.

Dot: To toss small bits of butter, cheese, etc., over food.

En brochette: Cooked on a skewer.

Filet: Boneless piece of meat or fish.

Flambé: Aflame, from burning spirits.

Macedoine: Mixture of cut fruits or vegetables.

Marinade: Liquid used for pickling or seasoning, a soaking mixture.

Marinate: To let stand in a marinade.

Pâté de foie gras: Goose-liver paste.

Purée: Food forced through a sieve to produce smooth consistency.

Ramekin: Individual casserole or serving dish.

Render: To melt fat from connective tissue.

Roux: Thickening mixture of fat and flour.

Roulade: Rolled meat.

Sauté: Cook or brown over low heat in small amount of fat or butter.

Scallion: A bulbless onion; a green onion

Shallot: A small onion-garlic hybrid.

Stock: Canned consommé or bouillon cubes dissolved in water may be substituted for stock, which is actually broth in which meat, poultry, fish, or bones have been cooked, and used as base in gravies, soups, and sauces.

Timbale: Pastry shell for creamed foods.

Temperature Guide
Very slow oven: 225° F.
Slow oven: 250° to 325° F.
Moderate oven: 350° to 375° F.

Hot oven: 400° to 450° F.
Very hot oven: 475° F. plus

Weights and Measures

Dash = less than ⅛ teaspoon
3 teaspoons = 1 tablespoon
2 liquid tablespoons = 1 ounce
4 tablespoons = ¼ cup
16 tablespoons = 1 cup
2 liquid cups = 1 pound
16 ounces = 1 pound
4 cups = 1 quart

Equivalent Weights and Measures

Butter: 1 lb. = 2 cups
Butter: ¼ lb. = 8 tablespoons
Grated cheese: ¼ lb. = 1 cup
Cream: ½ pint = 1 cup
Lemon juice: 1 lemon = 2-3 tablespoons
Potatoes: 1 lb. = 3 (about)
Raisins: 1 lb. = 3 cups
Rice: 1 lb. = 2 cups
Sugar: 1 lb. = 2 cups
Tomatoes: 1 lb. = 3 average

GOOD GO-TOGETHERS

This book has avoided menus on the theory that a man keeps his eye on the main dish, and what is served directly with it. If he wants a salad or a dessert, he knows it without being told, and can turn directly to the specific recommendations on this score. But there may be questions in your mind, from time to time, as to what goes with what on the entrée. Here again, you'll probably know your own preferences, but just in case, here are some useful combos:

When the main dish is meat

Steak	Parsley potatoes, spinach
	Mashed potatoes, peas
	Au gratin potatoes, green beans
Roast beef	Oven-browned potatoes, broccoli
	Baked potatoes, asparagus

Pot roast	Boiled potatoes, creamed carrots
	Macaroni, cole slaw
Hamburger	Potato salad, carrot sticks
Cheese hamburgers	On toasted buns with sweet onion rings
Meat patties	Hashed brown potatoes, braised carrots
Corned beef hash	Poached eggs, green salad
Spareribs	Horseradish sauce, julienne beets
(barbecued)	French-fried potatoes, pineapple wedges, tossed green salad
Boiled tongue	Buttered noodles, spinach
Meat loaf	Mashed potatoes, baked squash
Beef goulash	Buttered noodles, rhubarb sauce
Liver	Bacon, cream-style corn
Frankfurters	Sauerkraut or potato salad, pumpernickel
Baked ham	Sweet potatoes, spinach
	Parsley potatoes, asparagus
	Mashed potatoes, glazed pineapple

Ham steak	Fried eggs, corn muffins
	Fried eggs, hashed brown potatoes
	Hominy, fried bananas
	Buttered rice, apple sauce
Cold ham	Potato salad, dill pickles
	Baked beans, piccalilli, hot rolls
Bacon	Corn fritters, maple syrup
Canadian Bacon	Hot biscuits, pickled peaches
Roast pork	Horseradish or apple sauce
	Baked potatoes, cabbage au gratin
	Mashed potatoes, sauerkraut
Pork chops	Scalloped potatoes, apple sauce
Sausage	Mashed potatoes, cornbread
	Griddle cakes, maple syrup
Fried salt pork	Milk gravy, baked potatoes, string beans
Braised veal cutlets	Milk gravy, baked sweet potatoes, string beans
Lamb chops	Browned potatoes, succotash or spinach
	Baked potatoes, peas
Lamb stew	Dumplings, tossed salad
Roast lamb	Brown gravy, mashed potatoes, currant jelly
Creamed dried beef	Baked potatoes, cole slaw
	On toast, green salad

When the main dish is fowl

Roast chicken	Candied sweet potatoes, cauliflower
Fried chicken	Mashed potatoes, lima beans
	Corn on the cob, stewed tomatoes
Chicken fricassee	Dumplings, corn on the cob
Chicken pie	Green peas, mixed green salad
Chicken salad	Potato chips, peas, celery and olives
Duckling	Sweet potatoes, currant jelly, tossed salad

When the main dish is fish

Creamed salt cod	Boiled potatoes, cole slaw
	On toast, green salad
Fish chowder	Boston crackers, cole slaw or dill pickles

Baked salmon	Baked potato, tossed salad
Broiled salmon	Egg or hollandaise sauce, mashed potatoes, peas
Broiled halibut	Scalloped tomatoes, broccoli
Fried fish	French-fried potatoes, greens
Scalloped oysters	Hashed-brown potatoes, broccoli
Brook trout	Potatoes diced in cream, asparagus
Baked shad	Broccoli with hollandaise sauce
	Mashed potatoes, tossed salad
Lobster	Steamed clams, French-fried potatoes
Lobster newburg	French-fried onions, watermelon pickle
French-fried shrimp	Peas and carrots, tomato and onion salad
Broiled filets	Baked potatoes, scalloped tomatoes
Codfish cakes	Baked beans, salad
	Bacon, cole slaw

When the main dish is cheese or eggs

Welsh rabbit	Dill pickle or stuffed celery, beer, fruit salad
Cheese soufflé	Peas, green salad
Cheese omelet	French-fried potatoes, stewed tomatoes
French omelet	Consommé, asparagus tips
Scrambled eggs	French-fried potatoes, string beans
Scrambled eggs with cut-up ham	Rye bread, tossed green salad

Miscellaneous

Baked macaroni	Stewed tomatoes, lettuce salad
Split-pea soup	Crackers, Caesar salad
Lentil soup	Cheese soufflé, green salad
Cream of tomato soup	Tunafish salad sandwich
Turkey club sandwich	Cranberry sauce, potato chips
Ham-and-cheese sandwich	Tossed salad
Waffles	Broiled bacon, maple syrup, fruit salad
Chow mein	Buttered rice, pickled peaches
	Mashed potatoes, tossed salad

THE ART OF CARVING

It is no longer part of your masculine role to carve up your neighbor if he looks fondly on your love, or to skewer him on your rapier behind the cathedral if he suggests that facing dragons before you parboil them is not precisely your dish.

On the other hand, there is no more ineffectual sight than a male standing, carving knife and fork in hand—indecisive, timorous, fair prey for directions and advice from such guests as are always willing to take over in your own home.

So—balk these clowns. Study this major science of a competent host. And keep these things in mind to help you:

Both underdone and overdone meat are hard to carve. Medium is best (though in steaks or roast beef, you're apt to want it rare).

Allow a roast to "set" about fifteen minutes before bringing it to the table for carving. It will hold its heat; and the meat, meanwhile, firms up a bit.

You can't have your carving knife too sharp. Make sure that every bit of the blade is keen, especially the tip. Get a knife with a good husky handle—you're going to want something to get hold of. Ditto for the fork.

Use a very large platter and keep it clear. Don't crowd it with garnishes or vegetables. One slip, until you're an expert, and you're rolling potatoes and beans all over the place.

The carving knife awaits you at the right of the platter, the fork on the left. A tablespoon is also at your right for the service of vegetables, and/or others as needed for stuffing, etc.

Place the platter above the plates, so that you move the carved portions of the meat or fowl over the platter and directly to the dish. You may wish first to remove your carved pieces to a serving platter, and then take them from this for the plates. Remove all wine goblets, candles, and water glasses from the field of action. A good idea: to have a couple of slices of bread handy to serve as wedges in case your roast starts to rock.

Study the following directions on how to place the meat on your platter.

And now, *en garde!*

Let's start with a few simple ones:

Steak (T-Bone and Porterhouse):

1. Place before you with the small end to your left.
2. Cut around the bone and remove to side of platter.
3. Always cut a steak with the grain. Therefore, slice across both tenderloin and sirloin sections of your steak, i.e., straight out from where you're standing.
4. To save your knife blade, serve your steaks on a board cut to fit your favorite platter.

Leg of Lamb:

1. Place leg with small bone at your right.
2. Cut off a few thin slices from the side nearest you.
3. Turn the leg to rest on this flat cut surface.
4. Cut out a wedge shape at the base of the bulge, right. Then cut slices, from right to left, straight down into the bone.
5. Release slices by cutting along bone at right angles to the slices, from the wedge opening, right to left.

Rolled Roasts:

Easy. Place them flat on the platter, that is, on the end like a stump. Slice across the top, right to left, cutting out wheels.

Roast Beef: Pretty much the same.

1. Place the roast flat on the platter, with the rib bones to the left. (Carving's easier if you have the butcher separate the backbone from the ribs when you buy.)
2. Slice from the far outside edge right across the grain. Make vertical cut along bone to release each slice. Slices should be $\frac{1}{8}$ to $\frac{3}{8}$ inch thick. Lift slice to platter or plate.

Now we come to more delicate surgery. We'll leave the bird until last, because turkey seems to be the bête noir of every carver, and we mean to give you a real course in this operation.

For now:

Ham Slice: Cut it into three sections.

1. Put it before you, bone to the left.

2. Cut through the whole slice directly out from you, passing close to the right of the bone.

3. Then, bisect the remaining slice right down its middle, cutting parallel to your own stance.

4. Remove the bone.

5. Turn each section on its side and slice across the grain.

Baked Whole Ham:

1. Place shank end of ham at carver's right.

2. Take 2 or 3 thin slices off the edge toward you, the thinner side.

3. Turn the ham to rest on the cut surface.

4. Make a long cut, starting at the base of the bulge to the right; slice down to the leg bone and curve along the bone to the left as far as the knife can cut.

5. Now cut parallel slices straight down to the bone.

Note: If you do not plan to eat all of the ham at this sitting, make cuts 5 before 4, making cut 4 only as far as required.

Now for the Turkey:

1. Place the bird on the platter with the drumsticks to the right of the carver.

2. Go to work on the side nearest you. Insert the two-tined fork into the leg, one tine in the drumstick, the other through the joint. Make a clean cut between leg and body, using the fork as a lever to draw the leg away from the bird. (You can use your left hand for this if you prefer.)

3. Cut skin between leg and back.

4. Remove leg to serving platter. Cut slices of dark meat from the thigh and drumstick.

5. Next, remove wing. This is closer to the body than the drumstick, so hold the bird steady with a fork plunged into the wing, and start cutting about ¾ inch above where the wing seems to join the body.

6. Remove wing, cut in two pieces.

7. With your left hand, insert the fork across the ridge of the breastbone. Hold the bird firmly and squarely on the platter. Slice downward with long slices to cut the breast meat, angling against the grain.

8. To remove stuffing, cut an opening through the membrane where the leg was removed. Spoon it out.

9. For each serving have white slices laid over dark, with dressing underneath or alongside.

10. Turkey is usually completely carved off one side before starting on the other.

Duck or Goose:
Remove the legs and wings from both sides at joints. Cut down to breastbone. Then cut the breast slices free from the bone.

Suckling Pig:
Split up back, cut individual portions at right angles to backbone, serving 2 ribs to each chop.

Large Fish:
1. Place head left, tail right.

2. Using a silver (not steel) knife, cut a rectangle, with a right vertical line running from bottom to top of fish, just inside tail, where meat starts.

3. Cut horizontal lines joining verticals at top and bottom; horizontal line, top, close to spine; horizontal line, bottom, close to belly of fish.

4. Now cut individual vertical slices 1 inch to 1½ inches, holding knife across fish, cutting straight down.

5. Lift out pieces on knife and fork and serve.

6. Repeat on other side of fish.

Small Fish:
Cut rectangle as in large fish, then lift out entire fillet and serve in one piece as an individual portion.

And, now let's put down the weapons and get down to business—the cooking itself.

SIMPLE SURVIVAL:

the lone wolf

We know a man who cannot even boil water without getting into trouble. We know another guy who claims he's eaten dog food right out of the can and liked it—which isn't much of a boast when you come to think of it.

We also know a man who keeps his own collection of snail shells. Whenever he gets the urge to swallow a few dozen of the delicious little escargots, without so much as a walk in the woods, he buys them at the store, pops each little fellow into his shell (a home away from home) and they come from his oven with more piquant flavor than any hawk or jay can remember sampling.

Between these two extremes of low and high drama in the kitchen is a wide plains area where most of us live. We have nothing to fear but starvation itself. There is nothing quite so discouraging as to have to give up eating. Lack of money will do it. But there are even more subtle causes.

There comes upon every bachelor the time when he cannot be

civil to another haughty restaurant "captain" or bandy banalities with another waiter. He does not want to order another steak and wonder if it will be served to him rare, the way he wants it, or if he will have to send it back and discover that the management—which generously advertises that you don't have to eat your steak if it doesn't match the shade of red you selected on the menu—has replaced it with another, only one half the size of the original but twice as tough. Our man may be tired of dining with his tie on.

He may yearn to have just the number of drinks he wants before getting the meal going. You know how it is in restaurants: if you suggest to the waiter that you'd like to linger over your drink (you might have one or two more) he just nods graciously and disappears forever. If you order your food in response to his imperious thrust of the menu at you, the meal always arrives just as you've decided you'd rather have five more martinis, skip the food, and try to date the girl sitting by the window reading *The New Yorker*.

So you want to eat at home. Perhaps alone. You may want to lounge in your bathrobe, look at TV, listen to music, and eat on your own schedule. But a few banana slices on shredded wheat, while great in the A.M., soon take all the shine off the self-sufficiency of the evening. What you want is a good, tasty meal, which for quantity and quality will at least equal what you could have had by dining out.

That's what this chapter is for.

It is also for temporary bachelors—husbands whose wives have gone home to Mother for a while, to see whether Mother hasn't gone home to *her* Mother for a while. There are husbands whose wives may be kept late at the office—this works both ways, fellows, and you're supposed to be understanding about it—or possibly your wife was just held up at a bridge party, or a P.T.A. meeting and Dad was supposed to shift for himself. Or maybe she's gone to bed early, and you've seen the late, late show, and yawned so often you've worked up a colossal appetite. That's what this chapter is for, too.

For the moment, then, the keynote is a combination of speed and simplicity. There are even moments when this is more effective socially than a more handsome and complicated meal. Your girl agrees to stop by for a snack after the show. "But it must be fast," she says, as if virtue were a matter of speed. A friend gets off a late plane and you tell him to camp on the sofa for his first night in town. He's hungry, of course, after eating those carved pieces of soap in shapes simulating food that they serve on the airlines, but he's also tired. So, quick but good it must be.

Timely warning to sophisticates:

This chapter is probably not for you. To avoid the moment when you feel a slight curling of the lip coming on, and cries of "No, *no, NO!*" well within you, you should—if you will—move along to Chapter 4, where matters are a little more complex than 2 plus 2 equals 5, in the hopeful mathematics of the kitchen.

But, for the moment, there must be a beginning. And so that is where I shall start.

You should, if you have not already, discard any old-fashioned prejudices against canned foods, and a possible new-fangled dislike of frozen foods. This is an "out" statement rather than an "in," I realize, but status seekers will please forgive at least the next few paragraphs.

Of course, some canned foods are inedible, and some frozen foods are in no ways related to what God hath wrought in the fresh state of nature.

But many are remarkably good, and a few are great. For example, there are times when nothing but a plate of steaming soup will do, to tone up that Scotch-haunted stomach of yours, and you certainly are not going to spend hours or possibly days in the kitchen boiling and straining vegetables and distilling beef stock when your can opener and a selection of good old Heinz, S. S. Pierce, or Campbell's will turn the trick for you better than you'll ever learn yourself.

We do not, by the way, have any interest, financial or otherwise, in brand names, but in this chapter it's a point of information we'd like to pass on to you as you look for quality on the shelf. Possibly the best plan of all is to patronize a good grocery store where a bargain price isn't the only *raison d'être,* and then follow your grocer's knowledge in the matter.

For more exotic things than you can find in your local store, the can still will work for you. For example, hark to what you can pick up in Hammacher Schlemmer's specialty food shop. Here's what just at a quick glance the H. S. shelves turn up, and Charles & Co., Macy's, Altman's, Vendôme and Bloomingdale's in New York City, all have comparable inventories you can acquire by asking for a catalogue of their mail order goods:

Canned meat, fish, fowl	*Brand*
A whole cooked chicken in a glass jar	
A whole guinea hen in a glass jar (ready to eat)	Randall's
A whole cooked pheasant in a can (in natural broth with sherry)	Berkshire Game Farm
White meat of chicken in a glass jar	
Turkey meat in a glass jar	Randall's
Hickory-smoked breast of turkey	Hickory Valley Farm
Swedish meatballs	Kronobergs
King crab meat	
Lobster meat	Bonavita
Small Danish hams	Gala
English beef pie	A. C. L.
Wildschwein mit Pilzen in Aspik (Wild boar with mushrooms in aspic jelly)	
Ham	

Tongue
Veal
Brisket of beef   Englert
                                           (packed in Germany)
Tiny peeled shrimps   Golden Dane
Salads on a Shelf
Green beans pickled   Dilly Bean
Artichoke hearts   Cresca
Endives   Le Sueur
Asparagus stalks   Clos du Verdet
Asparagus tips   Roland
Hearts of palm   Bonavita
Artichoke bottoms   Rene Beziers (Francol)
Cheese dishes
Welsh rabbit   Golden Buck (H. S.)
Swiss fondue   Le Superbe (H. S.)
Specialties
Thin Swedish ginger cookies
Scottish oat cakes
Sherry pralines   Charlotte Charles
Marrons glacés (chestnuts preserved and
    candied with sugar and glucose)   Clément-Faugier
Miscellaneous
Yellow rice seasoned with saffron   R. M. Quiggs
Whole French chestnuts
Purée of French chestnuts   Clément-Faugier
Tarragon leaves in a jar (To flavor
    broiled chicken, poached eggs, seafood,
    Béarnaise sauce, marinate steak)   Classique
Mustards
Düsseldorf
Fine de Dijon poupon
Bahamian mustard
Herb-flavored mustard sauce   House of Herbs
Cheeses to send for
Colony Club private-stock aged Cheddar

Hormel's Famous Foods of the World, which your grocer probably already carries—and, if not, will get at your request—include
chicken cacciatore, beef Stroganoff, köttbullar, garbanzo soup, and
French onion soup!

But let's get going with the simplest dish of all, once you've
graduated from opening a can and eating what's in it.

It is

IN THE SOUP

There are several steps-within-steps to this. The simplest trick of
all is to try a few combinations, with no other effort required.
After that we'll move on to the addition of a few supplies of your
own, using the canned soup as a base, but creating a fuller and
more interesting dish. First, the combos:

ROSY BEEF NOODLE TWOSOME

1 can (10½ oz.) condensed beef
noodle soup

1 can (10½ oz.) condensed tomato soup or 1 can (10¾ oz.)
condensed tomato rice soup

1½ soup cans water

Blend soups and water in saucepan. Heat, stirring occasionally.

4 SERVINGS

TOMATO VEGETABLE SOUP

1 can (10¾ oz.) condensed veg-   mato soup or 1 can (10¾ oz.)
etable soup   condensed tomato rice soup
1 can (10½ oz.) condensed to-   1½ soup cans water

Blend soups and water in saucepan. Heat; stir occasionally.

4 SERVINGS

FARM KITCHEN KETTLE o' SOUP

1 can (10¾ oz.) frozen con-   densed green pea with ham
densed old-fashioned vegetable   soup
with beef soup   1½ soup cans water
1 can (10½ oz.) frozen con-

Blend soups and water in saucepan. Heat, stirring occasionally.

4 SERVINGS

PURÉE MONGOLE

1 can (11¼ oz.) condensed   1 cup milk
green pea soup   1 cup water
1 can (10½ oz.) condensed
tomato soup

Blend soups, milk, and water in saucepan. Heat, but do not boil.
Add a dash of curry powder, if desired.   4 SERVINGS

The next step is to add your own supplies to the soup from the
can. These are among the quickest and most palatable dishes to
prepare:

CHINESE EGG-DROP SOUP

This is just about the simplest, but it's also a great pick-up.

Heat 1 can chicken broth. (College Inn chicken broth is recommended for this recipe, because of its outstanding quality and flavor.
Other good brands will also serve.) Beat 1 egg with fork, stir hot
broth with circular motion, using fast stroke, then pour in egg in
fine stream.   2 SERVINGS

And now here is a line-up of others, slightly more complicated,
but none very difficult, to complete your repertoire in the soup line:

QUICK MINESTRONE

Add 1 No. 2 can kidney beans (undrained), 1 minced garlic clove, ½ cup snipped parsley, and 1 package frozen mixed vegetables to 2 cans College Inn chicken broth. Heat until all vegetables are tender. Serve in a casserole as a soup supper.   4 SERVINGS

GREEN TURTLE BISQUE

1 quart green turtle soup (canned)	2 egg yolks
	2 tablespoons dry sherry
½ pint heavy cream	Salt

Strain turtle meat out of soup and cut in fine pieces. Bring the soup to just below the boiling point. In a separate bowl, beat cream till thickened, but not stiff, add egg yolks and beat with the cream till well blended. Remove the soup from the flame and add cream-egg mixture (do not boil after the eggs have been added, or the soup will curdle). Add the turtle meat, sherry, and salt to taste and serve at once.   6–8 SERVINGS

OYSTER BISQUE WITH VEGETABLES

2 cans frozen oyster bisque	1 teaspoon Worcestershire sauce
1 small carrot	1 cup light cream
1 small turnip	Salt and pepper
1 small stalk celery with top	Chopped parsley
2 tablespoons butter	

Thaw and cook bisque according to directions on can. Meanwhile dice the carrot, turnip, and celery and cook in the butter until barely tender. Add Worcestershire sauce, cream, and a little salt and freshly ground pepper to taste. Stir until piping hot, but do not allow to boil. Pour into serving bowls and sprinkle with chopped parsley.

SENEGALESE SOUP

2 cups Campbell's cream of celery soup	1 package MTB instant broth
	1½ teaspoons curry powder
2 cups milk	3 tablespoons soft butter
1 cup heavy cream	Salt and pepper

Combine celery soup, milk, cream, and instant broth in a saucepan. Heat together slowly, stirring (do not boil). Add curry powder to butter, blend together, and add to the hot soup. Lastly add salt and pepper to taste.

This soup is good very hot. Also delicious served cold when made well ahead, strained after cooking, thoroughly chilled, and served with finely chopped raw apples sprinkled over the top.

CHILLED POTATO SOUP

Start with 2 cans Campbell's frozen cream of potato soup. Cook according to directions on can. Stir in one can chicken bouillon or MTB instant chicken broth. Add a little onion powder, salt, and pepper to taste. Stir in ½ cup heavy cream. Chill thoroughly for several hours, and sprinkle with chives or parsley.

QUICK NEW ENGLAND CLAM CHOWDER

Start with 3 cans Snow's New England clam chowder or Campbell's frozen New England chowder. Prepare according to directions on can. Then add 1 can minced clams (S.S. Pierce is good), a lump of sweet butter, 1 cup light cream, salt and pepper to taste, and a sprinkling of paprika when ready to serve.

CONSOMMÉ MADRILÈNE

2 cups beef bouillon
2 cups chicken consommé
3 cups unseasoned tomato juice
3 whole cloves
½ teaspoon onion powder

½ teaspoon dried celery flakes (well-muddled)
1 tablespoon fresh lemon juice
Freshly ground pepper and salt to taste

Mix all ingredients and bring to a boil, then simmer about twenty minutes. Remove the cloves. Serve with a very thin piece of fresh lemon floating on the top. If you prefer to serve the madrilène cold, allow to cool before refrigerating, and chill several hours until it jellies. Serve in chilled soup dishes.

COCKTAIL SHAKER TOMATO SOUP

Start with a good-sized cocktail shaker. Into it put 1 can unseasoned tomato juice, ½ teaspoon sugar, a couple of stalks of cut-up celery (with green leaves), 2 sprigs parsley, a few leaves of basil and chervil. If you can't get these fresh herbs, substitute the dried (about ½ teaspoon of each); but use some of the fresh if possible. Crumble them up a bit and let stand in the juice in a cool place about an hour. When ready to serve, add a heaping cup of sour cream, salt and pepper to taste, and as many ice cubes as the shaker will hold. Shake furiously and strain into chilled bouillon cups.

KING CRAB SOUP FLAMBÉ

1 six-oz. can frozen or canned Alaska king crabmeat

1 can condensed cream of mushroom soup

1 small can button mushrooms, drained

1 soup can water

½ soup can tomato juice

1 tablespoon butter

Salt and pepper

1 soup can medium cream

5 tablespoons bourbon

Combine all of the ingredients except cream and whiskey, stir well and simmer together until hot. Do not boil. Add the cream and simmer slowly another 2 or 3 minutes. Add salt and pepper to taste.

When ready to serve, warm your whiskey in a ladle or miniature saucepan, put a match to it, and pour it flaming into the hot soup. Obviously this is at its most dramatic when the last step is executed at the table.   4 SERVINGS

LEMON SOUP (AFTER THE GREEKS)

3½ cups strong chicken broth (College Inn brand, canned, is good)

3½ cups water

¾ cup rice

½ cup fresh lemon juice

3 eggs, well beaten

This is excellent hot or very cold.

Put the chicken broth and water into a saucepan. Bring to a boil and add the raw rice, which has been well washed. Continue to boil together about 15 minutes.

Remove ½ cup or so of the broth, and add to it the fresh lemon juice. Let this rest while you beat the eggs until they are a nice pale color. Now very *slowly* add the lemon and broth mixture to the eggs—beating all the while. This is important so the mixture does not curdle. If you perform this operation utilizing an electric mixer you're all set; otherwise you had better engage another pair of hands to beat as you pour.

Now all you have to do is to add this tricky little mixture to the rice and hot broth, and stir until smooth.   4 SERVINGS

CREAM OF CHICKEN BISQUE

4 tablespoons butter	¾ cup minced cooked chicken
4 tablespoons flour	Dash powdered garlic (if
1¼ cups chicken broth	desired)
½ teaspoon salt	1 egg yolk
1 onion, cut into halves	⅓ cup dry sherry
1 stalk celery, in halves	Whipped cream (if desired)
3 cups milk	

Mix butter and flour over low heat to bubbling paste. Add broth, salt, onion, celery. Stir until creamy; cover and cook over low heat 15 minutes, stirring as necessary to prevent lumping. Strain liquid into pot, add milk, minced chicken, garlic powder, if used. Cook until creamy. In a separate bowl, thin an egg yolk with a little of the hot soup; gradually add to broth. Add sherry and whipped cream just before serving.   3-4 SERVINGS

CRABMEAT A LA NEWBURG SOUP

1 can cream of mushroom soup	½ cup cream
1 can asparagus soup	1 can crabmeat
1 cup milk	3 tablespoons sherry

Mix all together and heat.   3-4 SERVINGS

EASY CLAM BISQUE

1 (7 oz.) can minced clams	1 cup milk
1 (10½ oz.) can condensed	1 teaspoon salt
green pea soup	Freshly ground pepper
1 (10½ oz.) can condensed	2 tablespoons sherry
tomato soup	

Combine clams, soups, milk, salt, and pepper. Heat, stirring until smooth. Add sherry. Ladle into bowls and serve with crisp crackers.

4 SERVINGS

MEDITERRANEAN SOUP

¼ pound ground beef
1 can (10¾ oz.) condensed min-
　estrone soup

1 soup can water

Shape meat into 12 small meatballs (if desired, add pinch of orégano to meat mixture before shaping). Brown slowly in saucepan (use a little shortening, if necessary). Pour off any excess drippings. Stir in soup and water. Simmer a few minutes.

2 TO 3 SERVINGS

CREAMY CHEESE SOUP

1 can (10½ oz.) condensed
　cream of mushroom soup
1 soup can water

1 cup shredded Cheddar cheese
Dash black pepper

In saucepan, stir cream of mushroom soup until smooth. Blend in remaining ingredients. Heat, stirring often, until cheese is melted. Worcestershire or Tabasco sauce may be added, if desired. This may also be made with other soups (green pea, tomato, cream of asparagus, celery or chicken).

3 SERVINGS

BEEF NOODLE DUET

1 can (10½ oz.) condensed beef
　noodle soup
1 can (10¾ oz.) condensed
　vegetable beef soup
1½ soup cans water

2 tablespoons butter
½ clove garlic, minced (or ¼
　teaspoon powdered thyme)
2 cups soft bread cubes

Combine soups and water in saucepan. Heat well. To make croutons: Melt butter in skillet; add garlic (or thyme). Lightly mix in bread cubes; cook over low heat, stirring constantly, until bread is crisp and brown. Place portion of croutons in each serving bowl; pour in soup.

4 TO 5 SERVINGS

COUNTRY SPECIAL

½ cup diced cooked ham

1 tablespoon butter or margarine

1 can (10½ oz.) condensed
  cream of chicken soup

1 can (10½ oz.) condensed

chicken vegetable soup or 1
can (10¾ oz.) condensed
cream of vegetable soup

2 soup cans water

1 tablespoon chopped parsley

Brown ham lightly in butter in saucepan. Stir in soups, water, and
parsley. Heat thoroughly.   4 TO 6 SERVINGS

And now, more soups but giving the can opener a rest:

CHEESE SOUP (HOT AND CHEDDAR), YOUR OWN

Make a white sauce by blending together 2 tablespoons melted
butter and 2 tablespoons flour. Add 3 cups hot milk all at once and
stir until smooth. Throw in a small clove of garlic. Set the saucepan
over boiling water, stirring frequently, while the garlic asserts its
influence on the sauce. Then fish out the garlic clove and toss it
out.

Slowly add to the white sauce 1 cup good dry white wine and 1
cup grated Cheddar cheese. Continue to cook gently over the hot
water until the cheese melts. (Keep stirring.) Add a pinch of
cayenne pepper (it's very hot, be careful), a pinch of nutmeg and
salt to taste. Just before serving add 2 lightly beaten egg yolks, and
3 tablespoons heavy cream. Keep on the fire about another four
minutes till blended through and piping hot.   3 SERVINGS

FRENCH ONION SOUP

Important things to remember with this soup:

1. The broth should be a rich golden color, well-blended with
the onion . . . not a watery, Milquetoast version with nasty little
specks of burned onion floating on top.

2. The bread should be French, if possible—not toasted, but
slowly *dried* to crispness in an oven after the flame has been turned
off.

3. The flavor of this soup is really better if it is made early and
reheated, the floating bread, cheese, and under-the-broiler part to
be done as a "just-before serving" operation.

With these primers in mind, the rest is easy. So, to the kettle
go we.

Take 4 medium onions and slice them ever so thinly. Into a heavy kettle or Dutch oven put 2 tablespoons butter and 2 tablespoons bacon fat. Melt it, and slowly sauté the onions in it, gently turning them until they are golden brown, but not blackened, please. Over this sprinkle 2 tablespoons flour and blend. Gradually add 6 cups good strong beef stock or bouillon (a combination of bouillon cubes and Bovril can be used too). Bring this to a boil, and simmer about half an hour. Season to taste with salt, pepper, and a dash of Worcestershire. Grate about ¼ lb. Parmesan or hard Gruyère cheese, or have your tinned version on hand. Slice medium-thick slices of French bread and "crisp" them in the oven following suggestion above. Float the bread on top of soup which has been transferred either to a large casserole or individual casseroles. Sprinkle liberally with the grated cheese and a few dots of butter.

Slip the whole thing under a preheated broiler till nicely brown. Serve at once.   4 SERVINGS

CLAM BROTH

Maybe you yearn for a really strong, fresh *Clam Broth*. Here it is:

Go to your fish market and buy 2 dozen steamer or cherrystone clams. Be sure the shells are tightly closed, which means the clam is alive. Take them home and scrub them thoroughly (a clean metal sponge is fine for this). Pop them into a large kettle and pour over them a light dribbling of olive oil (not more than a scant tablespoon), and 2 quarts water. Add a couple of chopped shallots or a small onion and 2 chopped scallions, plus about 5 sprigs of fresh parsley. Add *no* salt, as clams are usually salty.

Cover the kettle, put it over the fire and steam for about 10 minutes, until the clams open. Strain the broth, and it's ready to serve. You may want to have on hand a bowl of chopped parsley and one of whipped cream (½ pint). A little of each is delicious floating on top.

These ingredients thrown together will conjure up about 10 cups of strong broth. When cool, it can be successfully stored in a glass jar in the refrigerator for 2 or 3 days.

A minimum of effort for such a treat after all, *n'est-ce pas?*

CLAM CHOWDER

Or is real *New England Clam Chowder* what you crave? Buy

about 18 fresh chowder clams. Scrub them thoroughly with a good stiff brush or metal sponge. Put into a large kettle with a stalk of celery and enough water to cover. Steam 8 to 10 minutes or until shells are opened (don't overcook—it toughens the clams). Strain off liquid and reserve. Remove the clams from their shells and chop the hard part of the clam very fine; or put them through a food grinder. Reserve.

Dice ⅓ pound bacon. Fry it slowly in a heavy saucepan till half cooked. Pour off all but 2 tablespoons of the fat.

To the saucepan add: 2 onions (medium) that have been coarsely chopped. Cook these onions with the bacon gently till they are tender and just beginning to brown.

Add 1 cup boiling water, 2 cups potatoes, peeled and diced, some freshly ground pepper, and the clam juice. Bring to a boil and simmer gently about 20 minutes or until the potatoes are barely tender (don't let them get mushy).

Scald 2 cups milk and 1½ cups cream together in a saucepan and add to soup along with the minced clams and the soft part of the clams. Mix together and serve. This soup should never be allowed to boil after the milk is added.

A frugal lump of butter (very New England) and a delicate sprinkling of paprika over the top adds eye appeal to this soup. The taste speaks for itself.

OLD-FASHIONED SPLIT PEA SOUP, OR "DON'T THROW THAT HAM BONE OUT!"

Let us assume that you have already bought and paid a pretty price for the ham. You will feel a little more mellow about the whole thing when you discover that the bone will reward you with a delicious bonus.

Of course, if you like a little meat as well as flavor in your soup, don't carve off every last sliver. Even if you make the trip to the butcher especially to buy an end of ham to make the soup, it's well worth the effort, and not very expensive either. This is one of those hearty soups that makes a wonderful meal in itself with the addition of some good bread, perhaps a salad, and a bowl of fruit.

So then:

Get yourself a box of the quick-cooking dried split peas. They come usually in 1-lb. packages (or use 2 cups). Dump these into a very large kettle along with 3 quarts water. Put in the ham bone. The meat on the bone can later be sliced or cubed to be served with the soup.

Add 1 small grated carrot, 1 large or 2 medium onions, coarsely chopped, a sprig of parsley, and a couple of celery leaves.

Heat the soup to boiling, cover, and simmer very slowly 2½ to 3 hours, until the peas are tender and the liquid has thickened to a nice soup consistency.

Note here: Do not salt this soup before cooking. The ham may be very salty, so test-taste *after* cooking.

With the removal of the bone, celery, and parsley, the soup can be served just as the pot cooked it, or you can strain the whole kettle, add a little heavy cream, and top with toasted and buttered bread cubes.

MUSHROOM CHOWDER PROVINCIAL

2 tablespoons butter	2 cups boiling water
½ pound fresh mushrooms	½ cup diced carrots
¼ cup diced onion	½ cup diced celery
3 tablespoons butter	½ teaspoon salt
6 tablespoons flour	¼ teaspoon paprika
1 quart milk	Parsley, chopped
2 chicken bouillon cubes	

Melt butter in a skillet and sauté mushrooms and onion until tender. Set aside. Melt 3 tablespoons butter in a 2-quart saucepan, blend in flour, add milk gradually and stir constantly until liquid begins to thicken slightly. Dissolve bouillon cubes in boiling water and add to white sauce. Add carrots, celery, and seasonings. Simmer (do not boil) 10 minutes. Add onions and mushrooms and simmer 5 more minutes. Garnish soup with chopped parsley.

6 TO 8 SERVINGS

WINNING THE COLD WAR: FROZEN FOOD TRIUMPHS

There is one brand of instant coffee which is astutely advertised as not the best coffee—they point out that the *best* coffee is the same brand freshly prepared—but as mighty close to the perfection of the original.

And that isn't all marketing savvy: and the same type of reasoning can apply equally well to frozen foods. They are not just substitutes sitting in your grocer's locker for the day when you are too hurried or too lazy or too uninformed to do a better job. There are ways of making them taste mighty good.

And as with the higher types of canned foods, one of them is simply opening them.

You probably know all this, but one of the biggest packers, if not the biggest, has fully developed dishes which come in a laminated plastic envelope, heat-sealed and leak-proof and you don't even have to heat up your stove. You just drop the envelope in boiling water, and in a few minutes you're all set. These are no primitive dishes either: Seabrook Farms (to give them full credit for a terrific idea) numbers among their vegetable packages asparagus cuts and tips in hollandaise sauce, potatoes and peas in cream sauce, baby limas in cheese sauce, creamed spinach (you can add a few slices of hard-boiled egg on the top when you serve it) and peas in onion sauce. The Seabrook entrées include beef goulash with noodles, breast of chicken cacciatore, beef in red wine, and baked haddock filet bonne femme.

This is really going some, if eating is all we're talking about.

The other food packers, such as Mrs. Paul's with the fish products, Bird's Eye, and the Stouffer list—including escalloped cream and noodles, roast beef hash, Swiss steak with sauce, lobster newburg, king crab imperial, Welsh rabbit, baked breasts of chicken, spinach soufflé, potatoes au gratin—give you your food in the same dish you bake it in. Swanson's meat pies, chicken parts, and whole dessert pies are great.

You can help all of these dishes along with your own additions and inventions, if you like. A little fresh cream added to the ingredients of a newburg, for instance, with a spot of sherry and butter, then stirred for a minute more in your own saucepan, really gets things on the move. In every cream dish, adding your own fresh cream will enrich and loosen the preparation. The fish creams are helped by sherry and butter, the beef dishes with a spoonful of red wine. When the dish includes cheese, add a little of your own—Parmesan, Gruyère or Cheddar.

As you take these first steps beyond merely heating and eating the contents, you appreciate the fact that cooking can be fun, too, and the rewards great. So here are a few tips on the ways and means of getting the most out of your frozen food purchases. We have mentioned a few of the outstanding quality brands in an attempt to be helpful. These are nationally distributed; no doubt you will discover many others of quality which may be locally packed. When you find a good brand, keep an eye on your grocer's locker, as this frozen food business is expanding rapidly and almost every week something new and quite intriguing will appear in the cabinet. Besides, it's pleasantly cooling to stand there looking in.

There are a few simple techniques to keep in mind.

Check the frozen foods cabinet. It should be well stocked but not above the fill or safe line. Temperature should read zero or below.

Avoid frozen food packages which are dented or broken.

Shop for frozen foods last. Carry home in insulated bag.

Once home, immediately put frozen food into freezer or freezing compartment of refrigerator.

Top-of-stove: Most frozen prepared dinners may be heated on surface units of your range this way: Place foil-covered dinner tray directly on unit over low heat for 20 to 25 minutes. Move dinner around once or twice during heating so that all sections of the tray come in direct contact with the heat. Dinners are ready to serve when foil cover is hot all over to the touch. Dinners which give satisfactory results with this method are:

Beef	Macaroni and cheese
Creamed chicken	Meat loaf
Fried chicken	Swiss steak
Filet of haddock	Turkey
Ham	

Caution: Dinners with French-fried potatoes, such as chopped sirloin, should be prepared in the oven (not on top of the stove).

Electric skillet: Many cooks find a large electric skillet or frypan ideal for heating frozen prepared dinners. Follow directions in the manufacturer's booklet. Good to prepare this way are the dinners with fried chicken, sliced beef, and sliced turkey. Caution: Items with cream sauces (such as macaroni and cheese) and those with French-fried potatoes and crumb toppings are best prepared in the oven.

Outdoor grill: Outdoor chefs use their cooking ingenuity to heat frozen prepared dinners and "entrées and casseroles" over a charcoal fire, a good idea during warm weather when you may not want to heat up your kitchen. (Exceptions are the same as those listed above.) Follow these directions for good results: Build charcoal fire. When coals are ashen gray, place dinners or "entrées and casseroles" on grill rack 5 inches above coals. Move container occasionally so heat doesn't concentrate too long in one spot. Remember, source of heat is only coming from underneath the dinners or "entrées and casseroles," so allow a little more heating time than that given on label. Use a pair of heavy oven mitts to handle hot containers.

Here are ways to pick up frozen food flavors with a bit of garnish:

Frozen prepared dinners	*Garnish*
Beef	Turn back foil cover over meat and gravy. Spread with 1 tablespoon chopped chutney with syrup. Reseal; heat, following label directions.
Creamed chicken	Partially lift up foil cover over dinner. Sprinkle surface of creamed chicken with a little curry powder. Reseal; heat.

Frozen prepared dinners	*Garnish*
Fried chicken	Lift foil cover just enough to spread chicken with 1 tablespoon ginger marmalade. Reseal; heat.
Filet of haddock	Turn back foil cover to expose fish. Sprinkle with ½ teaspoon drained capers. Heat, following label directions.
Ham	Lift foil cover over ham and raisin sauce. Sprinkle with 1 tablespoon orange juice and bit of orange rind. Reseal; heat.
Macaroni and cheese	During last 10 minutes of heating, top macaroni and cheese with a red ripe tomato slice.
Meat loaf	Give an Italian flavor to this dinner. Turn back foil cover over meat loaf and sauce. Sprinkle ⅛ teaspoon crushed orégano over both. Reseal; heat.
Chopped sirloin	Fold back foil cover over meat and gravy. Insert 4 or 5 canned sliced mushrooms. Reseal; heat.
Swiss steak	Lift up foil cover over mashed potatoes. Sprinkle with onion salt. Reseal; heat.
Turkey	Slip 1 tablespoon currant jelly under foil cover, near sliced meat. Reseal; heat.

Frozen Entrées and Casseroles	*Garnish*
Chicken with noodles	After heating, top with a mound of whole cranberry sauce.
Fried chicken	Blend 1 tablespoon canned deviled ham and ¼ teaspoon prepared mustard. Turn back foil cover over meat; spread meat with mixture. Reseal; heat.
Seafood au gratin	After heating, garnish with a sprig of parsley and a lemon wedge.
Turkey	Lift foil over mashed potatoes. Sprinkle with chopped parsley. Reseal; heat.

Meat Pies	Garnish or Topping
Beef, chicken, and turkey	Top baked pies with toothpick kabob of olives and pickle wedge.
Chicken and turkey	Combine ½ cup whole cranberry sauce and ½ teaspoon grated lime rind; chill. Serve with 3 or 4 baked pies.
Beef and chicken	Top baked pies immediately with a slice of sharp process cheese.
Beef, chicken, and turkey	Melt 2 tablespoons butter, over low heat, in saucepan. Add 2 tablespoons chopped green onions and cook slowly 5 minutes. Spoon over 2 or 3 baked pies.
Beef and chicken	Spoon a little bottled barbecue sauce over hot baked pies.
Beef, chicken, and turkey	Fry several slices of bacon; drain; crumble. Mix with small amount chopped parsley. Sprinkle on tops of baked pies.
Beef, chicken, and turkey	Serve each baked pie with a dab of sour cream and a few toasted slivered almonds.
Beef	Combine ¼ cup apple butter with 1 tablespoon lemon juice in small saucepan; heat. Spoon over 2 or 3 baked pies.

Now, for some more extensive ways to stretch out from your frozen food base:

LOBSTER THERMIDOR

1 can (4 oz.) sliced mushrooms, drained
1 tablespoon butter
1 cup diced cooked lobster (or 6½-oz. can, drained)
1 can (10 oz.) frozen condensed cream of shrimp soup
¼ cup milk
¼ teaspoon dry mustard
Dash cayenne pepper
Grated Parmesan cheese
Paprika

Brown mushrooms lightly in butter in saucepan. Add lobster and cook a few minutes. Add soup, milk, mustard, and cayenne. Heat until soup thaws, stir often. Spoon lobster mixture into 3 individual baking dishes (or one large one). Sprinkle cheese and paprika on top. Bake in a hot oven (400° F.) about 15 minutes.   3 SERVINGS

CHICKEN LIVER BACON BROIL

1 pkg. (8 oz.) frozen chicken livers   4 slices bacon

Place livers in shallow broiling pan or on foil. Broil until thawed and lightly browned (about 15 minutes), turning often. Top with bacon, continue broiling, about 3 minutes, or until crisp.

2 SERVINGS

CHICKEN PAPRIKA OVEN STYLE

2 pkgs. (1 lb. each) frozen chicken breasts
Flour
2 tablespoons butter
1 medium onion, sliced
1 bay leaf

1 can (10½ oz.) condensed cream of mushroom soup
½ cup sour cream
2 teaspoons paprika
Dash pepper

Thaw chicken as directed on package; dust lightly with flour. Brown in butter, in oven-proof (all metal) skillet. Add onion and bay leaf. Combine soup and remaining ingredients, pour over chicken. Cover. Bake in a moderate oven (350° F.) for 1 hour.

4 TO 6 SERVINGS

SEAFOOD SOUP

2 cans (10 oz. each) frozen condensed cream of shrimp soup
2 soup cans milk

1 cup flaked cooked crab (or 6½-oz. can, drained)
1 teaspoon lemon juice
Minced parsley or chives (optional)

Combine soup and milk in saucepan. Heat until soup thaws; stir now and then. Add crab and lemon juice. Heat. Garnish with parsley or chives.   6 SERVINGS

BAKED PORK CHOPS WITH LIMA BEANS MORNAY

1 pkg. baby lima beans in cheese sauce	1 tablespoon flour
	1 cup milk
4 thick loin pork chops	¼ cup grated Swiss cheese
Salt and pepper	1 beaten egg yolk
1 tablespoon butter	Dry mustard, salt, paprika

Defrost baby lima beans in cheese sauce by boiling 6 minutes. Season pork chops with salt and pepper and brown on both sides in a skillet. Add ⅓ cup hot water. Stir in the brown bits in the pan and cook, covered, for 30 minutes, until pork is tender and thoroughly cooked. Melt butter, stir in flour, and cook for a minute or two. Stir in milk and Swiss cheese and continue to cook, stirring until sauce is thickened and smooth. Add a little hot sauce to the beaten egg yolk, then combine with sauce. Add half of sauce to hot lima beans and adjust seasoning with salt and pepper. Put the chops in the center of a shallow baking dish and spoon the beans around them. Season remaining sauce highly with mustard, salt, and paprika, and pour over chops. Bake in moderately hot oven (350° F.) about 20 minutes.   4 SERVINGS

EGGS BENEDICT, ASPARAGUS

1 pkg. asparagus cuts and tips, hollandaise style	4 eggs
Worcestershire sauce	2 English muffins, split and toasted
Salt, pepper	

Heat asparagus cuts and tips, hollandaise style, by boiling 12 minutes. Heighten seasoning by adding Worcestershire sauce, salt, pepper to plastic bag. Poach 4 eggs and arrange on toasted muffin halves. Divide the asparagus hollandaise evenly over the eggs.   2 SERVINGS

QUICK CLAM CORN CHOWDER

1 can (10¼ oz.) frozen condensed clam chowder (New England style)	1 soup can milk
	1 cup diced cooked ham
	1 cup cooked whole-kernel corn

Combine all ingredients in saucepan. Heat until soup thaws; stir now and then.   4 SERVINGS

BROCCOLI DEVILED EGGS AU GRATIN

1 pkg. chopped broccoli au
   gratin
12 hard-cooked eggs
1 can (4½ oz.) liver pâté

Salt, black pepper
Grated Swiss cheese
Paprika, chopped parsley for
   garnish

Defrost broccoli au gratin by boiling 6 minutes. Cool. Cut the hard-cooked eggs in half lengthwise, and carefully remove the yolks. Mash yolks with liver pâté and add salt and pepper to taste; pile mixture in whites of eggs. Place in casserole, pour defrosted broccoli au gratin over them, and sprinkle generously with grated Swiss cheese. Bake in hot oven (450° F.) about 10-15 minutes, to brown topping. Sprinkle with paprika and parsley. Serve as luncheon dish.

6 SERVINGS

LIMA SAUSAGE CASSEROLE

2 pkgs. baby lima beans in
   cheese sauce
1 lb. pork sausage
Salt and pepper

Few drops Tabasco
2 tablespoons grated Parmesan
   cheese

Defrost baby lima beans in cheese sauce by boiling 6 minutes. Shape sausage meat into 8 small patties and cook slowly until brown and thoroughly cooked. Season limas highly with salt, pepper, and Tabasco and turn into a 1-quart shallow casserole. Sprinkle with cheese, cover with sausage patties and bake in a hot oven (450° F.) until limas are hot and cheese browns.

4 SERVINGS

MARYLAND OYSTER STEW

2 tablespoons small thin green
   pepper strips
2 tablespoons chopped green
   onions
1 tablespoon butter or margarine

1 can (10 oz.) frozen condensed
   oyster stew
1 soup can water
½ cup cooked whole-kernel
   corn

Cook green pepper and green onions in butter in saucepan until tender. Add oyster stew, water, and corn. Heat until soup thaws; stir often.

3 SERVINGS

SALMON STEAKS IN ASPARAGUS, COLLÉE

1 pkg. asparagus cuts and tips, hollandaise style
4 cups water
1 teaspoon salt
1 carrot
1 onion
½ bay leaf
1 celery stalk
4 individual frozen salmon steaks
1 envelope gelatine
¼ cup cold water
½ cup mayonnaise

Defrost asparagus cuts and tips, hollandaise style, by boiling 6 minutes. Cool, bring the water, seasonings, and vegetables to a boil in a shallow pan wide enough to hold the salmon steaks side by side. Boil for 15 minutes. Put the salmon steaks into this stock and simmer for 10 to 15 minutes until the fish is no longer translucent and flakes readily at the touch of a fork. Cool the fish in the stock. Transfer the salmon steaks to a sheet of waxed paper. Reduce the stock to ¾ cup by boiling it hard, and strain it. Soften the gelatine in ¼ cup cold water and dissolve it in the remaining hot stock. Stir this into the asparagus hollandaise and cool until the mixture thickens and begins to set. Fold in the mayonnaise and adjust the seasoning with salt and pepper to taste. Spoon the asparagus collée mixture evenly over the salmon steaks and chill thoroughly. Transfer with a spatula to a serving platter covered with parsley. Garnish with green pepper rings centered with slices of hard-cooked eggs, mounds of cucumber salad.   4 ELEGANT SERVINGS

CHICKEN POT PIE

1 pkg. potatoes and peas in cream sauce
1 cup chicken broth
1 cup cooked chicken in pieces
1 slivered pimiento
Onion juice, celery salt, black pepper
½ cup biscuit mix
1 teaspoon chopped parsley
2-3 tablespoons milk

Defrost potatoes and peas in cream sauce by boiling 6 minutes. Stir in chicken broth. Add chicken to potatoes and peas. Fold in pimiento. Adjust seasoning to taste with onion juice, celery salt, and black pepper. Divide into 2 deep individual casseroles. Mix the biscuit mix with parsley, add milk, and pat out to make 2 thin crusts. Lay these crusts on the pie mixture and bake in a moderately hot oven (350° F.) for 20–30 minutes, until the crust is brown and crisp. 2 SERVINGS

CHICKEN DIVAN

1 pkg. chopped broccoli au gratin	4-6 slices cooked white-meat chicken
1 tablespoon sherry	3 tablespoons grated Parmesan cheese
1 tablespoon heavy cream	
Salt and pepper	

Heat chopped broccoli au gratin by boiling 12 minutes. Stir in sherry and cream and heighten seasoning with salt and pepper. Lay slices of white-meat chicken (or turkey) in buttered shallow baking dish. Cover with seasoned broccoli mixture and sprinkle with cheese. Bake in a moderately hot oven (350° F.) or brown cheese topping under broiler. 2 SERVINGS

TURKEY AND BROCCOLI AU GRATIN

1 pkg. chopped broccoli au gratin	Salt and pepper
1½ cups instant rice	8 slices turkey, or can of boned turkey
1 bouillon cube	¼ cup light cream
1 tablespoon chopped parsley	3 tablespoons grated Parmesan cheese
2 tablespoons butter	

Defrost chopped broccoli au gratin by boiling 6 minutes. Prepare instant rice according to package directions, adding bouillon cube to water. Toss with parsley and butter, adjust the seasoning. Spread rice on bottom of a buttered oblong baking dish. Arrange over-lapping turkey slices over the rice and pour the broccoli au gratin mixed with the cream over the turkey. Sprinkle with grated Parmesan, bake in hot oven (400° F.) 15 to 20 minutes, until sauce is bubbling hot and cheese browns. 4 SERVINGS

ASPARAGUS BEEF CHIPPER

1 pkg. asparagus cuts and tips, hollandaise style	½ cup diced celery
4-oz. jar dried beef slices	Salt, white pepper
2 tablespoons butter	Hot buttered toast

Defrost asparagus cuts and tips, hollandaise style, by boiling 6 minutes. Separate beef slices, pour boiling water over them. Let stand

2 minutes, drain, and repeat. Melt butter and sauté celery for 2 minutes. Add beef slices, brown lightly. Stir in asparagus, heat gently. Add salt and pepper to taste and serve on freshly made hot buttered toast.   2-3 SERVINGS

DINNER ALFREDO'S

Antipasto (details below)

4 pkgs. breast of chicken cacciatore

Linguine Alfredo (recipe below)

2 pkg. creamed spinach

Strawberries, powdered sugar (1 qt. berries)

Put water on to boil. Arrange antipasto: center serving plate with canned eggplant relish; surround with celery curls, radish roses, black and green olives, pimiento, green pepper, sardines, anchovies, salami and other Italian cooked sausages, prosciutto, provolone and other sliced cheeses, tomatoes, in any assortment to suit taste. Serve with cruets of vinegar and oil. Prepare linguine. Heat breast of chicken cacciatore and creamed spinach by boiling 14 minutes. Rinse strawberries, do not hull. Drain, serve chilled with bowl of powdered sugar for dipping.   4 SERVINGS

LINGUINE ALFREDO

½-lb. pkg. linguine (flat spaghetti)

¼ cup butter

¼ cup grated Parmesan cheese

Boil linguine in a generous amount of salted boiling water until barely tender, but still chewy. Drain and toss with butter and cheese. Season with salt and pepper to taste.

BEEF AND FRUIT KEBABS

1½ lbs. boneless sirloin (cut in 1-inch cubes)

1 can (1 lb., 1 oz.) unpeeled apricot halves, drained

1 can (1 lb., 4½ oz.) pineapple chunks, drained

1 can (10¾ oz.) beef gravy

1 tablespoon honey

1 tablespoon frozen concentrated orange juice

¼ teaspoon ground cloves

Arrange beef cubes, apricot halves, and pineapple chunks alternately on skewers. Combine beef gravy and remaining ingredients. Broil kebabs about 20 minutes, turning and basting with sauce about 4 times. Simmer remaining sauce; serve with kebabs.   6 SERVINGS

MEXI-CREOLE CASSEROLE

1 pkg. creole succotash	1 teaspoon chili powder
1 thinly sliced onion	½ teaspoon salt
6 frankfurters, sliced	¼ teaspoon pepper
1 can (16 oz.) kidney beans	½ teaspoon garlic salt
2 sliced tomatoes	1 tablespoon oil

Defrost creole succotash by boiling 6 minutes. Fill a 1½-quart casserole with alternating layers of succotash, onion, frankfurters, kidney beans, ending with tomatoes. Sprinkle each layer with the combined seasonings. Drizzle oil over top. Bake in a moderately hot oven (350° F.) 25 minutes. 4 SERVINGS

THE OLD SHELL GAME: EGGS COMING UP

An egg is one of nature's greatest miracles. It is flawless in outer design, and one of the most nutritious and easily digested of all foods. And think of the many ways it can be prepared—boiled, scrambled, fried, poached, or baked—you can't even do that to a chicken.

Eggs are simplicity itself to cook. So let's start with the very primary moves:

To soft-boil an egg, ease it into boiling water with a spoon. The water should cover the egg. Don't boil furiously and risk cracking the shell—keep the fire down to the minimum required to sustain actual simmering or boiling.

Your timing runs from 3 to 4½ minutes. Only experiment will tell you the exact way you like it. Then use your kitchen timer and stay with your choice accurately.

To coddle an egg, ease it into boiling water, then cover the pan, and shut off the flame. Let the egg stand in the water from 8 to 12 minutes. This method gives you a soft-boiled egg with the yolk very soft.

A second way to coddle an egg is to put it in cold water and remove when the water is boiling *over the entire surface.* I personally like this method and usually leave the egg in the water for about 20 seconds more before lifting it out, holding for a moment under the cold water tap, and then serving. The white now is very firm, and the yellow soft but not too runny. This method is

suggested for those who find distasteful the strands of uncooked
white or yellow egg often still remaining in soft-boiled eggs.

To hard-boil an egg, cook it from 5 to 6 minutes. That will leave
the yolk still a little soft. To hard-boil it more firmly, or for eating
cold later on, cook it for 10 minutes and no more. Any longer and
you might as well eat a tennis ball.

To poach an egg, break it into a cup and then ease it carefully
into a heavy frying pan ⅔ filled with boiling salted water. The
boiling will stop when the egg cools the water; keep your flame on
but don't let the water boil again. When the white has firmed and
enveloped the yolk, your egg is done. Remove it with a perforated
lifter.

Another way to poach eggs is virtually to fry them in water. Put about ½ inch of water in a frying pan. Boil. Slip the egg in. The white will set, and you may have the yolk soft. Or, if you'd like it a little firmer, cover the pan for a minute or so, or spoon some of the water over the yolk.

A third way to poach eggs, and the one I prefer, is with a poaching gadget. Actually it steams them—it is a tiny double boiler, with the egg cupped in the upper section, into which steam pours through vents when you boil the water in the lower base section. A tight cover guarantees poaching the top of the egg. It's a good idea to cover the egg-cup section with melted butter before using, so as to keep the white from sticking. Another advantage of this gadget is that it keeps the egg in a compact shape: in the other methods, the white sometimes begins to flange off into odd shapes, and you may want to use a cookie cutter to get the egg back into better shape.

To scramble eggs, country style, put 2 tablespoons butter in a hot frying pan, and drop your eggs into the melted butter. Break the yolks with the shell, or fork, and then, after whites have had a chance to set partially, stir and cook until both whites and yolks are set.

For regular scrambled eggs, beat the eggs in a bowl, but not too much. A few brisk turns with a fork will do it. You can add a teaspoon of cream or milk to the eggs at this time, if you want to tone down the egg flavor somewhat, and particularly if you like your scrambled eggs very soft in texture. Melt a couple of table-spoons of butter in the frying pan, pour in the eggs, and scramble over a very low heat. (Too much heat makes the eggs rubbery.) Stir constantly, scraping the egg as it forms from the bottom and sides of the pan. A large serving spoon is best for this purpose. Be alert and don't leave the eggs on the fire too long, or they'll be dry and bouncy. (If you're preparing bacon on the side, or ham, you can use the fat instead of the butter. The fats, of course, flavor the eggs; butter is recommended, if you want that nice, fresh, clean egg taste.)

To fry an egg, put 1 tablespoon butter (or ham or bacon fat) in the pan, melt, and then ease in your egg. (It's a good idea to open the egg first into a cup, rather than indulging in the gesture of breaking it on the side of the pan.) When the white is firm you're set, at least for sunny side up. If you're going to flip it and cook both sides, be sure there's enough butter in the pan where you plan to put it. If not, slip in a small pat over the spot. During cooking, if you'd like to set the yolk somewhat, spoon the butter or fat over the egg.

Shirred eggs (*baked eggs*) require individual baking dishes. Your dish is first buttered, then you ease the egg into it. Bake in oven at about 350° for 6 minutes, or until white is firm. Baked eggs have a characteristic and pleasant flavor.

How to make an omelet: Take 4 eggs, 4 tablespoons milk or cream, ½ teaspoon salt, ⅛ teaspoon pepper. Beat eggs, not too much, add milk and seasoning. Put 2 tablespoons butter into a heavy frying pan. Pour in egg mixture. After a few minutes over low fire, cautiously lift with a spatula, and let any loose, runny liquid trickle under the setting part. When the top is creamy, increase heat and brown underside quickly, being careful not to burn it. Then fold with spatula and serve.

That is the basic French omelet.

If you're yearning for one of those real fluffy jobs, which is the way Americans seem to like their omelets, the procedure is a bit different. Thus:

Oven omelet: Separate 4 eggs, beat yolks until thick, then add ½ teaspoon salt, ⅛ teaspoon pepper, and ¼ cup milk. Beat the whites until stiff. Fold the yolk mixture into the whites, and pour into a hot frying pan, in which 1 tablespoon butter has been melted. Heat over a low flame, and when the omelet seems set and starts to puff up, thrust it into the oven at 350°. Watch it carefully; it will turn light brown on the top in about 10 minutes. Fold over once with the spatula, keeping the brown parts outside, and serve.

Traditionally, an omelet is a test of the good chef, even in the finest restaurants. And a number of things contribute to your success.

Pan must be heavy, with sloping sides. The pan bottom should always be slidy, so keep it oiled always. Good idea: have a special omelet pan you use for nothing else.

Some connoisseurs believe that adding milk or cream is a mistake. A matter of taste. It's a necessity with the puffy American omelet. At any rate, don't forget the *fork* to mix the eggs, not a beater.

Pan sizzling hot before the butter is put in.

Butter foaming and just beginning to brown when eggs are poured in.

Some cooks *roll* the omelet with the spatula rather than folding it. As the omelet starts to cook, you poke it around once, as with scrambled eggs, then let set for a few seconds, then push and roll, with quick jabs of the spatula. As you roll, toss and poke tiny dots of butter under the omelet.

Serve omelets always on *warm* plate. Hot plate will cook it more.

Don't try to make a big omelet. Two small ones are usually more successful than one big one.

There are wonderful additions possible with an omelet. For instance, you can fold these separately prepared ingredients into the finished omelet, as follows:

Omelet aux Artichauts (with artichokes): Cut raw artichoke hearts in neat strips, cook in butter until soft; season. When omelet is dished on platter, make fairly deep incisions with knife, almost the length of each omelette, spread cut slightly, and stuff with the delicately flavored artichoke morsels.

Omelet aux Pointes d'Asperges (with asparagus tips): Prepare raw asparagus tips by cooking in butter until soft, and stuff omelet as above.

Omelet aux Tomates Concassés (with tomato cubes): Cut peeled tomato into small cubes, sauté these slowly in butter with a little scraped garlic and chopped parsley. Tomato must taste fresh, so don't overcook. Stuff omelet as above.

Other fillings:

Bacon: Diced and cooked.

Chicken: Cooked and chopped.

Jam or *jelly.*

Mushrooms: Sautéed.

Sausages: Cooked, sliced.

Spanish Omelet: Cook 1 tablespoon chopped onion, and 1 tablespoon chopped pepper in 2 tablespoons butter, add 1½ cups canned tomatoes, and simmer until almost dry. Add 1 tablespoon sliced mushrooms, ¼ teaspoon salt, and dash cayenne pepper. Fold in omelet, and use as sauce over it.

Cheese: Mix 3 eggs with tablespoon of mixed Gruyère and Parmesan. Sprinkle with cheese when served.

Ham: Add 2 tablespoons diced, cooked ham to 3-egg mixture.

Chicken Livers: Sauté in 1 tablespoon of butter 3 tablespoons of chopped chicken livers. Mix 2 of the tablespoons of livers in with the eggs, fold in the remainder after the omelet is done.

Au Fines Herbes au Fromage: Add chopped chives and parsley to the basic mixture before cooking, and sprinkle omelet after cooking with a tablespoon of grated Gruyère or Parmesan cheese.

Fluffy Omelet:

2 tablespoons quick-cooking	¾ cup milk
tapioca	1 tablespoon butter
¾ teaspoon salt	4 egg whites
⅛ teaspoon pepper	4 egg yolks

Combine tapioca, salt, pepper, and milk in saucepan. Place over medium heat and cook until mixture comes to a boil, stirring constantly. Add butter. Remove from heat and allow to cool slightly while beating eggs.

Beat egg whites until stiff. Beat egg yolks until thick and lemon-colored. Add tapioca mixture to egg yolks and mix well. Fold into egg whites.

Pour into hot buttered 10-inch skillet. Cook over low heat 3 minutes. Bake in moderate oven (350° F.) 15 minutes. Omelet is sufficiently cooked when a knife inserted comes out clean. Cut across at right angles to handle of pan, being careful not to cut all the way through. Fold carefully from handle to opposite side and serve on hot platter.   4 SERVINGS

Omelet Flambé: Mix 8 eggs with only a tiny pinch of salt. Also a tablespoon of sugar. Cook very fast and less than an ordinary omelet; this omelet must be very soft when rolled onto the platter, as when it is blazed later it will, of course, continue to cook. Sprinkle quickly with granulated sugar, place 4 thin slices of lemon along top of omelet, and then a small lump of sugar on each lemon slice. Pour ½ cup rum with ½ cup brandy (both previously warmed) quickly over the whole omelet; set on fire. Burn only 2 minutes for best flavor; extinguish flames by placing large lid (like clean roasting pan lid) over the platter, then serve.

The same procedure may be used, with kümmel or kirsch as the liqueur.

(Additional omelet recipes are given in Chapter 10, page 278, which can be mixed in your electric blender.)

POACHED PLUS

A la Benedict: Sauté rings of cold boiled ham, sized to fit on English muffin. Split and toast muffins, place ham thereon. Arrange a poached egg on each. Pour Hollandaise Sauce (page 000) over all. Top with broiled truffle* (optional).

Au gratin: Place poached eggs in baking dish. Sprinkle with Parmesan cheese. Cover with Béchamel Sauce (page 000). Sprinkle with another spread of cheese. Bake in oven until brown.

A la Reine: Over toast in baking dish pour small amount cream, cover with mushrooms sautéed in butter. Place poached eggs on top. Over this pour a cream sauce to which grated Parmesan cheese has been added. Sprinkle more cheese over entire dish and brown in moderate oven.

A la Suisse: What we're doing here is really poaching the eggs in cream. Melt a tablespoon of butter in your omelet pan, add ½ cup cream. Ease 4 eggs into cream, sprinkle with salt and pepper. Poach as usual. When nearly done, sprinkle with grated Parmesan cheese. Cook about another minute and serve eggs on buttered toast. Strain the cream sauce over the dish.

You can use about a tablespoon of sherry to flavor the cream, following the recipe above. Or follow the same recipe substituting white wine for the cream.

A more subtle recipe uses dry red wine. Take two cups, a bay leaf, a pinch each of dried thyme and tarragon, dash of salt and pepper, and simmer all this about 10 minutes in your skillet. Poach 8 eggs in this mixture and place on buttered toast. Melt a tablespoon of butter, blend with a tablespoon of flour, add the wine mixture to this and cook it, stirring gently, until it thickens into a sauce. Pour over eggs and serve.

SCRAMBLED EGGS PLUS

With mushrooms: Start with your basic recipe of, say, 8 eggs (for 4), ¼ cup cream, ¾ teaspoon salt, ¼ teaspoon pepper. Beat with fork. Melt 4 tablespoons butter in pan. Meanwhile, slice and sauté

---

* If truffles are not available to you, for this recipe or others later in the book, use slices of black olives.

in butter, in another saucepan, 1 cup mushrooms. Now pour in your egg mixture, and add mushrooms. Scramble as directed earlier.

With ham: 1 cup diced cooked ham, added to scrambled eggs as above.

With cheese: ½ cup grated Parmesan and Gruyère cheese, added to scrambled eggs as above.

With shrimp, crab meat and lobster: About 1 cup fish meat, flaked very fine, and added as above. Or toss in a half dozen anchovies, sliced into small bits so as to mix well among the eggs.

With onions: Sauté 1 medium-size onion, chopped small, in the same butter you are melting for the eggs. Pour eggs over onions, scramble as above.

A la Double Boiler: This is particularly for them as likes their eggs soft and creamy. Mix a package (3 oz.) of cream cheese, 2 tablespoons butter, ½ cup cream, ¼ teaspoon salt, a dash of pepper in the upper deck of the double boiler. Put over boiling water until cheese is softened, and mix ingredients gently. Now add 5 eggs, well beaten, and 1 cup diced cooked ham. Stir until set. Serve on English muffins, well buttered.

Number 2 in this technique is a cheese mixture. Melt 2 tablespoons butter in upper deck, using direct heat. Add about ⅓ cup grated Cheddar cheese, and 2 tablespoons water. Cook and stir until cheese melts. Add 5 beaten eggs, salt and pepper as above, and place over boiling water. Stir gently until set. Serve over toast or English muffins.

Number 3 Doubler is an old Southern dish. Melt 3 tablespoons of butter in the upper deck over direct heat, then add 1 tablespoon finely chopped onion and 3 large diced mushrooms. Let them cook awhile, then add 1 cup canned tomatoes, cover, and cook slowly for 10 minutes. Now place the upper deck over boiling water, stir in 6 eggs, lightly beaten, and season with salt and pepper. When eggs begin to set, serve over toast.

THE ONE-EYE EGG GRILL

Cut out a 3-inch circle from the center of a piece of bread, stale enough to be firm. Place the bread in a pan generously coated with melted butter. Drop an egg into the circle, season with salt and pepper, and fry for about a minute, or until the egg is set. Then, flip and fry on other side, adding butter if necessary underneath, for golden browning.

Another way to do this, but change the routine, is to cover the egg-in-the-hole with sour cream and sprinkle diced bacon on top. You do not fry but now bake it in moderate oven (350°) until egg is set, and the bacon crisp, which should run about 10 or 12 minutes.

BAKED EGGS PLUS

With cream: Melt one teaspoon butter in a small saucepan, and break in two eggs. Cook for one minute over a slow fire, then pour some hot cream over the eggs, just enough to cover them. Now, thrust the pan into a moderate oven (350°) and bake until the eggs are set.

With tomato juice: Butter shallow saucepan or flameproof dish, fill half full with hot tomato juice. Break the eggs into the juice and heat on the stove until the juice boils. Season with salt and pepper, dot with butter, and cook in a moderate oven (350°) until eggs are set.

In tomatoes: The tomato is the cooking vessel, almost. You cut the tops off ripe tomatoes, 1 per egg, per person. Scoop out the centers, and place in a buttered flameproof dish or saucepan. Break an egg into each tomato, add salt and pepper and a bit of butter, and bake in a moderate oven (350°) until the egg is set, which should be about 12 minutes. Then sprinkle the eggs with grated Parmesan cheese and brown under the broiler.

BEAU GESTE AUX OEUFS
(Big deal with eggs)

You may yet yearn to do bigger and better things with eggs. For this, try

ASPARAGUS A LA MILANAISE

36 spears of asparagus	¼ cup butter
6 eggs	Grated Parmesan cheese

Cook asparagus spears in boiling salted water until tender. Drain thoroughly. Arrange on a warm serving platter in the pattern of spokes on a wheel, points out, and keep hot. Poach or fry the eggs lightly and arrange them over the asparagus tips.

Melt the butter in a small saucepan and heat until it turns a dark golden brown. Pour the browned butter over the asparagus and sprinkle generously with grated Parmesan cheese. Place the dish under a broiler until the cheese has melted.

EGGS FLORENTINE

4 tablespoons butter	1½ pounds spinach, cooked and
4 tablespoons flour	puréed
1 cup hot milk	½ teaspoon nutmeg
1 cup hot cream	6 eggs, poached
Salt and pepper to taste	Grated Parmesan cheese

In a saucepan melt the butter and add the flour, stirring constantly. Gradually stir in hot milk and cream and cook, stirring constantly, until sauce is thick and smooth. Season to taste with salt and pepper.

Combine the hot spinach with ½ cup of the cream sauce and season it with the nutmeg. Pour the spinach mixture into a shallow flameproof casserole and arrange the eggs on top. Spoon remaining sauce over eggs, sprinkle with Parmesan cheese and brown lightly under the broiler flame.   6 SERVINGS

POACHED EGGS GRAND DUC

Fry bread in butter until golden brown, and cut out round pieces slightly larger than size of poached egg. Place poached eggs on rounds and then cover with lobster or crabmeat. Pour over this Sauce Mornay (page 260) and brown in hot oven (400° F.). Garnish with cooked asparagus tips.

EGGS MOLLET CHASSEUR

Melt 1 tablespoon butter in saucepan, and cook in it for about 5 minutes 1 minced green onion and 3 chopped mushrooms. Add ¼ cup chicken broth, and simmer 10 minutes more. Now, salt and pepper the mixture, and pour in about a tablespoon of sherry. Pour all this into shallow, flameproof dish. Now, ease in gently 4 poached eggs, and pour 2 tablespoons of heavy cream over the eggs. Sprinkle with grated Parmesan cheese, and thrust under the broiler until golden brown.

DEVILED HAM AND EGGS

8 eggs
½ cup of milk or light cream
½ teaspoon salt
½ teaspoon dry mustard

½ teaspoon Worcestershire
  sauce
Butter
1 can deviled ham

Combine eggs with milk and seasonings and beat slightly. Cook in butter over low heat until eggs are light and fluffy, lifting mixture from bottom of pan with spatula as eggs cook. Heap eggs onto 4 toast slices and center each serving with a spoonful of deviled ham.

4 SERVINGS

BREAKFAST HASH

Spoon contents of 2 cans corned beef hash into an 8-inch baking dish. Bake in 350° F. oven for 20 minutes. Remove hash from oven and with back of spoon make 6 "nests" in hash. Break an egg into each "nest" and continue baking for an additional 10 minutes, or until eggs are set.

6 SERVINGS

SCRAMBLED EGGS EL RANCHO

1 can corned beef hash
6 eggs, slightly beaten
⅓ cup milk
½ teaspoon salt

Dash of pepper
Freshly shredded Cheddar
  cheese or catsup

Brown hash in heavy frying pan. Combine remaining ingredients and blend into the hash. Cook over low heat until egg mixture is set. Stir only enough to break up the hash and eggs. Top each serving with shredded Cheddar cheese or with catsup.

SERVES 6

EGGS A LA CONSTANTINOPLE

You can't be in a hurry to do this. First, make some Turkish coffee by mixing finely pulverized coffee with an equal amount of sugar; add boiling water to this and bring to a boil three times, letting it set in between. You'll want about a pint of this, so use about 4 teaspoons of strong instant coffee. Now add an equal amount of olive oil to the coffee. Drop 2 or 3 eggs into the liquid, and cook them over a very low fire for about 10 hours. (You may have to add to the coffee-and-oil, but it should hold out if you don't heat it up too much.) What happens is that the coffee-and-oil mixture actually penetrates the shell during the long, slow cooking: the whites of the eggs turn to an amber color, and the yolks now have a nutty, quite delicious flavor.

SEVERAL BACONIAN THEORIES

You'll want bacon with your eggs, and simple as it is to cook there are a few pointers to keep in mind.

Buy the best bacon, in very thin strips, as lean as possible. Don't keep it too cold, or the slices won't separate without tearing. You can separate them best by using a rubber spatula—slip it under the end of the bacon slice and slither along lengthwise, lifting the slice at the same time.

To fry bacon, use a special skillet, with curved surface, or other device, to insure the drainage that means crisper bacon. If you haven't such a pan, spoon fat out of ordinary frying pan as you cook the bacon. Place your bacon strips flat, side by side, in an unheated skillet. Then turn your heat on, but keep it low at all times. Turn the bacon strips frequently to fry evenly. Drain on absorbent paper—a clean brown paper bag will do—before serving.

To broil bacon, put the separated slices on the rack of the broiler pan about 3 to 5 inches from the heat. Turn only once. It will broil quickly, so watch it, and move fast when the bacon is done.

To oven-bake bacon, put the separated slices on rack in shallow baking pan. Bake at 400° F. for about 10 minutes. No need to turn or drain; the heat moves in from all sides and does the work for you.

OTHER BREAKFAST MATTERS

After eggs, the next most popular breakfast dish for men is griddle cakes. Then French toast, I'd say, and finally waffles. All are simple to make, and have the added advantage of standing by for repeats that can be as fresh and hot as the first portion.

There's a knack to preparing all of these dishes that's somewhat similar to broiling steaks—no words can quite tell you the precise time when a flapjack should be turned, or the exact amount of butter that should be in your pan or on your griddle. Generally speaking, you should watch for bubbles to come through in your batter, and the underside will be brown at about that time. As for the butter, the recipes you'll have will include butter in the batter, and, therefore, grease the griddle only very lightly. Some cooks like to toss a dot or two of butter against the side of the flapjack as it cooks, to crisp it up a bit, but that's a matter of choice.

Here are a few recipes for gridders, and there are four more in Chapter 10 (Apple Flapjacks, Blueberry Pancakes, German Pancakes, and Sour Milk Griddle Cakes) which you can prepare in your electric blender. (See page 276–7.)

GRIDDLE CAKES

1¼ cups sifted all-purpose flour	1 egg
2½ teaspoons baking powder	¾ cup milk
2 tablespoons sugar	3 tablespoons melted butter
¾ teaspoon salt	

Sift dry ingredients together. Beat egg; add milk and melted butter. Add dry ingredients and mix into a batter with a large spoon. Drop batter by large spoonfuls on your griddle or into your pan. (Some cooks prefer to pour the batter from a pitcher, measuring the amount by eye.)

When bubbles form and break around rim of cakes, turn with spatula and bake second side until golden brown.

Makes 16-18 cakes, 3 inches in diameter, or fewer large ones, as desired.

BLUEBERRY GRIDDLE CAKES

Follow recipe for Griddle Cakes; add ½ cup washed, dried, and sweetened blueberries to batter or sprinkle 1 teaspoon fresh blueberries on each cake before turning.

BUTTERMILK GRIDDLE CAKES

2 cups sifted flour	2 tablespoons sugar
1 teaspoon baking powder	2 eggs
1 teaspoon soda	2½ cups buttermilk
½ teaspoon salt	¼ cup (½ stick) melted butter

Sift flour once, measure, add baking powder, soda, salt, and sugar and sift into a mixing bowl. Beat eggs; add buttermilk and butter and blend. Add to dry ingredients and stir only until dry ingredients are moistened. Meantime, heat griddle and grease lightly. Ladle about 3 tablespoons of the batter onto griddle for each cake and cook over moderate heat until bubbles break on surface. Turn lightly and continue to bake until golden brown. Transfer to warm plates and serve with butter and syrup, honey, or preserves. Makes 24 four-inch cakes.

BUTTERMILK PANCAKES

½ teaspoon baking soda
2¼ cups buttermilk
1 egg

2 tablespoons melted butter
2 cups pancake mix

Dissolve baking soda in buttermilk; add with unbeaten egg and butter to pancake mix, stirring lightly. Bake on hot, lightly greased griddle. If thinner pancakes are desired, add ¼ cup more milk.

STRAWBERRY SOUR CREAM FILLING

2 cups sliced fresh or frozen
  strawberries, sweetened

2 cups dairy sour cream

If using frozen berries, partially defrost, leaving some of the ice crystals in the berries. Add sour cream, stirring lightly and only enough to blend. Use as a filling between 2 pancakes and top with additional sour cream and strawberries.

WAFFLES

¾ cup flour
¼ teaspoon salt
1 teaspoon baking powder
1 teaspoon sugar

½ cup milk
2 eggs, separated
4 tablespoons melted butter

Mix dry ingredients and add milk, egg yolks, melted butter. Now beat egg whites medium stiff and add last. Bake on hot waffle iron. (Beware putting the batter on a cold iron and then heating. They'll stick until doomsday.)

Serve waffles with sour cream, fresh strawberries, jams, sweet butter, and bacon.

FRENCH TOAST

1 egg, slightly beaten	2 teaspoons shortening
¼ cup milk	4–6 slices stale or fresh bread
¼ teaspoon salt	

Combine egg, milk, and salt in pie plate or shallow dish.

Dip both sides of bread slices in egg mixture, being careful that bread is just moistened. Place 2-3 slices on each grid. Toast 3-5 minutes until golden brown on second side.   MAKES 4–6 SERVINGS

Serve with melted butter, maple sugar, or honey. French toast may also be baked. Prepare as above, then bake in a hot oven (400° F.) for about 12 minutes or until brown. Turn, to brown other side, and serve. You can sprinkle toast with sugar and cinnamon mixed after browning or sugar mixed with cinnamon and nutmeg. Then replace in broiler for a minute or two to caramelize sugar and let the flavor sink in.

SAY CHEESE AND SMILE

TYPES OF CHEESES AND THEIR USES

BLUE-VEINED CHEESES

Serve crumbled in salads; after the main course and before desserts with a crusty French or Italian loaf and red wine; with fruits such as pears.

Bleu de Bresse (France)
Danish blue (Denmark)
Gorgonzola (Italy)
Nazareth blue (Israel)
Pio crèm (France)
Roquefort (France)
Stilton (English)

SOFT-RIPENING CHEESES

Serve after the main course and before desserts with a crusty French or Italian loaf and dry red wine.

Brie (France)
Camembert (France)
Certosino (Italy)
Liederkranz (United States)

SEMISOFT CHEESES

Serve after the main course and before desserts with a crusty French or Italian bread and dry red wine. Fontina and mozzarella are excellent "melting" cheeses. Feta, served cold, goes well with watermelon when in season.

Beaumont (France)
Bel Paese (Italy)
Cantal (France)
Feta (Greece)
Fontina (Italy)
Gourmandise (France)
La Grappe (France)
Limburger (Germany)
Monterey Jack (United States)
Mozzarella (Italy)
Muenster (Germany)
Oka (Canada)
Pont l'Evêque (France)
Port du Salut (France)
Reblochon (France)
St. Paulin (France)
Tallegio (Italy)
Tête de Moine (France)
Tomme de Savoie (France)
Tilsit (Denmark, Germany)
Wensleydale (England)

FIRM CHEESES

Serve after the main course and before desserts with a crusty loaf of French or Italian bread and dry red wine. Gruyère is the best of all cheese for fondues. Gruyère, Swiss, Cheddar, and Cheddar-type cheese in this category are excellent for soufflés and in cheese sauces.

Black Diamond (Canada)
Caciocavallo (Italy)
Caerphilly (England)
Cheddar (England, United States)
Cheshire (England)
Chevre or goat cheese (France)

Christian IX (Denmark)
Coon (United States)
Double Gloucester (England)
Edam (Holland)
Gouda (Holland)
Gruyère (Switzerland)
Irish Blarney (Ireland)
Kasseri (Greece)
Lancashire (England)
Leicester (England)
Noekkelost (Norway)
Pineapple (United States)
Provolone (Italy)
Sage (United States)
Swiss or Emmentaler (Switzerland)
Vacherin (France)

CREAM-TYPE CHEESES

Serve after the main course with berries and champagne or sweet, well-chilled white wines.

Costello (Denmark)
Cottage cheese (United States)
Cream cheese (United States)
Crema Danica (Denmark)
Crème chantilly (France)
Double crème Gervais (France)
Petit Suisse (Switzerland)
Ricotta (Italy, United States)
Saint Florentin (France)
Triple crème (France)

HARD OR GRATING CHEESES

These cheeses are principally used grated over pasta such as spaghetti or lasagne. They may also be used sparingly in cheese sauces to produce a sharper flavor.

Parmesan (Italy)
Pecorino (Italy)
Repatoe (Sicily)
Romano (Italy)

Sbrinz (Switzerland)
Sap Sago (Switzerland)

Note: Many of the above cheese types are manufactured in the United States. The countries of origin are in parentheses. There is controversy among cheese experts as to whether Tallegio, Reblochon and Pont l'Evêque are soft-ripening or semisoft cheeses but they are generally considered semisoft.

SWISS FONDUE

This is the "friendliest" of cheese dishes as it requires the diners to sit around and all dip from the one steaming dish of fondue. Each diner has some squares of bread and a long fork with which to work. He spears the bread on the fork, and dunks it with a stirring motion into the bubbling pot of cheese. Along with the cheese it is good to sip a little chilled white Swiss wine (a Chilean Riesling is good also), and later to follow with a crisp green salad.

Here is how the fondue is prepared: Rub the inside of a chafing dish or earthenware casserole with a cut clove of garlic. Pour 2 cups dry white wine into it and place it over a low flame. Let the wine become very hot. When it is just below the boiling point, add 1 pound grated cheese. The cheeses vary with the enthusiasts. Emmentaler and Gruyère are a good combination. Some prefer plain good aged Wisconsin Cheddar. One good cook makes his fondue with Wisconsin Cheddar plus ¼ lb. Borden's Vera-sharp cheese. Add the cheese a little at a time to the hot wine while stirring constantly with a wooden spoon. When the cheese is all melted, stir in 1½ teaspoons cornstarch, which has first been mixed to a paste with a little of the hot wine. When the fondue begins to bubble, season with a pinch of nutmeg and some fresh ground white pepper to taste. Set the dish over an alcohol burner at the table. Now stir in 3 tablespoons kirsch. (The Swiss often sip kirsch too along with the white wine while they are eating the fondue.) Prepare the bread cubes early. They should be cut bite-size from French bread. They can be covered with a damp cloth till serving time to keep them from drying out.

The fondue should be kept at a low bubble all during the meal. If it stops bubbling, turn up the heat. If it gets too thick, add a little warm wine. Traditionally, the one who loses his bread first in the cheese pays for the wine. The crust that forms at the very bottom of the dish is considered quite a prize. It can be lifted out with a fork.   4 SERVINGS

SPECIAL CHEESE TOAST

Make a white sauce by blending together 2 tablespoons butter and 1½ tablespoons flour. Bring ½ cup milk to just below the boiling point and add all at once to the butter and flour. Stir vigorously till thick and smooth. Cool for about 15 minutes. To the cream sauce add ½ cup natural grated Emmentaler cheese, 3 tablespoons dry white wine, ½ teaspoon dry mustard, 1 clove garlic, minced, 1 beaten egg and salt and white pepper to taste. Mix together well. Toast some slices of diagonally-cut French bread on one side. Spread the untoasted side of the bread with the cheese mixture. It should be about ½ inch thick. Place the slices under a medium broiler until the cheese is heated through and lightly browned. Serve with well-chilled dry white wine.   5 SERVINGS

GOLDEN BUCK

2 tablespoons butter	Buttered French bread toast
½ lb. natural Cheddar cheese, grated	4 eggs, poached
	Anchovy filets
⅓ cup milk	Chopped parsley
Salt, pepper, dry mustard	

Melt butter in top of double boiler over direct heat. Add cheese, and heat until melted. Add milk, and cook until thickened. Put over boiling water, and add seasonings to taste. Serve on toast, topping each portion with a poached egg and 2 anchovy filets. Garnish with chopped parsley.   4 SERVINGS

WELSH RABBIT (RAREBIT) with BEER

1 tablespoon butter	1 egg, well beaten
1½ lbs. sharp Cheddar cheese, diced	1 tablespoon Worcestershire sauce
⅓ bottle beer (4 oz.)	Toast
¼ teaspoon salt	

Melt butter in top of a double boiler, add cheese and beer, and allow cheese to melt. Stir in salt, egg, and Worcestershire sauce. Serve at once over toast on heated plates.   6 SERVINGS

RINK TUM DIDDY RABBIT (RAREBIT)

½ lb. grated cheese (2 cups)   1 tablespoon Worcestershire
½ teaspoon salt   sauce
1 can condensed tomato soup   Toast or toasted crackers
3 tablespoons water

Stir and melt cheese in double boiler over hot water. Add salt, tomato soup, water and Worcestershire, and heat, stirring constantly until thick and bubbly. Serve over toast or toasted crackers.

SHARP CHEESE RABBIT (RAREBIT) with MILK

Melt ½ lb. old sharp crumbly American cheese, broken in small pieces, over hot water. Stir in 2 tablespoons flour, 1 tablespoon Worcestershire sauce and ½ teaspoon dry English mustard. Blend well, add 2 cups milk slowly. Cook and stir until thick and bubbly, about 10 minutes. Serve over toast or toasted crackers.   4–6 SERVINGS

KIDNEY BEAN RABBIT (RAREBIT)

Melt over hot water or in a chafing dish 2 cups diced Cheddar cheese (½ lb.). Stir in 2½ cups heated cooked kidney beans (No. 2 can), ½ cup diced green pepper, 1 tablespoon Worcestershire sauce. Keep hot. Serve on crisp toast or crackers.   4–6 SERVINGS

FACETIOUS AND FARINACEOUS: MAN
WITH A PASTA

The Italians, a joyous and creative race, have made a little world out of their pasta, no less piquant in its nomenclature than the sphere of French wines.

The extrovert of this family is *spaghetti,* known to everyone. *Macaroni* has been curiously immortalized in our folklore by "Yankee Doodle"—today one of our own patriotic ditties, but once a passage sung by the redcoats deriding a Yankee so stupid he thought a feather in his cap gave him the air of an Italian dandy, or *macaroni.* Yet no amount of feathers in any Yankee cap have ever been linked with *spaghettini* (which is finer than spaghetti), *vermicelli* (which is finer than spaghettini), *vermicellini* (which is finer than vermicelli), *capellini* (which is fine as a child's hair), *fidelini* (which is fine as an angel's hair), or *sopracapellini* (which is as fine as a cherub's hair). On the other end of the scale are *bucatini* (slightly thicker than spaghetti) and one step up in size, *perciatelli.* There is *fettucini* (ribbon-shaped and broader than spaghetti), and *fetucci,* even broader. And they have taken fettucini

and dyed it a lovely green with spinach juice to create *pasta verde.*
Then there is *taglietelli,* a wide noodle.

Italian inventiveness has outdone itself in the myriad shapes of
pasta. There are birds' wings (*penni*), bow ties (*cravatte*), little
bow ties (*tripolini*), chicken crests (*crest di gallo*), rings (*annelini*),
spirals (*rotelle*), the horns of plenty (*riccini*), jelly beans (*piperini*),
stars (*stellini*), tiny stars (*pastina*), dots (*acini di Pepe*), little oats
(*orzo*), seeds (*seme di mellone*), alphabets (*lettere*) and one shaped
like a tongue (*lingue di passeri*). And then there are the lovely
shells: large (*maruzze*), small (*maruzzelle*), nut-shaped (*gnocchi*),
and peanuts (*cavatelli*).

The words flow like a song as we move into the flat macaroni
family: very wide (*lasagne*), not so wide (*mafalde*), medium size
(*fettuccelle*), medium with a twist (*margherite*), small spaghetti
(*linguine*), and flat spaghettini (*linguine fini*).

The more familiar tubular *maccheroni* (home-town spelling) includes *manicotti* (stuffed and baked), *rigatoni* (grooved), *ziti* (cut
in lengths), *ditali* (ziti cut in ½-inch pieces), *diralini* (small ditali),
mostaccioli (cut on the diagonal), *mostaccioli rigati* (mostaccioli
with grooves), *mezzani* (thinner than ziti), *mezzani rigati* (mezzani with grooves), (we're getting the swing of this now, wot?)
maccaroncelli (thin macaroni), *tubetti* (maccaroncelli cut in pieces),
tubettini (tiny tubetti), and the most popular of all, elbow. *Cannoli*
is a 5-inch macaroni stuffed with spinach and meat. Empty, cannoli
becomes *calzoni. Ravioli* is the square of the family, stuffed with
meat or cheese. *Angolotti* is dwarf ravioli.

Their names are legion, and there are many more than I have
catalogued. But the water's boiling now and time to put the pasta
in. All of these varieties are cooked in about the same way. But
spaghetti being the most prized of all, let's talk about that for your
own spread. Here are some of the points which will guarantee you
the delicious results this grand food deserves. To begin with, use
the biggest pot in the joint to boil your water. Use no less than 6
quarts for every pound of pasta and more if you can. Put in a
couple of teaspoons of salt, and ½ cup of olive oil (an Italian
secret) to keep the pasta from sticking to itself or the pot. But,
mostly, keep that water boiling furiously, and don't drop your
pasta in until the hurly-burly is at its height. Even then, with the
water creating its own mixing currents, you'll want to stir it occa-

sionally with your biggest spoon, probing especially to make sure that none of the pasta is stuck to the bottom, where the heat is greatest.

The different kinds of pasta take varying lengths of time to cook, running from 10 minutes to twice that, depending on the thickness. The Italians like it barely tender—*al dente*. The best way to test your progress is not, of course, to risk taking out the whole amount. Take one or two samples out with your spoon, and cool under your cold water tap—don't try to get away without doing this, or you'll burn the roof of your mouth to vermicelli-like ribbons. When your pasta is done, lift it out of its water with a special spaghetti hefter, since, if you drain it in a colander, the starch-filled water will pour over the pasta and coat it. At this point many cooks prefer to rinse the pasta with a blast of cold water, to further reduce the starchy surfacing. But this obviously cools the pasta, no matter how quickly done, and then you have to go back into a reheating deal that threatens the texture of your dish.

You may now want to pour a little butter over the pasta to keep it from sticking together, although if you've done it right (and not overdone it, particularly) there should be no clinging.

Now for the sauce.

Here we have a bit of a problem. For this dish, which is so simple to prepare, must be eaten with sauce, and the sauce is a complicated and time-consuming specialty to prepare. That causes me to pronounce a heresy, to wit, that if you're lucky enough to find a practically home-made sauce in your locality, prepared in some nearby Italian kitchen and put on your grocer's shelf by the same hand that raised the tomatoes, utter a short prayer of thankfulness and buy it. It takes years of practice to make sauce as good as you enjoy in your favorite little Italian restaurant. An equal heresy is the suggestion that you buy one of the commercially packed brands and give it a couple of booster shots of your own: broil and add mushrooms; if it's a meat sauce brown a bit of ground beef and add; and—after tasting first—probably you can spice it a little by adding a speck of orégano, a bay leaf, and simmering gently to meld these goodly flavors with your boughten product.

But, lest heresy wax too eloquent, let us pause and reflect on what you must do if you would attempt the flight.

Here's the list of ingredients:

1 onion	½ cup water
¼ green pepper, diced	½ teaspoon salt
1 tablespoon olive oil	¼ teaspoon sugar
½ lb. ground hamburger	1 tablespoon chopped parsley
½ cup broiled sliced mushrooms	½ teaspoon orégano
1 garlic clove, minced	¼ teaspoon thyme
1 can (1 lb.) tomatoes (2 cups)	1 bay leaf
1 can (8 oz.) seasoned tomato sauce	½ pound cooked spaghetti
	Grated Parmesan cheese

Sauté the onion and the pepper in the olive oil. Then add the meat, mushrooms, and garlic, and stir until the hamburger is somewhat browned. Make sure that the bits of meat are well separated and not clinging together in lumps. Now add tomatoes, tomato sauce, water, salt, and sugar. Let simmer for a short time, to combine ingredients, then add remaining seasonings—parsley, orégano, thyme, and bay leaf. The latter is not just window dressing, but lends a most important bouquet and flavor to your sauce. Simmer without covering for from 2 to 3 hours, or until thick.

Remove the bay leaf, then ladle the sauce, piping hot, over your spaghetti, and sprinkle with grated cheese over all. *Bene.*

To make meat balls and spaghetti, follow the same procedure (omitting the ground meat) up to the point of removing the bay leaf, with the sauce done. Now take four slices of bread, and combine with 2 eggs, a pound of hamburger, and ½ cup grated Romano cheese, and give the meat a touch of garlic and orégano for itself. Shape into small balls, making sure that the ingredients are well distributed, and brown in hot oil. Add to the sauce, and cook together for another 30 minutes. Serve over spaghetti. *Molto bene.*

To make Marinara Sauce:

3 garlic cloves	Salt and pepper
1 sprig parsley	Orégano
½ cup olive oil	Bay leaf
1 large can tomatoes	

Chop the garlic fine and fry it and the parsley in the olive oil for a few minutes. Add tomatoes, season with salt, pepper, orégano, and a bay leaf. Simmer for about an hour, stirring from time to time, until thick. Serve over spaghetti. Top with grated Parmesan or Romano cheese.

To make Caruso Sauce:

6 chicken livers	1 can mushrooms
	Butter

Slice livers and mushrooms, not too fine, sauté in butter until nicely browned, and then add to marinara sauce as above. Test livers to make sure they are done before serving the sauce.

A Clam Sauce is given later, in Chapter 7, page 183, as prepared by Romeo Salta.

Macaroni Musing: It is hardly playing the gourmet to note that macaroni is superb with just sugar and butter over it, but 'tis so. Try it, and to sophisticate it a touch, if you wish, top it all with grated Parmesan cheese. Elbow macaroni is easy to handle and prepare (cook it the same as directed for spaghetti) and here are a couple of recipes for this family member, if such is your bent:

ELBOW MACARONI CREOLE

1 lb. sausage	1 teaspoon salt
1 medium onion, chopped	⅛ teaspoon pepper
1 green pepper, chopped	1½ teaspoons sugar
4 tablespoons sausage fat	½ lb. macaroni
1 No. 2½ can tomatoes (3½ cups)	Buttered bread crumbs

Fry sausage and cut into small pieces. Sauté onion and green pepper in fat until soft, add tomatoes and seasonings and simmer 15 minutes. Cook macaroni and arrange in alternate layers with sausage and tomato mixture in baking dish. Top with buttered bread crumbs and bake 30 minutes in a moderate oven (350° F.)

6 SERVINGS

EASY-DO MACARONI AND CHEESE

1 eight-oz. package elbow
  macaroni
1 teaspoon salt
2 cans cream of chicken soup
⅓ cup chopped onions
2 tablespoons chopped pimiento

4 hard-cooked eggs, diced
½ lb. Edam or Cheddar cheese,
  diced
½ lb. fresh mushrooms
2 tablespoons butter

Cook macaroni according to package directions except reduce salt to 1 teaspoon. Rinse and drain. Combine undiluted soup, onions, pimiento, eggs, and cheese with macaroni in 2-quart casserole. Sauté mushrooms in butter to garnish top of casserole. Bake 25–30 minutes in preheated 350° oven.   6–8 SERVINGS

And with your pasta what better than garlic bread?

Cut a loaf of French bread into thick slices, diagonally, cutting as deeply into the loaf as the bottom crust but not through it. Crush a garlic clove and cream it into a quarter of a pound of butter, and then butter each slice of bread on both sides, taking care to keep the loaf intact as it accordions out for you. Shut the loaf in a paper bag, twist or staple the bag shut, and bake in a 450-degree oven for 10 minutes. A variant on this is to mix butter with grated Parmesan cheese, instead of garlic.

COFFEE

There isn't much doubt that coffee is the national drink at present. Employers curse at it; hangover-ees bless it; employees send out for it while waiting for their coffee break; it is standard procedure to offer a business caller a cup of coffee if the matter at hand has any significance—meaning money—one way or the other.

The National Coffee Association, a parcel of energetic parties, claims that the universal coffee break is a happy custom in or out of the home. Of course, they *would* claim it was a happy custom. But just the same they have a point to make, and in this fact-ridden world they make it with unexpected charm.

An Ancient Arabian legend ascribes the discovery of coffee to a goatherd named Kaldi who noticed that his goats became very frolicsome after eating berries from a certain shrub. Kaldi told the abbot of a nearby monastery, who experimented by boiling the fruit in water. Its effect, he found, was so exhilarating that he ordered the decoction served to his monks to help them stay awake during their nightly prayers. This might be called the origin of the coffee break, a popular custom in the U.S. today. In fact, in a survey among industrial plants, 62 per cent credited the coffee break with a rise in productivity; 82 per cent reported a reduction in worker fatigue; and 32 per cent reported a decline in accidents.

Regardless of this, if the number of people who are not themselves until they've had a cup of coffee in the morning were lined up end to end, it would be quite a passel of strangers. In Turkey at one time a husband's refusal or neglect to give his wife coffee provided legitimate grounds for divorce, if you'll pardon the expression. So, learn to make good coffee and others will appreciate it—and so will you. If you use cream, make it fresh and heavy. Give the men sizable mugs, and the girls something dainty and figured. And give them coffee made like this:

Start with a thoroughly clean coffeemaker. Rinse coffeemaker with hot water before using. Wash thoroughly after each use. Rinse with hot water and dry.

Fresh coffee is best. Buy coffee in the size can or package which will be used within a week after opening.

Fresh water is important too. For best results start with freshly-drawn cold water.

For best results, use the full capacity of your coffeemaker. For lesser quantities use a smaller coffeemaker. Never, in any case, brew less than ¾ of the coffeemaker's capacity.

Consistent timing is important. After you find the exact timing to obtain the results desired with your coffeemaker, stick to it in order to get uniform results.

Coffee should *never* be boiled. When coffee is boiled an undesirable flavor change takes place.

Serve coffee as soon as possible after brewing. Freshly brewed coffee always tastes best. If necessary to let brewed coffee stand before serving, hold at serving temperature by placing the pot in a pan of hot water or over very low heat on an asbestos pad.

VACUUM METHOD

1. Measure fresh cold water into lower bowl. Place on heat.
2. Place filter in upper bowl. Add measured amount of "fine grind" or "drip grind" coffee.
3. When water boils, reduce heat or turn off electricity. Then insert upper bowl into lower bowl. Twist to insure a tight seal.
4. Let most of water rise into upper bowl. Stir water and coffee thoroughly. In 1 to 3 minutes, remove from heat, exact time depending on grind and strength desired.
5. When brew returns to lower bowl, remove upper bowl and coffee is ready to be served.
6. If a cloth filter is used it should be thoroughly rinsed after each use (no soap), and kept immersed in cold water until used again.

DRIP METHOD

1. Preheat pot by rinsing with hot water.
2. Measure "drip grind" coffee into filter section.
3. Measure fresh boiling water into upper container and cover.
4. When dripping is completed, remove upper section. *Stir brew* to mix before serving.

PERCOLATOR METHOD

1. Measure fresh cold water into percolator. Place on heat until water boils. Remove from heat.
2. Measure regular grind coffee into basket.

3. Insert basket into percolator, cover, return to heat, percolate slowly 6 to 8 minutes.

4. Remove coffee basket and serve.

STEEPED METHOD

Measure coffee into clean, scalded pot. Bring freshly drawn water to a boil; pour over the coffee; stir well. Cover and let stand on an asbestos mat over low heat or in a warm place 4 to 6 minutes. Strain.

Here are the amounts of ground coffee and fresh water needed to make any given number of servings of coffee. These proportions apply to all methods of brewing coffee. The basis is one Coffee Brewing Institute standard measure of coffee and ¾ of a measuring cup (6 fluid ounces) of water to yield approximately 5½ ounces of beverage. (A standard coffee measure equals 2 level measuring tablespoons.)

Average 5½ oz. Servings	Standard Coffee Measures of Coffee	Level Tablespoons	Standard Measuring Cups of Water	Ounces of Water
2	2	4	1½	12
4	4	8	3	24
6	6	12	4½	36
8	8	16	6	48

FOR LARGE QUANTITIES OF COFFEE

20	½ lb. coffee		1 gal. water
40	1 lb. coffee		2 gal. water

There are other ways to serve coffee than the everyday "straight" variety. If you'd like a little fun and some taste variations, try these.

Breakfast coffee cannot be used in recipes with satisfactory results, because the strong flavors of the other ingredients "drown" any but dark-roast Italian coffee. (A recommended brand is Medaglia d'Oro.)

Café Royale: Place lump of sugar in teaspoon filled with cognac and hold over demitasse cup of steaming coffee until cognac is heated. Ignite cognac and lower spoon into cup slowly, thereby firing the entire surface of the coffee.

Café grog: In a small vessel, put the following ingredients: 6

lumps sugar, 2 slices lemon, ½ pint fine rum, 1 pint coffee. Heat this mixture until it almost boils, then add a pony of brandy and serve.

Zabaglione caffe: Here is a dessert using coffee. For each serving take the yolk of 1 egg, 1 tablespoon sugar, and 3 tablespoons demitasse coffee. Place in top of double boiler over hot water and whip with a wire whisk until thick and light. Do not boil. Serve immediately.

Cappuccino: Start the day the Continental way. To ¾ cup of black coffee add a cinnamon stick and a dash of warm milk. Sugar to taste.

Café Soirée: Brew enough coffee for 6 demitasse cups. Place in saucepan 6 teaspoons sugar, 1-inch stick cinnamon, 4 cloves, 1 small curl orange peel. Add the coffee, heat to just below boiling point. Add 4 oz. rum, strain and serve. Top each demitasse with unsweetened whipped cream, if desired. Your guests will be enchanted!

Viennese coffee frost: Brew 6 cups double-strength coffee. While it is still hot, pour it over 4 crushed cinnamon sticks, 8 cloves, and 8 allspice berries. After an hour, strain the beverage and pour over ice in tall glasses. Sweeten to taste with sugar syrup and top with whipped cream.   4 GENEROUS SERVINGS

Turkish coffee: Although Turkish coffee is traditionally made in a tall, tapering pot open at the top, a conventional saucepan may be used. Mix 4 tablespoons powdered sugar with 2 tablespoons pulverized dark-roast coffee (if unavailable, fine grind vacuum coffee can be used in double strength). Add two cups of very cold water, and heat until it froths to the top of the pot. Allow the beverage to froth up three times in all, removing from heat each time. Let it settle, then serve in demitasse cups.

Café brûlot diabolique (as prepared at Antoine's Restaurant in New Orleans): 1 one-inch stick cinnamon, peel of 1 lemon, cut thin, 8 whole cloves, 3 lumps sugar, 3 jiggers brandy, 3 cups strong coffee. Place cinnamon, cloves, lemon peel, and sugar in a chafing dish. Place brandy in large ladle, ignite and pour over ingredients in bowl. Keep ladling brandy over ingredients until sugar is dissolved. Gradually add coffee, ladling the mixture until the flames fade. Serve immediately. For a dramatic effect, Antoine's dims the dining-room lights whenever Café Brûlot Diabolique is served.

Café cacao: Take a large cup of freshly brewed coffee, add jigger crème de cacao, top with whipped cream.

Café Cointreau: Place one teaspoon freshly grated lemon peel in large cup, add coffee until up to two-thirds full, add one jigger Cointreau.

Café au lait: Hold a pot of coffee in one hand and a pot of hot milk in the other and pour simultaneously.

Choco: Make hot chocolate with milk; to each quart of milk add 1 cup very strong coffee, 1 tablespoon sherry, pinch of salt. Serve with dash of whipped cream.

Hot coffee rum: Make 6 demitasse cups of very strong coffee. Rub 6 lumps of sugar on the rind of an orange, and place them with 6 cloves, a stick of cinnamon, and some thickly peeled orange rind in a chafing dish. Cover with rum and bring to a boil, stirring until sugar is dissolved. (Do not let it catch fire.) Add coffee, bring again to a boil, and serve at once.

And never forget that no one has ever spoken more eloquently of coffee than Talleyrand:

> *Pure as an angel,*
> *Sweet as love,*
> *Black as the devil,*
> *Hot as Hell.*
> Serve it that way, sir.

TEA

Something interesting is happening to tea. I don't mean that I am particularly impressed by the wash of English accents over TV and radio urging tea on us as if Rudyard Kipling were the midnight news broadcaster, giving us the lowdown on the Empah.

But perhaps the Madison Avenue boys are the hope of the Tea Party after all. Have you noticed how Mr. Big now asks his secretary for his *tea*—complete with Oriental china—while the wage slaves are busy quaffing their java? It seems to be something about status—it's in the bag.

Anyway, here's how to make it without having it taste as if you boiled up old sneakers and pieces of hickory bark to flavor your brew.

One to 2 teaspoons tea and two 8-ounce measuring cups boiling water make 3 cups of tea. Put the tea leaves in a warm teapot, pour the boiling water over them, and let steep about 3 or 4 minutes.

Then draw off immediately into the serving pot.

If you use tea bags, follow the same procedure, pouring the water over the tea.

There are many, many brands of tea, and dedicated tea drinkers will fight to the death to defend their favorite. If you—as I—drink tea, but not regularly, I recommend Constant Comment brand, which has orange and spices in it to achieve a really fragrant result. It'll remind you of those nights in Darjeeling, old boy, with the Lancers. Come in, Rud, you're on.

FAST MAN ON THE KITCHEN DRAWER: 21 QUICKIE DINNERS

Blessings on cannery row, the frozen tundra, on the bovine and poultry and farinaceous families for their by-products—but now you should be set for more extensive excursions into cooking with fresh chicken, meats, and fishes.

This is big-league stuff, but a chef has to be brought along as gradually as any ballplayer, and therefore your first expeditions will be carefully calculated both as to speed and complexity. All of the recipes in the following section wind up with a delectable dish: none of them, however, will involve an excessive amount of time in preparation, and the process is reasonably simple. This is still part of the cooking schedule we have created by which you can elude starvation, and so none of these is particularly recommended for entertainment purposes. But who are we to say what is your idea of making merry? These dishes might turn the trick precisely for you sometime. At any rate, they are recommended for your close study. These are fundamentals. This is a repertoire of survival, with just a first blush of the true chef-a-borning within you rising to the surface.

There are really two approaches to so-called "fast" cooking. One is where you do the initial preparation and cook it through from start to finish—fifteen minutes to an hour—stirring, adding, etc.

The second approach to fast cooking is a very brief preparation of 10 minutes or so; then leaving it to cook itself on top of the range or in the oven for the next 30 minutes to an hour, while you make a phone call, read the paper, drink your cocktail or what have you.

We give you a few examples of each:

FOIL-WRAPPED CHICKEN AND BACON

Buy some chicken legs or breasts. Wash and dry each piece, and sprinkle over a little salt, a touch of dried tarragon or orégano, a squeeze of fresh lemon. Encircle each piece of chicken with uncooked bacon. Wrap each chicken piece in foil, sealing it well. Tumble the pieces into a baking dish and put in a hot (425° F.) oven (preheat this as you start getting the chicken ready). Allow them to bake for 25 minutes. Remove from the oven, take off the foil, and slide the chicken back for 10 minutes to brown.

FRESH LIME BROILER

Buy small broiler chickens and have them quartered. Wash, dry, and rub with salt. Now mix this sauce (enough for three whole chickens): ½ cup lime juice, ½ cup peanut or corn oil, 3 tablespoons chopped scallions, 2 teaspoons dried tarragon, 3 squirts Tabasco sauce.

Place the chicken pieces on the broiler, skin side up. Brush with the lime sauce. Cook them slowly until tender. The rack should be 6 inches from the broiler flame. The cooking time will be about 1 hour, and the chicken should be turned and basted occasionally.

You can put in some potatoes to bake while this is going on, or some whole acorn squash, which can be split after baking, descooped of seeds, buttered, and seasoned. Add a salad, and you have a dinner.

SPECTACULAR FLAMING SQUABS

Allow 1 squab chicken to each person (ready to cook weight about 1 lb.). Leave chickens whole, wash, dry and rub with salt. Stuff with a small, peeled onion, a few sprigs of fresh washed parsley and a lump of butter.

Put the chickens on a rack in an open roasting pan. Roast in a moderate oven (350° F.) for about an hour till tender and brown. During the last half hour, brush several times with a little butter.

Transfer the chickens to a serving dish along with the pan drippings. Heat some brandy (allow 1 ounce per chicken) in a ladle or saucepan over the gas flame or alcohol burner. Pour the warmed brandy over the chickens and blaze them with a match. Continue to spoon the liquid over the chickens till flames die down.

ENTRECOTE AU POIVRE (PEPPER STEAK)

Buy ½ lb. sirloin steak per person (or more; those bones, you know). Trim off the fat. Take several whole peppercorns and roll them until they are coarsely cracked. (You can also buy coarsely cracked pepper in jars at fancy grocery stores.) Press the pepper into both sides of the steak. Heat half oil and half butter together in the heaviest frying pan you own. Allow about 2 tablespoons per steak. Get the pan good and hot till oil sizzles. Sear the steak quickly on one side then the other in the hot pan. Reduce the heat a bit and cook it to your individual taste. Remove to a hot platter and quickly make this sauce:

Add 3 tablespoons beef bouillon and 2 tablespoons cognac, plus ¼ teaspoon arrowroot to the pan drippings. Scrape the bottom of the pan, season to taste, and let the sauce bubble about 4 minutes. Pour it over the steak and sprinkle with a little finely chopped parsley if that's on hand.

BEEF TARTARE

Top honors in the uncooked school. Earned, obviously, by uncompromising insistence on the best beef you can buy.

About ½ pound of lean chopped beef per enthusiast is the order here. Avoid frozen beef like the plague for this one. Have your butcher grind the beef as near as possible to serving time, or, if you have to get the beef early, buy it in lean chunks and put it through the food chopper at the last minute.

Add whatever you like to the beef. Salt, freshly ground pepper, paprika, a little prepared mustard, or a little Tabasco sauce—all to your taste—are a few suggestions.

Take an onion and cut a couple of thin slices. Peel off a couple of the outside rings. Chop coarsely the middle part of the onion slices. Make a nice mound of the meat, and make a circle of the chopped onion around the outside. Inside of this make a circle of capers if you like. Put the onion rings in the center of the meat, encircling a fresh raw egg—an attractive way to serve Beef Tartare.

CHOPPED STEAK SKILLET SUPPER

Peel and chop a good-sized onion and a clove of garlic. Sauté in a heavy skillet in 1 tablespoon each butter and oil. Add 1½ lbs. lean chopped beef. Stir around with a fork till the meat is broken up and browned. Add salt, pepper, and a few drops of Worcestershire sauce to taste. Drain a medium-size can kidney beans and add these, plus a medium-size can stewed tomatoes. Simmer gently about 15 minutes till piping hot.

(If you prefer, cooked macaroni can be substituted for the kidney beans.) The above recipe will serve 6 persons. It can be easily adapted for a lesser number.

BRAISED PORK CHOPS

Buy some loin pork chops about an inch thick. Trim off the fat. Use some of the fat to rub the bottom of a heavy iron skillet. Season and brown the chops in the skillet over slow heat (about 3 or 4 minutes on each side). Top each chop with a thin onion slice, a thin lemon slice, and a light sprinkling of brown sugar. Pour 6 tablespoons bouillon into the skillet. Put a tight-fitting cover on the skillet. Continue to cook slowly on top of the stove about 35 minutes till chops are very tender.

SKILLET-BROILED GLAZED HAM

Buy a center slice of ready-to-eat ham about an inch thick. Cut off some of the excess fat and rub the bottom of a heavy iron skillet. Preheat your oven to hot or 400°. Cut slashes around the edge of the ham slice. Brown the ham in the skillet on top of the stove. About 5 minutes on each side should do it. Remove from fire and spread this glaze over the top: Mix together ½ cup brown sugar, 1 teaspoon prepared mustard, ¼ cup spiced fruit juice or sweet pickle juice.

Currant jelly can also be spread over the ham slice as an alternate glaze, or here is a really fancy and delicious one: To ½ cup Persian pomegranate seeds (purchased in health food stores or fancy grocery stores) add ½ cup honey, juices of ½ orange and ½ lemon, a little grated peel of each, and a pinch of cinnamon.

Whichever glaze you decide to use, spread it over the ham slice, and slide the skillet under the broiler for about 10 minutes or until hot and browned.

COUNTRY SAUSAGES, ETC.

The etc. consists of Polish sausages, Knockwurst, Bratwurst, or any fat sausage that you like. A combination isn't bad either. The procedure is:

Cover the sausages with water. Simmer for 20 minutes. Drain, and brown the sausages over a low flame. Turn from time to time. Do this carefully with a spatula or a couple of spoons so as not to break the skin. That's it. Good flavor mates with sausage are hot potato salad, hominy, or sauerkraut, and of course, cold beer.

BAKED LAMB CHOPS WITH STUFFING

Buy shoulder lamb chops about ½ inch thick. Season and brown them in a heavy skillet that can go in the oven a bit later. Preheat your oven to moderately slow or 325° F. Make a little bread stuffing: as many crumbs as necessary to cover nicely the number of chops you are cooking, a little chopped onion sautéed in a generous amount of butter till soft, a little chopped celery or celery flakes (dried), a sprinkling of dried rosemary, salt and pepper to taste.

Mix the stuffing together and spread it over the chops. Pour a little orange juice over the whole thing. Cover, and bake about 45 minutes till tender. Baby lima beans are particularly good served with this dish.

BROILED HERB LAMB CHOPS

Buy double lamb chops. Preheat the oven to very hot or 450° F. Make a slit in the thickest part of the chops. Cream some butter with a little finely chopped parsley or dried parsley flakes, a few finely chopped chives or scallions, and a sprinkling of rosemary. Caress the surface of the chops with a freshly cut clove of garlic, and rub in a light coating of olive oil. Pack opening in chop with seasoning. Seal the slit in the chops with toothpicks and place the chops on a rack about 2 inches under the broiler flame. Cook the chops 8 minutes for rare, 15 medium and as charred as you like for well done. Turn once to brown both sides, season and serve.

Hot matchstick potatoes and a few sprigs of washed and chilled watercress are good with the chops.

VEAL SCALLOPS

A perfect answer to short, short cooking. The scallops can be prepared in many different ways. Attention should be given to the veal, as the end result should be scallops tender enough to cut with a fork. Ordering ahead is necessary if you want to be assured of a good cut of veal and the proper preparation by the butcher. The loin is considered the best cut of veal for the scallops. The leg is the second choice. The scallops should be pounded *paper thin*. No matter how much you impress this fact upon your butcher, they usually never are, so be prepared to do a bit more beating when you get home. This can be done with any heavy object like an iron pan . . . or an antique flat iron . . . or a *real* meat pounder, if you're a stickler for the professional touch. If your butcher looks too glazed about the whole thing, seek out a good Italian butcher. They understand such things. Oh, yes! If you're pounding the scallops, place them between wax paper. The Italians call the meat "scaloppine," the French, "escalopes."

The meat is the important thing here. Now you can do all sorts of fancy but quick things with it such as:

SCALOPPINE ALLA MARSALA

A classic dish of southern Italy. For 6 people, order 1½ lbs. loin or leg of veal pounded paper thin and cut into 4-inch pieces. Get a heavy skillet good and hot, and to it add 3 tablespoons butter and 3 of olive oil. Dip the scallops in flour and shake off the excess. Brown in the sizzling oil quickly on both sides. (You may want to use two pans for this, or remove the first-browned scallops to a hot covered dish till all are browned.) Next pour in enough Marsala to barely cover the veal. Simmer over a low flame about 5 minutes. Remove the scaloppine to a hot serving dish. Lay paper-thin slices of lemon over them. Simmer the Marsala another minute or two while scraping the bottom of the pan. Add a bit more Marsala, if necessary. Sprinkle the scaloppine with salt and fresh pepper and pour the hot sauce over all. Top with a little chopped parsley.

ESCALOPES WITH CUCUMBER

Order a pound or so of veal scallops cut from the loin or leg and pounded paper-thin. Dry the pieces on a paper towel. Dip them in flour, shaking off the excess, and salt and pepper. Peel 3 medium cucumbers and cut in 1-inch slices. Place these in a saucepan with boiling, salted water and cook for 15 minutes or a little under till just tender. Put about 3 tablespoons each of butter and olive oil in a heavy skillet. When the pan is very hot, brown the veal pieces quickly on both sides. Put those browned first on a covered, heated plate to keep them hot. When all are browned, scrape up the brown residue in the bottom of the skillet and dissolve it with a little dry vermouth or dry white wine. Boil a couple of minutes, and slowly add 1 cup heavy cream. Continue to stir and bring to a boil. Remove the skillet from the flame and let the boiling sauce subside. Then bring to a boil again. Do this 3 times in all so the sauce reduces to a better consistency. Add a pinch of salt, fresh ground pepper, ½ teaspoon dried dill, and a dash of Worcestershire. Put the escalopes back in the cream to heat very slowly 3 or 4 minutes. Arrange the cooked cucumbers around the edge of a serving dish. Place the veal in the center, and pour the sauce over all. Sprinkle with a little paprika, and serve.

BREADED VEAL SCALLOPS

Buy 6 slices veal that have been pounded very thin. (Follow general advice for ordering scallops as given earlier.) Season with salt and pepper and dip in flour, shaking off all the excess. Beat 2 eggs till light in color. Dip the slices in the egg. Crumble up enough bread or soft rolls to make 1 cup of crumbs. Dip the veal slices in the bread crumbs. Two suggestions to help them stick: (1) tap them lightly with the flat edge of a knife, (2) chill before sautéing.

Cook the veal slices in a hot pan to which have been added 4 tablespoons butter and 4 of olive oil. Brown them nicely (about 5 minutes on each side).

Here are some garnishes for the scallops which can be prepared earlier, and at the last minute put onto the edge of the serving platter: Chopped hard-cooked white of egg, chopped hard-cooked yolk of egg, capers. (A little dab of butter, chopped parsley, thin lemon slices, and anchovy-wrapped olives pile up in that order on top of the scallops.)

BROILED FRESH BROOK TROUT

Clean the fish and leave whole. Make a couple of slits on each side to allow for skin shrinkage during the broiling. Season with salt and pepper and roll in flour and salad oil. Preheat your oven to moderate or 350° F. Place the fish on a hot buttered pan and broil them 9 or 10 minutes on each side, till the flesh flakes easily. Serve with a wedge of lemon, and a little melted butter. If you like, add some slivered almonds to the melted butter. Most any small fish can be broiled in this manner.

SHAD BAKED IN CREAM

For 6 people, buy a 3-lb. boned shad. Preheat your oven to moderately hot or 400° F. Place the shad in an oiled baking dish. Sprinkle with salt and pepper, and dot with butter. Bake for 20 minutes. Add 1 cup heavy cream and bake 10 or 12 minutes longer. Baste occasionally, sprinkle with chopped parsley and serve.

SWORDFISH GARNI

Buy 1 swordfish steak for each person. Preheat your oven to moderate or 350° F. For each swordfish steak, fry 2 pieces of bacon until crisp (crumble and set aside), 2 teaspoons slivered almonds (brown lightly in a little butter), and 1 teaspoon finely chopped onion or scallions. Put these all aside till later.

Make a butter sauce for the fish like this: melt 2 tablespoons butter, add ½ teaspoon chopped parsley, 1 teaspoon lemon juice, 1 teaspoon grated lemon rind.

Put the fish on a broiler pan that has been covered with foil. Top with a sprinkling of fresh pepper and a spoonful of the butter mixture. Broil for 10 minutes. Carefully turn the fish, and dribble over it another spoonful of the butter mixture. Broil another 10 minutes and remove to a hot serving platter. Pour over any remaining sauce and sprinkle with the bacon, almonds, and onions that you have prepared earlier. Serve with wedges of lemon.

SOLE IN VERMOUTH

Buy 2½ lbs. fresh sole filets. Pour 1¾ cups dry vermouth into a large skillet. Poach the fish in the vermouth about 9 minutes. (You can keep them from falling apart and they are much easier to extract from the steaming broth if you wrap them in a couple of thicknesses of cheesecloth and twist the ends so that the whole thing can be lifted out.) Put the fish on a broiler-proof platter, and preheat the broiler to hot or 450° F. Continue to boil the vermouth till it is reduced by ⅓ its original measure. Pour into the top of a double boiler. To it add 5 egg yolks which have first been blended with a little of the vermouth, ½ cup butter, and 2 tablespoons heavy cream. Cook this over hot but not boiling water and continue stirring till it is thickened. Season with a pinch of dry mustard, salt, and pepper to taste. Pour the hot sauce over the fish and brown it quickly under the broiler. Sprinkle with finely chopped chives and serve.

COQUILLES ST. JACQUES (SCALLOPS)

Buy fresh sea scallops . . . allowing 4 or 5 per person. Quarter them with a sharp knife. Wash the scallops under running cold water. Cover them with a dry white wine and cook gently about 6 or 7 minutes till barely tender. In another saucepan sauté half the contents of a small can of mushrooms in 2 tablespoons butter (or 6 chopped fresh mushrooms). Add 1 tablespoon finely chopped parsley and 2 tablespoons finely chopped scallions or shallots. Stir around a bit till bubbly, then blend in 2 tablespoons flour. Slowly add a cup of the hot wine in which the scallops were cooked. Stir until the sauce is thickened and add 2 tablespoons cream. Season with salt and pepper to taste. Add the scallops to the sauce and put the mixture in individual baking ramekins. If you have some of those baking shells that are sold in gourmet departments, you can be very authentic or perhaps you'd like to bake your own, using the ready-made, frozen variety. Sprinkle the top with bread crumbs and a few dots of butter and put under a hot broiler to brown.

On another occasion you might try the scallops in a curry sauce: Omit the mushrooms and parsley and add a tablespoon curry powder. Instead of bread crumbs, sprinkle with grated Swiss cheese.

BAKED FISH WITH OLIVES

Gently boil filet of flounder in salted water with 2 bay leaves and a few whole peppercorns. When cooked, drain off water and flake fish; put in casserole. Make cream sauce by blending 1 tablespoon flour with 1 tablespoon butter. Add 1 cup hot milk all at once and stir till thickened and smooth, season with a little grated onion, pinch of mace, salt and pepper; pour over the fish. Slice a few pimiento-stuffed olives and place on top. Bake in oven until a light brown, approximately 15 minutes.

MAKE MINE RARE:

from hoof to platter

This chapter calls for a meating of the minds.

It is about steaks, and that is a most difficult subject to bring about such a meeting. Every man seems to be his own expert on the subject of steaks.

Fine. No argument.

But here we will summarize the scene for you. This will be your Baedeker of beef.

And so I shall take you on a sentimental journey with a good friend of mine, John Bruno.

In person, John resembles Ezio Pinza when that great man appeared in *South Pacific*. John is built like a wrestler. He has a full head of hair. His eyes betray the fact that he is a devotee of grand opera, and he listens to it in the grand Continental style, sipping champagne in the lounge of the Metropolitan in between favorite arias, before returning to his center box. John has a baritone voice, not to be mentioned in connection with Pinza's, but in his own way he is also a perfectionist: at his restaurant in New York, the Pen & Pencil, you will get without a doubt the best steaks in the country.

I make this specific reference, not only because it is true, but because it is necessary for us to have a standard of quality.

Now, the U.S. Government has its own standards. The beef you eat is graded, starting at the top and moving down: *Prime, Choice, Good, Standard, Commercial, Utility, Cutter,* and *Canner.*

We are interested only in prime beef. Of all the cattle in the U.S. only about 3 or 4 per cent are prime. Out of this 3 per cent or so, about one-third of the cattle are known as "low prime." The other two-thirds are high prime.

And it is to go shopping for some good high prime steaks that we are going down to the New York City meat market with John Bruno. This is a modern hunt for the best piece of steak on the plains.

First a few statistics:

Each U.S. citizen eats a total of eighty-one pounds of beef on the average per year. If you multiply this by the population of the country, you'll realize how many pounds of meat that is, roughly, nearly thirteen billion pounds.

(Incidentally, you also consume an average of 354 eggs, 29.8 pounds of chicken, and 16.3 pounds of coffee.)

Of this huge total, we have noted that only the merest percentage is prime beef. And of this, about 90 per cent finds its way to the New York market. The necessity of fresh meat for the kosher market is partly the reason for this, and in addition the hotel and restaurant buyers in New York are willing to pay the same high prices.

The animals (about 20 per cent Black Angus and the rest Herefords) that find their way to this luxurious end, just before the final wreath of parsley is applied, start out in the great cattle-breeding areas of the country—Texas, California, Montana, Indiana, Iowa, Utah and the like. At the age of six or seven months, they are shipped to feeding lots in the Midwest, and put on a diet of grass, corn, and food additives. Each animal requires an acre of land on which to grow, on the average, so that if you're thinking of going into the feeding business don't start it in your own back yard. And furthermore, since the feeders now complain that the cost of the food for the steers, including the chemicals which are now all the rage, costs more per pound than they're able to get for the animal itself per pound, you might not think at all of becoming a feeder.

The steer, who is mercifully unconcerned with economics, thrives on his balanced diet to the tune of gaining at least 80 to 90 pounds per month. He arrives weighing about 500–600 pounds; he hits 1200–1300 when he graduates. If the lucky fellow is heading for the New York market, he gets a reprieve in Chicago, and is sent along alive to New York to be slaughtered there.

This is the beast we encounter now, as we follow John into one of the largest markets in the group clustered together on Manhattan's West Side, on Fourteenth Street, right by the Hudson River.

John and I stop by two suppliers—Gotham Hotel Supply and Davis & Co.—to buy his meat for the Pen & Pencil. We put on white butcher coats. John wears a Borsalino hat and a fur-lined coat to keep out the cold. Unforewarned, I wear a Knox hat and a trench coat, and do not keep out the cold. I should have worn my ski clothes, because we step into a refrigerated storage vault as big as an armory where the temperature is around thirty degrees all the time. I use the word "vault" advisedly, since one glance at all the beef stored here suggests that the value might be somewhere in the neighborhood of Fort Knox.

The meat in this particular section is hung in hind quarters, where the best steaks are. John is about to prove his reputation. The only restaurateur in New York who personally shops for his steaks, he carries with him a brass stamp with his Pen & Pencil mark on it. He's about to look at the one per cent or so which is at the top of the prime list, and he's prepared to be choosy.

At a signal from the manager, a couple of perspiring heavy-weights (they don't seem to mind the cold) swing the quarter in such a way that John gets a quick look at the cut across the bottom: the meat is strung up by the shank (the point just above the hind hoof) on a hook, and John judges from the look of the outside loin cut how all of the meat inside will be.

Both John and the men from the supplier's office wear the dreamy, rapt look of men judging a beauty contest. They like their work, obviously. No judge at a Miss America contest ever surveyed the entrants with a more critical or affectionate eye. They speak knowingly to each other of youth, conformation, and grain. They refer to the "bloom" still on certain carcasses recently slaughtered, and not subjected very long as yet to the refrigerator's cold. John looks with disfavor on one quarter which has an orange rather than a red hue. The suppliers explain to me that the beast was a glutton for grass and didn't pay enough attention to his corn. Bad habits will out in the end, you see.

Each time our Vic Tanny boys hoist the quarter, John stoops, casts a quizzical look at the open loin, and bellows *yes* or *no.* If *yes,* they whack the carcass with his stamp, and it's his for keeps. If *no,* and it's no most of the time with him, the heavyweights look a little hurt and rejected, and swing another quarter along on the overhead trolley, and heave it up for another look. It would not be entirely fair to the suppliers to tell how many John selected out of the hundreds he looked at, because the truth of it is that everything they have is the best, and he is not rejecting anything, but merely skimming the cream off the top of the cream. I can say, though, that there were times when the heavyweights looked downright blue, like girls not asked to dance for quite a series of numbers.

I cannot say precisely what John was looking for, because I have not been in the restaurant business for forty-six years, starting in the Savoy as a lad, and becoming the foremost authority on meat in the business, as John is. But in general he refines what the suppliers were looking for in the whole carcass—he looks at the inside shape of the steaks, the relationship of fat to meat, and in particular for the distribution of fat in the sinews of the meat. This is called "marbleization" and it has a lot to do with how the meat will cook, supplying its own fat in just the proper amounts, and also how it will taste. A coarse marbling suggests that possibly a really thick vein of fat will ruin a steak at the other end of the loin, so John yells no. An even, not too heavy, yet perceptible marbling—all else being considered—gets a yes from him.

Now, let us carry this search just a little further, until you see at length why I have not saved this experience for my autobiography or a novel, rather than wishing it on a cookbook.

John has now selected his meat. He buys by the "shell," each weighing about twenty-five pounds. He will get only about nine steaks from each shell. Here we get into some interesting mathematics.

John ages his meat, usually about three or four weeks, in the same refrigerator where he purchases it. He has his own special racks for this, and a fan continually plays upon the meat, a special Bruno drying process which hardens the outside into something of a shell, and preserves every drop of goodness inside.

So, *attendez:*

John has to buy his meat with the fluctuating market prices in mind. The price for prime has varied from a low of $1.55 per pound in recent years to a high of $2.30 a pound. Let us say he buys today somewhere in a middle bracket, at $1.95 a pound. Thus, for one shell he pays $48.75—and he gets nine steaks from each shell. Since each steak weighs one pound, where does the rest of it go?

1. During the aging process, the evaporation of excess moisture (and the fan trick increases this) causes a loss of from three to four pounds.

2. Then, when the bone is trimmed out and the excess fat cut off, everything over the actual nine pounds of steak served is waste.

The per-steak cost has now reached $5.42. When you add overhead to this basic price, you can begin to understand the problems of a restaurateur trying to ask a fair price for his steak.

You have to realize that steak of this quality never filters down into the market where you buy your meat, and so you must dine out if you want the finest Delmonico cuts, and appreciate the economics which went into setting its price level. The suppliers told me that many of the buyers for the big restaurant chains simply walk over and buy the rest of any carcass John Bruno stamps to reserve his shells. After that, they buy on their own, generally not taking the trouble to be as selective as John.

If you do find a small meat market in your neighborhood, the butcher there might have a small chance of getting a Delmonico cut or shell steak, if he's got friends in the supplier's who can let him in from time to time on a large purchase. Supermarkets will never have this quality in their cuts at any time, no matter how appetizingly it may be wrapped. In your shopping, however, you must appreciate in advance that there's no such thing as a bargain in buying steaks. The grading down the line comes out in the price: if your butcher is honest, the best meat is the most expensive every time. Your only "bargain" will happen if he gets a special purchase of some better-than-usual meat—and then your bargain will cost you more!

That's the scene in the market, then.

Now, let's apply it to your own skillet.

All of the best cuts for steaks come from the loin. The tenderloin, or filet mignon, is the highest-price steak, and the pin-bone sirloin the lowest. The others you'll want are in between.

You'll want to buy about a pound each for men, if they're your guests, and if there are women (the more fragile sex?) aboard you can figure them for closer to one-half pound each. The statistics should go up a little if your steak has a bone in it, since you're going to have that weighed in (and pay for it) and only pooches look kindly on a bone as a proper diet.

Usually have your steak cut for broiling from one to two inches thick. If you want to have it extra rare, you can go another inch, and cook it longer.

Here are the steaks you'll want to know about:

Delmonico (club or shell) is the smallest cut that can be taken from the loin and is therefore excellent for you alone or for a couple. It contains little or no tenderloin, but is consistently tender and yet firm throughout.

Filet mignon comes from a long strip of meat lying directly under the chine, or backbone. (The tenderloin is sometimes served entire as a roast, and is naturally very delicious.) Men as a rule find filet mignon a little too soft and pliable in texture, and usually prefer the more pronounced flavor of a sirloin cut.

T-bone steak comes from the loin, next to the Delmonico, but is larger and contains some tenderloin. Identified by the T-shaped bone. Well marbled.

Porterhouse steak is often confused with T-bone. Actually, it is a T-bone with a larger proportion of tenderloin. It is well marbled, with a characteristic portion of fat.

Sirloin, from the loin end. (The name did not come, as in the aprocryphal tale of an English king knighting the loin because he liked the meat so much. It originated as the sur-loin, that is, above the loin; it is above the other steaks.) Sirloin steaks vary in size, shape, and bone size. The wedge-bone steak is largest. Others are round-bone, pin-bone, and double-bone steaks.

Round steak is not cut from the loin at all, but obtained from the leg. It is practically all lean meat. Oval in shape with small round bone. He had to use this steak to run with, while those above went along for the ride, so, for broiling purposes, better pick the passengers. However, bottom or top round makes good enough hamburger. I personally prefer to have chopped meat made out of the best steak meat, to get that wonderful quality meat flavor, and believe that the hamburger has been degraded by being made of the lesser cuts. They make it out of the flank ends of the steak (the "tail" on your steak) part of the rump, and from the chuck (which is the shoulder section of the steer), as well, and these are all good to steer clear of, although edible.

Chuck steak is a shoulder cut. Let it go.

Flank steak is a piece of muscle with the meat fibers running lengthwise. Nyet.

And, for your further disinterest:

Short ribs. These are cut from the ends of the ribs and from the plate, the area just above the navel.

Brisket. Aft and forward of the front leg, on the bottom of the beast, forward of the navel.

Corned beef consists of various of the less tender cuts, usually preserved in brine, at the market. Some housewives do it themselves to save money. Never mind, it ain't worth it.

And while we're about it, the liver, heart, tail, and tongue of the steer are also consumed by humans.

Tripe is the muscle of the first stomach of the steer. It is boiled and then pickled to make it, as they say, palatable.

Sweetbreads are the thymus and thyroid glands of the calf (located in the throat) or the pancreas (located in the hold).

Salisbury steak is a melange of chopped meat, formed into an oblong or steak shape, and then pan fried.

Among the roasts of beef:

Rib roast beef is the best. It sets amidships, on the top of the animal, where you'd put a saddle, and is his chest cage. The *prime* ribs are the best—that is, these are the ones closest to the loin of the beast. Starting from the back, the first three ribs are the best, and then they run all the way through to the front of the animal, the "prime" area including the eighth rib, but stopping there as the remaining ribs, up to number thirteen, run into the chuck.

Rump roast beef comes from the spot between the loin and the bottom round. This meat is very good in flavor, and juicy, but not tender unless the beef itself is in prime condition.

And now to the business of broiling your steak:

As I explain in Chapter 8, on outdoor cookery, I am of the opinion that you should charcoal-broil your steak at every possible opportunity, even if you have to stand out in the snow to do it.

Second to that I am for ceramic broiling, which a restaurant such as the Pen & Pencil employs, since the heat intensity is distributed evenly by the ceramic blocks, which function in the oven as do your charcoal blocks outdoors. But this is impractical in the home, and such equipment hardly exists (although certain ceramic portables are now available for outdoor cooking).

That brings us to pan broiling vs. the oven broiler.

Most kitchen broilers have only a ring of flame, or wiring, to bring the heat to the meat, and although this is adequate for providing oven heat for casseroles, pies, etc., it does not offer the even distribution of heat needed to sear the meat equally in all its parts and start the proper breakdown of that marbling we've been talking about, or an even cooking of the meat. However, if you're for this, here's how to go about it (I'll concede the point that with a large porterhouse or T-bone, it might be necessary):

1. Preheat the broiler with regulator set at *broil*.

2. Slash the fat edge of the steak so that it won't curl up when the heat reaches it.

3. When you preheat the oven, preheat the broiling pan and rack too. When hot, rub down the broiler rack with a bit of fat from the meat to prevent the steak from sticking.

4. The steak should be at room temperature, not chilled, when you put it in. Lay it on the broiler rack with top of steak 2–5 inches from source of heat: A 1-inch steak goes 2-3 inches from the source of heat. A 2-inch steak 3-5 inches from source of heat.

5. Broil until top side is browned. Season.

6. Turn until second side is browned. Season.

Broiling time depends upon thickness of steak and degrees of doneness desired. Authorities differ on this, but a fair table of broiling time is (minutes per side):

Thickness	*Rare*	*Medium rare*	*Well done*
1 inch	5 min.	6½ min.	7 min.
1½ inches	8 min.	10 min.	11 min.
2 inches	15 min.	18 min.	19½ min.

The truth of the matter is that such a table can, at best, only be an estimate. You can't explain how to broil a steak with a chart, like tying a knot. It becomes a matter of trial-and-error for a while, which is described more usually with the uptown word "experience." You won't spoil the steak if you give it an incision close to the bone to have a look, about midway along your broiling. Keep your eye on it as it cooks, too. A steak talks back to you, makes signs at you, and these you must commit to memory, so that when you have your first brilliant success, you'll know how you did it. It will

be different the next time after that, nevertheless, because each piece
of meat is different. But you're in the heartland now: you know
what's to be done, and you can ride with the punches as any small
exceptions begin to take place.

Pan broiling is for me, however. A good heavy iron skillet, solid
enough to translate the heat below it into an evenly tempered
broiling surface, is incomparable for working on the fats and sinews
of the meat, the same way at the same time.

There is a school of thought that suggests rubbing the bottom of
the pan with a bit of fat, just enough to keep the steak from stick-

ing, and then waiting until the fat begins to smoke over a hot fire. Then you place your steak therein, with the fat well trimmed off beforehand, and broil until one side is brown. Season, then turn with tongs to prevent piercing the meat, and brown the other side.

Others suggest searing meat on both sides immediately, and then cooking over reduced heat on both sides.

This method of hot blast to sear, low fire to cook is the one I prefer. John Bruno's own method is the best I know for this. He takes the pan, runs some cold water into it, and then empties out the water, leaving the inside just moist. The steak goes in, and now the first side is seared over a medium fire. Turn, and sear other side. Now, turn again, and cook over a low fire until brown. Turn again, and cook over a low fire until desired doneness is achieved. Season.

Since a man must take some stand in this world, I take it against seasoning the honest meat before it is broiled. This is not only because it may affect the cooking deleteriously by blocking up the follicles of the meat, but because the kind of steak we've been talking about is just about the finest flavor a man can eat in this world without any outside help. I'm excepting salt and pepper, of course, which seem to be a permanent part of our civilization.

Seasoning after cooking is a little more sensible. I prefer a butter sauce. Cream a quarter of a cup of butter for each steak, and into it mix 2 tablespoons each of chopped parsley and green onions, and perhaps a tablespoon of paprika or catsup. The parsley alone does very nicely, by the way. You can also mix a mashed clove of garlic in with the butter for a nice seasoning. Another way to get your garlic taste is to sprinkle the steak with garlic juice or garlic sauce.

Some men like mashed Roquefort or bleu cheese spread lightly on top of their steaks. Others prefer to squeeze a bit of lemon over the well-buttered steak.

In the field of prepared seasoning, you can cream your ¼ cup of butter once more, and mix it with a tablespoon of Worcestershire sauce for a neat flavor. There are a number of prepared seasonings that you might do well to have on the table, to permit your guests a choice.

And lastly, put a bit of Escoffier Sauce Diable on the side of your plate, and touch every other piece of meat to it, lightly.

And, as accompaniments, packaged frozen French fries will do beautifully, and the French Fried Onion Rings, prepared as follows. If parsley is not used in your steak seasoning, place a few sprigs over the steak itself—looks fine, and lots of people like to chew on the stuff, straight.

FRENCH FRIED ONIONS BRUNO

Use Bermuda, Chilean, and Idaho onions—mixed is best, but singly if you must—and slice about ⅛ of an inch thick. After the slices are cut, separate and place in a container, covering them with milk. Allow them to soak until well impregnated. Then remove from container, place on a cloth, and toss in flour until the milk-soaked onion rings have absorbed the maximum of flour. Then place them in a deep fryer and cook for five minutes at 350°. The Pen & Pencil uses melted suet, but you can use Crisco or other pure vegetable shortening made from hydrogenated vegetable oil. After the five minutes are up, transfer the onion rings to another deep fryer bubbling at 500°. The cooking of the onion rings is complete when they turn a golden brown. They will be hot, crisp, grease-less, and perfect for your steak dinner. And—although there's a probability on this just short of a guarantee—onion rings prepared this way are kinder to your digestion. My experience has been that they seem to like you: and you'll like them, without a doubt. This is an art perfected at the Pen & Pencil, where a special chef fries onion rings exclusively.

If you want to reach the heights in steak artistry, then set your sight for

PLANKED STEAK

This is a steak that has been broiled or pan broiled for about 8 minutes. Then it is placed on a hardwood plank, which has been well-buttered. Mash potatoes and to each 2 cupfuls add 4 teaspoons milk, 1 tablespoon butter, and 1 egg. After these materials have been mixed well into the potatoes arrange a border of potatoes around the edge of the plank. Then garnish the steak with a combination of cooked vegetables—asparagus tips, string beans, peas, tiny onions, small carrots, mushrooms, stuffed peppers, etc. (If onions, mushrooms, or carrots are used, sauté them first in a bit of butter in a frying pan to make sure they are thoroughly cooked and a bit brown.) Garnish the steak with the selected vegetables. Then place the plank in a hot oven or under the broiler and allow it to lie there long enough to brown the potatoes, cook the steak a little more, and thoroughly heat all the vegetables. Butter the steak well when removed, season with salt and pepper, and serve.

MAIN EVENT:

host with the roast

In the argot of the sports world, a football coach often tells the sportswriters: "We're stressing fundamentals this year." Translated, this means: "The lead-footed clowns I'm stuck with won't win a game. All I can do is teach 'em to block and tackle, and then try to keep the scores down."

In the argot of the culinary world, there are certain similar symbolic phrases, such as: "That was a lovely little casserole you gave us tonight, Scraghead old boy. Thanks ever so much." Translated, this means: "Too bad you can't really cook. Maybe what you fed us used to taste great back in the reformatory, but we were really expecting something solid—like a roast."

In other words, a fundamental.

These are the classic dishes, the basics, the ones you have to know how to cook before you can say you're a chef. Up until now, we've been hedging a little on the main brace: we worked with prepared foods, or flexed our muscles in short-time short orders. But now is the time to face the realities. This is not the ultra-style cooking— that we'll get to later. But this is the heart of the matter: so now, take heart.

POT ROAST

A basic which demands little of the cook in preparation time or $ outlay. A combination of meat, vegetables, and gravy slowly cooked together. The meat may be any cut of beef, lamb or veal that is not tender enough for roasting, but lends itself beautifully to browning and flavorful *slow-cooking*. That latter part is important; as the point is to soften the tough connective tissue, which is achieved only through moist heat—given time.

For a beef pot roast weighing from 3 to 5 lbs., the cooking time is 3½ to 4 hours.

BEEF POT ROAST

For this roast it is best to use the chuck or round. For a 4-lb. roast (bone in), rub the meat with a combination of flour, salt, and pepper and brown it on both sides in a little fat. Heat the fat first in a heavy kettle or Dutch oven. You don't want the meat to burn while cooking, so it is best to place the meat after browning on a rack or on 3 jar covers which you have punched with holes.

Add a little less than 1 cup water to the kettle plus 1 small bay leaf, 1 clove garlic, minced, ½ cup sliced onions, ½ teaspoon dry mustard, ½ teaspoon paprika. Cover tightly and cook very slowly 3½ to 4 hours on top of the stove. Turn the meat once or twice during the cooking. The liquid should be kept at ½-inch depth during the cooking, so add more water if necessary. If you wish to add vegetables to the roast, do so about 40 minutes before the meat is done. Scraped whole carrots (about 8 small), peeled and quartered potatoes (8 small), celery stalks (6 or 7 cut the same length as the carrots), and small white onions (8 or 9, left whole).

8 SERVINGS

One of the best accompaniments for a roast or braised meat dish is plenty of good brown gravy. Perfect gravy is easy to make. After a little experience, you can do it without even a sidelong glance at a measuring cup. But at first it pays to measure ingredients carefully.

POT ROAST GRAVY

Remove meat from pan to hot platter.

Pour all liquid and fat into separate container. Meat juices and cooking liquid will settle to bottom. Fat will rise to top. Skim off fat with spoon, returning only 4 tablespoons of liquid to pan. Heat and stir in 4 tablespoons flour gradually.

Cook over low heat, stirring constantly until smooth and thickened. Scrape bottom of pan to loosen any meat particles.

Season to taste with salt and pepper and, if desired, a dash of Worcestershire sauce, pinch of herbs, or a spoonful of horseradish.

ROAST LEG OF VEAL

Buy a 4-lb. leg of veal—boneless. Have your butcher tie it securely. (Serving generality: here allow ½ lb. of meat per person for a roast with bone; ⅓ lb. meat per person for a *boneless roast*.) With a sharp knife make about 6 deep thrusts evenly spaced over the roast. Into each cut place a very thin sliver of garlic and a little anchovy paste (or anchovy filets that have been pounded to a paste). Rub the roast with olive oil, salt, and freshly ground pepper. Roast in a slow oven (325° F.) about 2⅔ hours till tender. In the roasting pan surround the meat with 1 coarsely chopped carrot, 1 coarsely chopped onion, a small bay leaf, a pinch of thyme, and 1 cup dry white wine. Baste occasionally during the cooking.

CROWN ROAST OF PORK

Have crown made at market from strip of pork loin containing 10 to 12 chops. (For easy carving, have backbone removed.) Season with salt and pepper. Place in roasting pan, bone ends up; wrap bone ends in aluminum foil to prevent excess browning. Roast uncovered in slow oven (325° F.) 35 to 40 minutes per pound of meat. An hour before meat is done, fill center with 1 cup coarse dry bread crumbs, ¾ cup chopped apples, 3 tablespoons chopped raisins, ½ teaspoon salt, 2 tablespoons sugar, 2 tablespoons minced onion, dash of pepper and sage, 2 tablespoons melted butter or margarine.

To serve roast, replace foil wraps with spiced crab apples or paper frills. Garnish platter with parsley. To carve, slice between the ribs. 10 to 12 servings.

Note: If stuffing isn't used, place roast in pan with bone ends down so fat from roast bastes rib ends. At serving time, center may be filled with roast potatoes or other vegetables.

To roast potatoes, peel and quarter them; parboil for 12 to 15 minutes and spread out in roasting pan 30 to 35 minutes before meat is done.

Place any remaining stuffing in pan around roast, or place in greased casserole and dot with butter; cover; bake with roast for last hour of cooking time.

ROAST LEG OF LAMB

If you like your lamb cooked pink as the French do, cook it at 375° F. for 12 minutes to the pound. If you prefer it well done, cook it about 18 minutes to the pound. Allow the meat to arrive at room temperature before you begin the roasting.

Cut small slits in the leg of lamb and insert very thin slivers of garlic. Rub the surface of the fat with 1½ teaspoons dried rosemary (which you have muddled about a bit), salt, freshly ground pepper, and a good squeeze of fresh lemon juice. Turn and baste occasionally while cooking.

After roasts are cooked, they slice easier if you let them stand about twenty minutes.

GRAVY FROM OVEN ROAST

In making gravy from an average-sized rib roast of beef or pork, veal and lamb roasts, the procedure is this:

As no water is added to the roast during cooking, only fat and drippings are left in the pan. Skim off all but 2 or 3 tablespoons fat; stir in 2 or 3 tablespoons flour and slowly add 1 to 1½ cups water. Cook over low heat until well thickened, stirring constantly. Season to taste. (When a rib roast of beef is cooked to the rare stage, there will be few drippings and it will not yield much gravy. In this case use less fat, flour, and liquid.)

STUFFED BREAST OF LAMB

2-lb. lamb shoulder roast cut "cushion style" and boned	3 tablespoons butter
	2 cups bread stuffing mix
1 teaspoon rosemary	1 cup dairy sour cream
⅔ cup water	½ small garlic clove

Preheat oven to 325° F. Wipe roast with damp cloth; sprinkle with rosemary. Fasten three sides of roast together with metal skewers.

In saucepan combine water and butter; bring to boil. Stir in stuffing mix; blend in sour cream. Fill pocket of roast with part of stuffing; fasten open edges together with metal skewers. Cut slits in fat side of roast; insert slivers of garlic. Place roast fat side up on rack in shallow roasting pan; insert meat thermometer in meat. Spoon extra stuffing into 2-cup casserole; bake along with meat. Roast meat 1¾-2 hours, or until thermometer indicates 182°. Remove skewers and garlic from roast; place on platter with extra stuffing.

ROAST PRIME RIBS OF BEEF

Start with the best and manipulate as little as possible. Look for the United States Department of Agriculture stamp indicating the quality of the meat. When you've gone far enough to choose this cut of beef, you'll surely want to go all the way and demand prime beef or the second best, which is choice. This is a costly treat, especially if you go on to the top strata and demand *aged beef* and the first three ribs.

If you have followed the rules above, you have just purchased the best beef available, so let's go on to the best possible cookery for said beef.

(Fresh rather than frozen beef is recommended, but if you do use frozen beef and are going to roast it unthawed, allow 15 to 20 minutes more time per pound than for a thawed roast.) If you like *rare* roast beef, cook it about 18 minutes to the pound. *Medium* will require about 22 or 23 minutes to the pound and *well done* can go to 33 or 34 minutes per pound. The really accurate way to test is with a meat thermometer. A reading of 130 would indicate rare, 140 for medium, and 160 means your meat is well done.

The roast should be removed from the refrigerator at least an hour before it goes into the oven so it will be close to room temperature; and the oven should be preheated to slow (or 325° F.). This modern way of roasting meats at low temperature prevents great shrinkage and spattered ovens and the finished result is a juicier one.

Rub the roast with salt and pepper and place it fat side up on a rack in an open roasting pan. If you use a meat thermometer, insert it through the outside fat in the thickest part of the muscle. The point should not rest on bone.

Roast the meat till the thermometer or your clock indicates the desired state of doneness has been arrived at. Remove the roast to a hot platter, and let it rest about 20 minutes before carving. To make the gravy, follow the recipe given earlier for Gravy from Oven Roasts. You may, however, prefer only the natural juice spooned over the beef with no thickening whatever added. Then carefully pour off the fat from the roasting pan, scrape the bottom and sides of the pan to loosen the nice dark drippings, add about 1¾ cups boiling water and some strong stock or 2 bouillon cubes. (Bovril is good too.) Boil this up, and if you have used the bouillon cubes, stir till dissolved. Serve in a separate bowl, and as you carve the roast spoon the juices that exude over the slices as well.

Be sure that your roast beef slicing knife is very sharp. So that the appetite will match the anticipation, it is suggested that only a cup of clear, hot consommé be served before this rare treat.

ROAST TURKEY

Roasting the bird at high temperature wrapped in heavy-duty foil cuts the roasting time nearly in half and produces a delicious moist turkey. Here is how you do it: Choose your bird weighing in any- where from 6 to 24 lbs. Go over the surface with a sharp eye and pick out any pin feathers. A tweezers is helpful here. Singe the bird over a gas flame if necessary to remove fine fuzz. Wash the turkey and thoroughly dry inside and out. Salt the inside and stuff. You can get very creative over a stuffing. It can consist of chestnuts, sausage, giblets, wild rice, herbs, and many such tempting things mixed together with bread. Or you can fill the cavity with several sprigs of fresh vegetables and herbs like parsley, onion, celery, tarragon, etc. A good and simple bread dressing dry, rather than soggy, goes like this:

Break a loaf of good-quality bread into small crumbs. It should be a day or two old. Add 2 tablespoons fresh chopped parsley, a light sprinkling of water, 1 teaspoon dried thyme and ⅔ cup melted butter. Dribble the butter over the other ingredients, add salt to taste, and mix lightly. Don't pack the stuffing tightly into the tur- key—just spoon it in loosely, as it will expand while cooking. To truss, fasten the opening together with small-size skewers, then, using a strong white string, lace it between the skewers till the opening is closed; or if you have a very large needle and some stout thread, sew the opening closed. Tie the leg ends and the tail together. Pull the neck skin up and fasten to the back with a skewer.

Tie the wings close to the body of the bird. Don't make the string so tight that it will break the skin when the turkey begins to roast.

Preheat your oven to hot or 450° F. If you are roasting a frozen turkey, defrost it completely before cooking.

The turkey must be carefully and properly wrapped, so that you do not puncture the foil. First of all, the foil should be heavy duty. If the bird is not more than 16 lbs. (ready to cook weight), an 18-inch width will do. If it is larger, you will have to splice two 18-inch widths. First, in order to prevent puncturing the outside foil, take several small pieces of the foil and cover the wing tips, the ends of the legs, and the tail. Tear off a long piece of foil about three times the turkey's length and place it on a table. In the center of the foil, place some fresh celery leaves and some rings of onion. Place the turkey on top of these, breast side up. Spread some soft butter all over the bird, and overlay a few more onion slices on the breast and legs. Bring the foil up and over both ends of the turkey, making sure it overlaps at least 3 inches. Press this top foil down close to the turkey, securing the ends. Then bring the foil from the sides of the bird up over the top, letting it extend up 2 to 4 inches. Fold it over lightly, but do not secure it tightly, as the circulation of air is important.

Put the turkey in a roasting pan and cook according to this time-table:

Ready-to-Cook Weight (lbs.)	Total Cooking Hours at 450°
6 to 9	2¼ to 2½
10 to 13	2¾ to 3
14 to 17	3 to 3¼
18 to 21	3¼ to 3½
22 to 24	3½ to 3¾

Open the foil 20 minutes before the cooking time is due to expire. Test for doneness. Move the leg joint up and down. If it moves easily or breaks, it is time to brown the turkey. Fold back all of the foil and spoon over the bird the juices that are in the bottom of the foil. Let the turkey brown to a deep golden color.

A nonthickened gravy can be made very successfully with turkey that has been roasted by the high temperature because there are sufficient brown drippings to make a rich sauce. After you have removed the bird to a hot platter, pour all the juice from the foil into the roasting pan. Skim off as much of the fat as possible. Add 2 cups boiling water to the pan and simmer, scraping any crustiness off the bottom of the pan. Season to taste with salt and pepper.

ROAST CHICKEN

A 3- to 5-pound chicken will take from 2 to 3 hours to roast. Small broiling chickens or frying chickens can be deliciously roasted in about 1½ hours by this method:

Wash and dry chickens inside and out. Remove any pin feathers. The chickens may be stuffed with any good bread stuffing; but just placing fresh vegetables and herbs in the cavity gives a wonderful flavor and aroma. Rub the inside of the chicken with salt. Wash and dry several sprigs fresh parsley, and place them in chicken together with an onion cut in half and a good tablespoon butter. When fresh tarragon is obtainable, it can be used instead of the parsley.

Place the chicken on a rack in an open roasting pan. *Do not* oil the outside of the chicken. Don't do a thing with it at this point. Put the chicken into a *cold oven* and roast at a low temperature— 325° F. Roasting the chicken in this way will take a bit longer, but the taste and juiciness are superb. About the time the chicken should be done, test it by piercing thigh with a fork. The juice should run out clear with no touch of pink. At this point, pour melted butter and salt over the surface of the chicken. Turn the oven to 400° F. and allow the chicken to brown about 10 minutes.

Sometime try spreading the chicken with Escoffier sauce instead of the butter at this last cooking stage. The sauce can be purchased at fancy grocery stores, and is very good with chicken. Serve the chicken with only the natural juice spooned over it. Wild rice, glazed carrots and a salad help to make it a memorable meal. A good bottle of wine helps too.

A CLASSICAL DUCKLING
Sauced with Vermouth and Oranges

5- to 6-lb. duckling	2 oranges
Salt	¾ cup sweet vermouth
2 tablespoons flour	2 tablespoons lemon juice

Rub duckling with salt inside and out. Truss and roast in hot oven (400° F.) 30 minutes. Remove bird from pan. Pour off all but about 2 tablespoons of the fat in pan. Add flour and stir over heat to form a well-browned paste. Add juice from 1 orange plus water sufficient to measure 1 cup. Cook to a smooth sauce. Add ½ cup sweet vermouth. Return duck to pan, baste with the sauce; cover. Roast in moderate oven (350° F.) 1 to 1½ hours. Remove skin from second orange and parboil this skin. Scrape out the inner white lining and discard. Cut skin into very thin strips and add to sauce in roaster shortly before duck is done. Section the orange pulp.

To serve: Remove duckling to platter and garnish with orange sections. To sauce, still in pan, add remaining ¼ cup sweet vermouth and lemon juice. Heat gently to blend, pour small amount over the bird and serve remainder in a sauce boat.   4 OR 5 SERVINGS

DOUBLE PORK CHOPS WITH STUFFING

Buy 6 double loin pork chops. Wipe them with a damp cloth and cut a deep slash or pocket in the meaty side of each chop. Preheat your oven to 350° F.—or moderate.

Mix this stuffing: Wash and dice 2 medium cooking apples, leaving the peel on. Chop 2 medium onions and 2 stalks celery (leave some leaves on) fairly fine. Mix with apples, plus 2 teaspoons salt, a grating of fresh pepper, and ½ teaspoon poultry seasoning (sage could be substituted for the poultry seasoning).

Fill the pockets in the chops with as much of the stuffing as you can get in. Let it bulge out a bit, as this looks interesting. Place the chops in a baking dish and sprinkle with salt, pepper, and poultry seasoning. Cover the baking dish with a tight cover and bake the chops about 1¼ hours or until tender when they are pierced with a fork. Remove the cover and allow to bake an additional 20 minutes or so till very brown. Pork should be very well done. Cooked red cabbage is a perfect flavor mate for the chops.

BRAISED OX JOINTS

2 oxtails	1 bay leaf
Flour, fat	4 cloves
2 medium onions, chopped	1 cup canned tomatoes
½ teaspoon celery salt	1½ cups water
Salt	Cooked noodles

Have meat man cut oxtails into 2-inch pieces. Wipe with a damp cloth and roll in flour. Brown thoroughly in several tablespoons fat in Dutch oven or large, heavy kettle. Add onions, seasonings (including 1 teaspoon salt), tomatoes, and water. Cover and cook slowly for 3-4 hours or until meat is nearly falling from bone. Add more water during cooking as necessary. Remove ox joints to platter and keep warm. Skim fat from gravy and stir in 1 tablespoon flour blended with 2 tablespoons cold water. Add water to gravy to dilute to strength desired. Season to taste. Serve ox joints with buttered noodles and top both with gravy.   4 SERVINGS

OLD-FASHIONED BEEF STEW

Buy 2 lbs. chuck or bottom round and have it cut in 2-inch pieces. Roll the meat in flour that has been seasoned with salt and pepper. Shake off the excess flour. Put 2 tablespoons cooking oil in a heavy pot with a tight-fitting cover (a Dutch oven really functions perfectly here). (Don't cover the pot yet; you're just being forewarned.) Cut a small onion into rings. Sauté these in the fat and remove. Add the beef and brown the pieces well on all sides. Add 1 quart boiling water in which you have dissolved 3 bouillon cubes. Add also ½ teaspoon Worcestershire sauce, 1 small bay leaf, the onion rings which you have browned, ½ teaspoon paprika, 1 clove garlic, and 2 sprigs fresh parsley. Cover tightly and simmer slowly for 1½-2 hours or less till meat is barely tender. (It will have to cook another 30-40 minutes after you add the vegetables, and although you want it to be tender, it shouldn't fall apart.) Check after the first hour or so to see whether more water should be added to the meat. The cubes should be nearly covered.

While the meat is cooking, prepare these vegetables: 4 medium potatoes, cut into quarters, 3 carrots, scraped and cut into 1-inch pieces, 2 parsnips cut in 1-inch pieces, 1 cup diced celery, 1 cup diced turnips, 10 or 12 very small white onions.

Remove the garlic clove, bay leaf, and parsley sprigs from the kettle. Add the vegetables and cook until tender—30-40 minutes. When cooking is complete, the liquid can be thickened a little if you choose. To do this, remove vegetables and meat from the pot. Blend 2 tablespoons flour with a little water and add it slowly to the liquid, stirring all the while. Let it boil together a bit to remove the raw flour taste. Test taste, add salt and pepper. Re-add vegetables and meat. The flavor of stew seems to improve each time it is reheated. It can be made with great success the day before you plan to serve it. One word of warning, however: in this case do not overcook the vegetables as they will have to be heated still once more before serving. If you have cooked the stew in a Dutch oven (one of the iron ones) do not store the stew in this overnight, as the pot will rust.   6 TO 8 SERVINGS

LAMB STEW WITH DUMPLINGS

Buy 2 lbs. lean, boneless lamb shoulder. Have it cut in 2-inch pieces. Roll the meat in flour that has been seasoned with salt and pepper, shake off excess flour, and brown in 2 tablespoons hot cooking oil. It is best to use a heavy kettle or Dutch oven. Add 1 clove minced garlic, 1 bay leaf, 1 tablespoon lemon juice and 4 cups water. Cover and simmer the stew very slowly about 1½ hours till the meat is almost tender. Add 8 tiny white onions, 4 small potatoes, halved, and 4 carrots cut in 2-inch lengths. Cook until vegetables are done—about 20 minutes. Add one 10-oz. package frozen peas and 3 tablespoons chopped parsley. Cook 5 minutes longer and add dumpling batter (see below).

If you wish to thicken the stew liquid more, blend ¼ cup flour with ½ cup cold water. Remove meat, vegetables, and dumplings from the pot and keep warm. Gradually add flour mixture to liquid, stirring all the while. Boil together a bit to eliminate raw flour taste. Season with salt and pepper. Return meat, vegetables and dumplings to pot.

To make dumplings: Sift together 1½ cups flour, 2 teaspoons baking powder and ¾ teaspoon salt. Using 2 table knives, cut in 3 tablespoons shortening. When the flour and shortening are mixed, stir in ¾ cup milk. Don't do a lot of stirring—just barely blend. Drop the dumpling batter by spoonfuls right on top of the stew. Cook slowly for ten minutes with kettle uncovered, then cover tightly and cook an additional ten minutes.

BARBECUED SPARERIBS

Buy the loin-back ribs. Allow ½ side per person (or at least ¾ pound). For 2 sides spareribs, mix together ½ cup catsup, 1 minced garlic clove, 1 cup water, ½ teaspoon chili powder, 1 teaspoon dry mustard, 1 tablespoon sugar, 1 teaspoon salt, 2½ tablespoons vinegar, 1½ tablespoons Worcestershire sauce.

Place one side ribs in large roasting pan. Cover with thin slices from 1 medium-size onion. Spoon over half the sauce. Repeat with second layer of ribs, onion, and sauce. Cover the pan and bake in a slow oven (or 325° F.) for two hours till very tender. Uncover for the last half hour of baking to crisp and brown chops. Slice between each rib and serve.   4 SERVINGS

MIXED GRILL

Allow 1 lamb chop and 1 lamb kidney for each guest; large mushroom caps, white sausages (Bratwurst style), lean, thick-sliced bacon (Canadian bacon is good too), and firm, medium-size tomatoes. Separate large mushroom caps from the stems. Wipe the caps with a damp cloth. Wash and split the kidneys. Remove the fat and membrane. Wipe the lamb chops with a damp cloth.

Preheat the broiler to medium. Place the broiling rack so that the food will be 4 inches from the unit. Place the kidneys, split side up, on broiler rack. Sprinkle with salt and pepper. Place the mushroom caps, rounded side up, on broiler rack and sprinkle with onion salt. Brush both kidneys and mushrooms with melted butter. Place the sausages and bacon on the broiling rack. Turn the foods as they brown and brush the mushrooms and kidneys again with melted butter. When cooking is complete, remove from broiler and keep warm. Place the chops and tomatoes under the broiler. Sprinkle both with salt and pepper, and brush the tomatoes with melted butter and chopped parsley. Turn chops when brown. When cooking is complete, serve the chops on triangles of toast, surrounded by the kidneys, bacon, sausage, mushrooms, tomatoes, and a few fresh sprigs of watercress. (Note: the mushroom caps and kidneys may be sautéed in butter on top of the stove if you prefer.)

LIVER BASICS (calf, lamb, beef, and pork)

Calf liver is the most delicate, but baby beef liver is often as tender. To pan fry calf, beef, or lamb liver:

Have the liver sliced ½ inch thick. Remove membrane and veins from slices of liver and dip them in flour, shaking off the excess. Brown the slices in ½ butter, ½ hot cooking oil in a heavy pan. When brown, reduce the heat to low and cook 10 to 15 minutes longer, turning once. Season with salt and pepper and serve.

To broil. Have veal or lamb liver sliced ⅓ to ½ inch thick. Remove membrane and veins (a kitchen scissors does a neat job of snipping these out). Place the liver slices on a cold broiler pan and brush with melted butter. Broil 3 inches from heat for 3 minutes. Turn and broil 2 to 3 minutes longer. Brush with melted butter. Season with salt and pepper.

To braise (this is only necessary for older beef or pork liver). Cut liver into ½-inch slices and remove membrane and veins. Roll the pieces of liver in flour that has been seasoned with salt and pepper. Brown quickly on both sides in ½ butter, ½ cooking oil. Dissolve 1 bouillon cube in ½ cup water, and add to pan. Cover and cook very slowly till tender (about 1 hour).

To serve bacon with liver. Allow 2 thick slices bacon for each serving. Fry slowly, turning constantly till crisp. Remove the slices from pan, drain on absorbent paper, and keep hot while you fry the liver. It imparts a wonderful flavor to the liver if you fry it in the bacon grease.

To serve onions with liver. Peel and slice sweet onions. They can be either sliced into thin rings or chopped. Cook them slowly in bacon fat till golden and tender. Remove from pan, drain, season with salt, and keep hot. If you like a real oniony flavor, fry the bacon in the same pan.

REAL BAKED BEANS

Great baked beans are started the night before like this: Buy a 1-pound package of dried pea marrow or navy beans. Wash and pick them over, discarding any of the imperfect ones. Cover with cold water, and let them soak overnight. Drain the beans in the morning, cover them again with water and let them simmer at a very low heat till the skins burst when blown upon. Drain again, and save 2 cups of the bean water. Peel and quarter 1 medium onion and place it in the bottom of the bean crock. Cut ½ pound salt pork on top of it. To the 2 cups of bean water add 5 tablespoons brown sugar, 1 teaspoon salt, 5 tablespoons molasses, and 1½ teaspoons dry mustard. Bring the bean water to a boil and pour it over the beans in the crock. Add more boiling water if necessary to just cover beans.

Start your oven at 325° F.—or slow. Cover the beans and bake from 6 to 7 hours till the beans are very brown and taste tender. The secret of perfect beans is long, slow cooking and to keep them covered with liquid except during the last hour when you want the water to boil away. You will have to keep watching the beans while they are baking and every once in a while add more boiling water so they stay covered with liquid. During the last hour of cooking remove the cover from the bean pot. Beans like these need little else to recommend them. Perhaps just the complement of pickles, catsup, cold beer, and thin-sliced brown bread (½ cup dark rum dribbled over the beans the last thing before putting them in the oven is also a good idea).

BAKED HAM

Try to find a flavorful, dry-textured ham. If you buy a whole ham, you'll have to leave this to your butcher's discretion, that is, till you find a brand you favor. If you buy a half ham, you can see the texture, and avoid the wet, stringy-looking fibers. A whole ham, un-

cooked, will require 19 to 20 minutes per pound (meat thermometer—160°). A whole ham "ready-to-eat" requires 10 minutes to the pound (meat thermometer 130°). The ham should be baked in an uncovered baking pan in a slow oven (or 325° F.). Half an hour before the ham is done, remove it from the oven and cut off the rind. The ham may then be scored, that is, angled cuts are made through the fat in two directions so they form a diamond pattern. A glaze can be spread over the ham at this point if desired. The ham should then be placed back in the oven for about 20 minutes for browning, and the oven should be turned to high heat or 400° F.

To glaze ham, mix together 1 cup brown sugar with ¾ cup apricot, pineapple, or spiced fruit juice. Spread over scored fat and stud each scored square with a whole clove.

Instead of a glaze here is a sauce that can be served with the ham.

MINCEMEAT SAUCE FOR HAM

1 cup mincemeat
4 cloves
½ cup brown sugar
1 tablespoon cornstarch
1 tablespoon vinegar

¾ cup water
¼ cup sherry wine
¼ teaspoon Worcestershire
   sauce

Combine all ingredients and cook until slightly thickened. Serve hot on slices of ham. Note: Wine may be omitted.

GREAT ADVENTURES:

there's a man in the kitchen

Meat eaten without either mirth or music is ill of digestion.
—Sir Walter Scott

As a chef, you owe it to yourself to make the preparation of your food as much of an adventure as eating it. A chafing dish is in reality only a small stove, and you can prepare most of the characteristic dishes just as well back in the battered old frying pan on the iron duke in the kitchen. But the gesture is a handsome and uplifting one, and the psychosomatic truth is that the food literally tastes better for it.

You have now progressed in your culinary journey from the first axioms of the skillet—not to mention the can opener and frozen locker—to a plateau of ability that should make you a pretty good host. But there are peaks ahead of you well worth scaling. These are dishes notable for unusual content, for bravura preparation, and for adventuring into new tastes. In this chapter we shall introduce you to some epic achievements, and in the following one go on to learn from the world's greatest chefs some of their recipe secrets.

But don't let this scare you. After all, Boeuf à la Mode is just a pot roast at heart, and Beef Stroganoff is a simple stew with a few extra ideas added.

You can't eat *à la haute cuisine* every night in the week. You'd go nutty and break out in spots. Champagne every night will soon have you reaching for that bottle of red-eye whiskey.

But there are times when the host wants to pull out all the stops and start them talking, or throw a party based upon such a special dish that for weeks afterward that greatest of compliments, envy, will flourish, with the tag line: "Why didn't *I* think of that?"

Invitations for such festive occasions should always mention the key food. Some people are squeamish about eating odd foods. Or, perhaps too accustomed to thinking that meat is something that comes from the butcher's case, they are unequal to the reproachful look in the eye of a suckling pig or a lobster about to be ducked into boiling water. Not all such eating adventures are so close to nature, but it *is* wise to give fair warning to the tender-hearted who have not pondered the philosophical truth that all of life is bound up in the active and passive forms of the verb *to eat*.

And here let me bring out the traditional warning about too many cooks and what they can do to the broth. Be firm about this. Guests are guests, and not hosts. Any helpful suggestions from them should be received with a dreamy smile and a slight nod— and then immediately forgotten. The worst pest of all, of course, is the guest who wants to barrel in on the act and do things *his* way. (In a gallant gesture, I have refrained from saying *her* way, but watch out for that, too, unless she's so appetizing herself it's worth messing up the meal just to have her in the kitchen all the time as your "tweenie.")

If your little helper (unwelcome variety) is too pressing, give him a spiked drink or two, put him to work on some unneeded and unpleasant task—like dicing peanuts, shredding coconut, or squashing squash—and then overlook that ingredient when serving the meal. Stronger measures include getting a touch careless with boiling water, or a friendly suggestion to get the hell out of the kitchen.

At any rate it is time for you to pursue the grail.

Here is your library of the magnificent.

Excelsior!

MAGIC WITH A CHAFING DISH

If your chafing dish has been collecting dust on a top shelf, drag it out of there and make it earn its keep. It is a festive utensil, both for serving and cooking, and needs only a little thought on your part to live up to its reputation.

The secret of chafing-dish cookery is the preparation **that** has been done before the in-front-of-your-guests cooking begins.

CHAFING-DISH SCRAMBLED EGGS TARRAGON

14 eggs	3 tablespoons butter
6 tablespoons water	2 tablespoons heavy cream
1 teaspoon Worcestershire sauce	2 tablespoons finely chopped
1½ teaspoons salt	fresh tarragon (or 1 tablespoon
Freshly ground pepper, a	dried tarragon)
generous amount	

The eggs will be cooked double-boiler fashion (over hot water) in your chafing dish. Assemble all the ingredients beside the chafing dish. Break the eggs into a bowl, and beat them lightly with a fork. Add the water, Worcestershire, salt, and pepper.

Melt the butter in your top cooking pan, add eggs and cook slowly, stirring them with a wooden spoon. Cook until lightly firm but still soft. Add the heavy cream and tarragon and stir around quickly and serve.   6 SERVINGS

FROGS' LEGS IN A CHAFING DISH

Melt a generous amount of butter in the blazer of a chafing dish. Dust the frogs' legs with flour, shaking off any excess. Sauté them in blazer over high heat until they are crisp and brown. Sprinkle with a liberal amount of freshly chopped parsley and serve on toast with lemon wedges.

This makes a delicious appetizer or main course.

CHAFING-DISH SAUSAGES WITH ALE

Parboil a couple of dozen small link sausages. Drain them on paper toweling. Pile them on a plate and carry to your chafing dish. Brown them in butter in the chafing dish, pour a bottle of ale over them, cover, and simmer gently about 25 minutes. Sprinkle with parsley and serve immediately.

SHRIMP NEWBURG IN A CHAFING DISH

Start with 2 lbs. frozen or fresh shrimp, cleaned and cooked. Make a Basic White Sauce like this: Blend 3 tablespoons butter with 3 of flour. Add 2 cups hot milk all at once and stir constantly over low heat till the sauce is smooth and thickened. Add salt to taste, a pinch of cayenne pepper, a pinch of dry mustard, some freshly ground pepper to taste and ¼ cup Madeira. Prepare the shrimp and the white sauce ahead up to this point. Transfer the white sauce to your chafing dish and cook over boiling water about 12 minutes. Stir in 2 egg yolks that you have lightly blended with one cup heavy cream (warm the cream before combining). Blend and add the cooked shrimp. Turn off the burner on the chafing dish, but leave the dish over the hot water. Stir around a few times till the shrimp are heated through. Add 1 tablespoon Madeira and serve on triangles of hot buttered toast.   6 SERVINGS

SHAD ROE IN A CHAFING DISH

Allow 1 pair of shad roe for two people. Into the chafing dish put a generous amount of sweet butter. When it is hot and foaming add the shad roe and cover. Cook over low heat 12 to 15 minutes. Turn once. Be on guard as the roe can "pop" while cooking. Season with salt, pepper, and chopped parsley. Serve with lemon wedges and slices of crisp bacon. If you add boiled potatoes and a salad, you have a very special kind of meal.

CHAFING-DISH KIDNEY STEW WITH CHAMPAGNE

To prepare the kidneys, wash, remove outer membrane, split in half lengthwise, remove white centers, fat, and tubes. Sliver into ¼-inch slices. To prepare 8 lamb kidneys, melt 5 tablespoons butter in the chafing dish. Dredge the kidneys with flour and brown evenly in the butter. Add 1 cup champagne, and 1 pound sliced fresh mushrooms. Add 1 teaspoon salt. Cover and cook for 10 minutes. Stir in 1 cup heavy cream and another cup of champagne. Blend and serve over fluffy rice. Sprinkle with chives.

7 OR 8 SERVINGS

HOW TO PREPARE A SMÖRGÅSBORD
(for 8–10 people)

Along the line of impossible direct translations *smörgåsbord* in Swedish means bread-and-butter table. But, if you've ever seen such a table set with the great varieties of fish, vegetables, salads, cheeses, and meats, the name would imply a considerable frugality in view of such a lush repast. The custom of the smörgåsbord is said to have originated long ago at country parties, when a food dish was brought along by each guest attending. All dishes were placed on a long table for one and all to walk around, plate in hand, and sample their neighbors' cookery.

Traditionally, one begins the first "round" of the table by sampling only bread, butter, and herring. This, augmented by a glass of ice-cold schnapps. (Akvavit is popular throughout all of the Scandinavian countries; also Kronbrannbin for those who prefer a blander schnapps.) On the second round of the table, other cold fish dishes are chosen, followed by cold sliced meats, salads, and vegetables. The famous Swedish hot dishes follow this, then the cheese. And to drink with all this? Beer throughout.

The password at one of these superb table feasts is "gauge yourself," as the eye can easily overpower the appetite.

But now you want to serve a smörgåsbord:

Planning is the principal thing here. The amount and variety of the food to be served can be very simple; or as elaborate as time and pocketbook will allow. You should, however, serve some food from each of the five basic categories mentioned above. On your shopping list you may find that the local delicatessens with good prepared salads play an important part. If you plan to do it all yourself, however, you will find that a couple of days' preparation for shopping and cooking are a great help. Therefore, a lazy Sunday is about the best time for a smörgåsbord invitation for the host who will need a weekend of preparation.

We list below some suggestions on our classic theme:

Begin with the bread and butter:

The bread should be interesting and special. Consider limpa, the traditional Swedish bread, usually available in Scandinavian deli-catessens throughout the country. It is made with the basic in-gredients of rye and wheat flour, malt and spices, and has a slightly sweet taste. It should be sliced very thin. Borrowing a little from the famous breads of the nations, pumpernickel is also excellent, especially with the fish course. Salty rye, crusty loaves of home-baked white, or Jewish rye bread are to be considered, plus the crackers: Swedish ones (crisp bread), dark and light. Ry-King is an excellent brand, and is available in gourmet shops and many supermarkets across the country. The breads are interesting served as whole loaves on a large bread board with a good sharp knife. The pre-sliced kind and the crackers are served in baskets.

As for the butter, make it a good one. Danish butter is mar-velous. Supermarket whipped butters have a considerably better flavor than the run-of-the-mill varieties. Serve with a flourish: heaped in a crock, rolled into butter balls, European style (by a guest who likes to work, of course), or smoothed into small, small pottery ramekins—one to each guest.

Now to the fish:

Sill is the Swedish word for *herring*. It is tinned and exported from Sweden in a great variety of marvelous sauces. There are:

Lok-Sill (onion herring)
Herring in fruit sauce
Herring in dill sauce
Herring in catsup
Polar Matjes herring
Swedish herring tidbits in wine sauce
  (Skansen is a delicious brand, packed in Sweden and
  imported by many food specialty shops. It is famous for
  converting non-herring eaters.)

Then there are the Swedish fresh anchovies (sprats) and the smoked and jellied pickled eel. Sardines: packed in tomato sauce, mustard sauce, chili sauce, curry sauce, sherry sauce (Knorden, Fjord, Princess Astrid, Norwegian Girl Brand) mackerel: fillets in wine sauce, Worcestershire sauce, or tomato sauce (Knorden, Lindesnes, or Fyens brands).

The fish is usually served right in its container on the smörgåsbord table. Just remove the tops of the cans and arrange them on a platter. Leave the labels on the cans so that the fish is easily and attractively identifiable.

A BOWL OF CHILLED SHRIMP

Buy three pounds of large fresh shrimp. Put a pot of water on the stove with only enough water to cover shrimp when they are added later. Throw into the water a potpourri of soup greens (a few sprigs of parsley, a sliced carort, a medium-sized onion, a stalk of celery), two tablespoons of vinegar, one teaspoon of salt. Boil together about twenty minutes, until the water is well met with the seasoning. Now wash shrimp in cold water and plunge them into the pot. Cook for ten minutes after the water comes to a boil again. Turn off flame and allow shrimp to cool in broth.

When cleaning shrimp, remove shells only up to the tail. Remove the black vein running down the back. Now hang the shrimp around the edge of the serving bowl, or arrange in parallel rows on a platter. Sprigs of fresh watercress or fresh dill make a fitting garnish.

It is not necessary to serve a sauce with your shrimp for smörgås-bord, but if you're a real "sauce" man, make it a delicate one for this occasion. Perhaps a *Mayonnaise and Sour Cream Sauce* (half and half); the whole thinned with a little cream, spiked with salt, pepper, a touch of lemon juice, a pinch of sugar, and a pinch of dry mustard, all to your taste. Pour into a serving bowl, put a sprinkling of scallions (or chives) on the top and place bowl in the center of the shrimp.

A PLATTER OF SMOKED SALMON

Neatly arrange a pound of sliced smoked salmon on a serving platter, or use two cans of the frozen smoked salmon (the Norwegian is good). Toss a liberal amount of capers over all, and layer several thin lemon slices at each end of platter.

A WHOLE SMOKED WHITEFISH

A medium to large whitefish for this, depending on size and appetite. Usually, one fish for two portions. (These can be purchased in fish markets, food specialty stores, or Jewish delicatessens.)

Before serving, debone like this: Take a scissors and gently make two cuts under the top layer of skin only: one next to the tail, the other next to the head. Now carefully peel back the top skin, and with a blunt knife remove the top layer of flesh (it is very soft and easy to do). Now the large bone will be revealed. Pick up the scissors again and clip either end of the bone. Pull it out. Trim out any other bones. Replace the top layer of flesh, then fold the skin back. All ready to serve now as the "whole" fish complemented with wedges of lemon and sprigs of parsley.

A FISH SALAD . . . Lobster, Crab, or Shrimp

Canned or frozen lobster may be used with excellent results for this salad. Its success story consists of using large chunks of the seafood, both for taste and eye appeal, and serving it really well iced. Begin with 1 lb. lobster meat, shrimp, or Alaska king crab. Add about ½ cup tender chopped celery (including a little of the tops), 2 tablespoons capers, enough mayonnaise to hold it all nicely together, salt to taste, and a couple of tablespoons fresh lemon juice. Garnish around edges with sliced hard-cooked eggs.

FISH IN ASPIC

(This is complicated to prepare, but we can't let true smörgåsbord lovers down by not including it.) Basically, it is a mold containing fish, tomatoes, shrimp, and hard-cooked eggs—bound together and given a shiny form by the aspic.

Start with 2 lbs. fresh salmon or mackerel. Clean fish, cut in 1-inch chunks and set aside. Now put into a pot 1½ quarts water, 1 tablespoon salt, 7 whole peppercorns, 2 tablespoons vinegar, 4 sprigs fresh dill (or 1 teaspoon dried dill), 7 allspice, 1 medium bay leaf. Boil together 15 minutes. Now add fish. Cook 10 minutes longer. Take out chunks of fish and allow the stock to cool.

Now for the aspic:

Into a saucepan put 2 tablespoons plain Knox gelatin. Pour a little cold water over it and let soak till softened. Now stir in gradually 3 egg whites and 3 cups of the strained stock in which you have cooked the fish. Blend well and slowly bring the mixture to the boiling point, stirring all the while. Turn off the flame, cover the mixture, and let stand for about 15 minutes. Now strain it, add pepper (the Swedes use white), and salt to taste. Cool the mixture.

Now take a round mold. Over the bottom of it spread some small cooked shrimp (you can use canned or frozen ones for this), some hard-cooked eggs cut in wedges, and some deseeded tomato wedges. Arrange in some symmetrical pattern that will make for an appetizing-looking top when it is unmolded. Perhaps the tomatoes in the center, surrounded with the egg and shrimp wedges. Next slowly pour over enough aspic to cover well, and chill in refrigerator until the aspic jellies. Lastly, arrange the cold fish chunks on top of the jellied aspic and pour over remaining aspic. Refrigerate the whole until well jellied. To serve, loosen a bit around the edge of the mold with a blunt knife, dip the mold quickly in hot water and invert onto a serving plate. This accompanied by a bowl of mayonnaise.

COLD SLICED MEATS

Thin-sliced ham, salamis, goose-liver sausage, cold sliced roast pork, veal tongue, or chicken. Arrange in neat rows on serving platter.

SALADS AND VEGETABLES

A bowl of radishes, white or red. No need to cut these into fancy shapes. Leave whole with about an inch of the green stem intact. Scrub well or scrape a little where necessary, soak overnight in the refrigerator in salted, cold water to cover. When ready to serve, drain, and pile them cold and crisp into your serving bowl.

Tomatoes: If they are in season, a bowl of the tiny whole tomatoes, sometimes known as "love apples," is most attractive. Just wash the tomatoes (leave the stem on), chill, and serve.

Large tomatoes well-ripened can be peeled (dropping into boiling water for a few seconds facilitates this), sliced thick, overlaid with thin slices of Bermuda onion, arranged on a platter, and seasoned with salt, pepper, vinegar, oil, and chopped parsley.

Pickled beets: If you plan to cook the fresh ones, buy them small (about 18 or 20), and cook 30 to 40 minutes in boiling, salted water until tender (or pressure cook according to chart). They should be washed and deleafed before plunging them into the boiling water, but leave on about ½ inch of stem. When tender, drain, cool, peel, and slice thin.

For the dressing:

4 tablespoons sugar
1 cup vinegar
4 tablespoons water

1 whole clove, or a pinch of
    powdered cloves

Mix all ingredients. Place beets in a glass bowl and pour dressing over all. Allow to marinate three hours or more before serving. (Note: There are several very good brands of canned pickled beets on the market.)

Pickled fresh cucumbers: Choose two large, firm cucumbers. Wash well and slice very thin without peeling. Put slices into a glass bowl.

For the dressing:

4 tablespoons sugar
1 cup vinegar
3 tablespoons water

½ teaspoon salt
A dash pepper
2 tablespoons chopped parsley

Mix together. Marinate three hours or more before serving.

A platter of cold cooked vegetables: Good frozen and canned brands are available of all the vegetables listed below.

Asparagus spears: Wash well, break off tough ends at bottom of spears. Tie stalks together, and cook standing up if possible (a coffee pot is perfect for this). Plunge the spears into boiling water which reaches to just under the asparagus tip. (The tips are much more tender, and the steam will cook them just fine.) Cover and cook till tender but still firm (about 8 minutes after the water resumes boiling). Cool, cover, and refrigerate.

Whole small carrots: Scrape and plunge into boiling, salted water to which a teaspoon of sugar has also been added. Cook about 20–25 minutes or until tender. Cool, cover, and refrigerate.

Whole green or yellow string beans: Snip off ends of beans. Wash well, and cook in boiling, salted water until tender (about 15 minutes).

Tiny whole beets: Wash well, remove leaves, but leave about 1 inch of the stem intact. Cook in salted, boiling water until tender (about 30 minutes). Cool, peel, cover, and refrigerate.

(In cooking fresh vegetables it is well to remember to use only enough water to barely cover vegetables. You can always add a little more if necessary before the cooking time expires. Otherwise, a lot of vitamins are tossed out with excess water.)

The sauce for the vegetables can consist of half mayonnaise, half whipped cream with a little salt and pepper and a touch of fresh lemon added to taste. Or, here is a good one made in your electric blender:

¾ cup melted butter
¾ cup olive oil
Juice of two fresh lemons
1 teaspoon capers
2 teaspoons coarsely chopped
   parsley

2 teaspoons coarsely chopped
   scallions or leeks
A pinch dry mustard
2 pinches sugar
1 teaspoon hard-cooked egg
   white
Salt and pepper to taste

Put all ingredients into the blender and whizz on high speed a minute or so till well blended.

A bowl of greens: Well washed, drained, and crisped in the refrigerator in advance is the formula here. The greens are more interesting if you shun the knife on this occasion. Consider gently separated whole leaves of Boston lettuce, Belgian endive, a bed of watercress, each sectionalized to retain its identity . . . . one of the mayonnaise sauces standing nearby, or a bottle of oil and vinegar.

HOT DISHES

Boiled new potatoes with dill: Allow two small new potatoes per person. Peel and toss into cold, salted water. Be sure they are covered by the water, or they will turn brown. Cook about 25 minutes after the water boils or until tender when tested with a fork. Pile into a serving bowl, and sprinkle with fresh chopped dill.

Swedish Meat Balls

⅔ cup bread crumbs
1 cup water
1 cup cream
2 tablespoons finely chopped
   onions
5–6 tablespoons butter for frying

½ lb. ground fat pork
1½ lbs. ground beef
2 tablespoons melted butter
3 teaspoons salt
½ teaspoon white pepper
1 teaspoon sugar

Take a large mixing bowl. In it put the bread crumbs, water, and cream. Allow to soak. Now cook the chopped onions very slowly in a little of the frying butter, stirring constantly till they are a golden-brown color. Now add the onions and all the other ingredients except frying butter to the bread crumbs in the mixing bowl. Blend until the mixture is smooth.

Prepare a small bowl of ice water. In it place two tablespoons. Use these to shape the meat into very small balls. Place the balls on a bread board or on sheets of wax paper as you make them up, and every so often redip the spoons into the ice water. Place a large, heavy skillet over a low flame till hot. Put in the frying butter. When melted, add enough meat balls to cover three-quarters of the bottom of the pan. Now shake pan continuously to make balls round and brown evenly. As they brown, pile into a warmed dish and keep hot.

Creamed Mushrooms

¾ lb. mushrooms	2½ cups cream
3 tablespoons butter	1½ tablespoons sherry or
Salt and pepper to taste	Madeira
3 tablespoons flour	

Wash mushrooms thoroughly (it is not necessary to peel them). Trim the stems, leaving about one-half inch remaining. Slice the mushrooms through lengthwise. Melt the butter in a heavy skillet, being careful not to brown it. Add the mushrooms, white pepper, and salt, and cover. Cook slowly for about 30 minutes. When tender, remove mushrooms from pan, leaving remaining butter and liquid. Into this, blend flour gradually. Put aside. Heat the cream to just below the boiling point. Add all at once to the butter and flour mixture. Now put back over low flame and stir with a wire whisk until thick and smooth. Return the mushrooms to sauce, and test-taste for seasoning. Add the sherry or Madeira just before serving.

CREAMED LOBSTER, CRAB OR SHRIMP

3 tablespoons butter
3 tablespoons flour
2½ cups cream (may be half
  milk or fish stock)
Salt and pepper to taste
1 tablespoon fresh lemon juice

½ teaspoon dry mustard
Worcestershire sauce, a short
  dash
1 lb. cooked lobster, crab or
  shrimp, cut into chunks

Melt but don't brown the butter; blend in the flour. Bring the cream to just below the boiling point. Add all at once to the butter-flour mixture. Stir over low flame till thick and smooth. Add salt, pepper, lemon juice, mustard, and Worcestershire. Add the cooked shellfish. Pour into warmed serving bowl, a fine sprinkling of parsley over all.

On cooking fresh lobster: In a large pot bring to a boil water (enough to cover or about 3 quarts), ½ cup salt, a few sprigs of fresh dill or 1 tablespoon dried dill. Plunge 2 live 2-lb. lobsters headfirst into the boiling water. Cook 25 minutes. Turn off flame and allow to cool in the stock. Split the lobsters, remove stomach and the dark intestinal vein. Crack the claws. Remove all the meat from the shell and cut into chunks. Try to keep one side of the lobster claws intact and use them stuck upright as a garnish around the outside of the serving bowl. The bright red is very attractive and immediately communicates the content. (If you cook 1-lb. lobsters, allow 15 minutes instead of 25.)

(The directions for cooking shrimp are contained in an earlier smörgåsbord recipe under "A Bowl of Chilled Shrimp.")

Creamed Sweetbreads: Funny how rumors get started, and in some circles the true identity of the sweetbread has been falsely represented for years. So I would like to state the case for the sweetbread once and for all. They are the throat glands and the pancreas of calves.

Check with your butcher ahead on these, as you may have to place an order for the fresh ones. Many good butchers have the frozen ones available at all times. Note: sweetbreads spoil very quickly; therefore as soon as they are brought into your kitchen, put them in very cold water, and leave them there for about an hour. Then put them to cook in boiling water for 20 minutes. Plunge again into cold water, and when cool remove all of the thin membrane encasing them. Slice into fairly thick slices (about

⅓ inch), and carefully remove heavy veins and stringy parts. Cut into large cubes and keep cool.

For this recipe you will need:

3 tablespoons butter
3 tablespoons flour
2½ cups cream
Salt and white pepper to taste

Lemon juice, sherry or onion juice—make a choice here. Just a few drops of one or the other, added at the last minute, for a little zip.

2 small pairs sweetbreads

Blend melted butter and flour. Heat cream to just below the boiling point and add all at once to flour and butter. Stir until thick and well-blended. Add seasonings and the cubed sweetbreads. If you like, you can combine the sweetbreads with some cooked mushrooms, a simpatico partner.

Oven-Baked Omelet with Sauce:

6 eggs, well beaten
1½ teaspoons salt
2 cups cream or milk

1½ tablespoons melted butter
A dash of white pepper

Preheat oven to 350° F. Get ready an omelet pan or baking dish, well-buttered (one that can go right from the oven to the smörgåsbord table is preferable). Now mix all ingredients.

This is the basic formula. If you want to add cubed cooked ham, bacon, or some chopped chives, parsley, or herbs to it, now is the time before you pour it into the baking dish and slide it into the oven. Or maybe you would rather bake it plain, and adorn it when it emerges from the oven with minced, creamed chicken, creamed mushrooms, or creamed spinach (use any of the basic cream sauce recipes given before). The baking time is 15–20 minutes or until it is a lovely, golden brown.

Swedish-Style Brown Beans:

2 cups dried brown beans
1½ quarts water
2½ teaspoons salt

Molasses
White vinegar
Mor salt

Wash the beans thoroughly and soak overnight in the 1½ quarts water. Cook very slowly in the same water about 2 hours till tender.

Now add to the beans the molasses, vinegar, and Mor salt to taste. The beans should have a thick consistency, and a well-seasoned sweet and sour taste. Some very thick bacon is good layered over the top of the beans.

CHEESE

Really good aged cheeses are important to round out a smörgåsbord. One or two of excellent quality are far better than a large assortment of inferior ones. The cheeses should be served in chunks on a bread board or platter for guests to cube or shave off with a cheese knife.

Below are listed some of the typical smörgåsbord cheeses:

> Danish caraway cheese
> Tybo (Danish)
> Nøkkelost (Norwegian)
> Tilci (Swedish)
> Herrgardsost (Swedish)
> Svecia (Swedish)
> Esrom (Danish)

THE GOOSE HANGS HIGH

There's something tremendously festive about the idea of a goose, something harking back to olde Englishe countrysides, and the villeins—tugging at their forelocks—come around to serenade the master on the feast day with lutes and viols. Your guests will regard the occasion in much the same light. Chicken, turkey, and occasional duck eaters they may be, but goose rarely.

The goose should be plump and young, another one of those assignments on which your butcher stakes his reputation and continues to collect your cold cash. A 10–12 lb. one would be fine to serve 6 or 7 people. Don't try to stretch the goose to too many people. Appetities are usually well-whetted for this occasion and generous portions are in order.

After the goose has arrived *chez vous,* singe it if necessary over a gas jet to remove any pin feathers, then wash and dry it well inside and out with paper toweling or a clean cloth. Now you are ready to stuff it. Any number of delicious stuffings might be used, but we offer here a fruit one with Scandinavian leanings that is unusually delicious.

The stuffing is composed of:

Pitted prunes—about 22 of them, which have been cooked till they are barely soft and not mushy.

Raw apples—8 of medium size that you have peeled, cut into quarters, and seeded.

Salt—2 level tablespoons.

Pepper—a good grating; use the white pepper if possible.

Rub the goose inside and out with a little salt, pack the stuffing loosely into the cavity, sew up the opening, and prepare to roast.

The roasting will take about 2½ hours or possibly a little less. Your oven should be fairly hot or about 425° F.

The end result is that the goose should be a deep brown color, with a crackling crisp skin.

Since there is a lot of fat in the goose, it is advisable to keep draining this off during the roasting so that it will not be greasy. When most of the fat is drained off, start basting from time to time with a little strong stock of bouillon. During the last few minutes of roasting, when the goose is almost done, spoon over the top 3 tablespoons very cold water, and leave the oven door a little ajar. This will help make the skin brittle, and help in the carving.

When tender to the fork-and-leg test (the leg joint should move around very easily when the fingers push it into a little circular motion), transfer the goose to a hot serving platter, cut the string and remove the fruit stuffing, and pile this in neat rows around the goose.

To make the gravy:

Strain the pan juice and remove the fat. (This can be quickly done by pouring the juice through 2 or 3 layers of cheesecloth that has been wrung out in ice water, to trap the fat.) Mix 2 tablespoons cornstarch with a little cold water and add to the juice. Keep stirring and bring to a boil. Add a little more water if necessary. Season to taste, and serve the gravy in a heated separate bowl.

Small browned potatoes and sweet-and-sour red cabbage are very good served with the goose. You will find many brands of red cabbage on the grocery store shelves. (Lohmann's is one of the better brands.)

THINK BIG WITH BEER

Beer, priced at the low end of the liquid totem pole, rises above the mediocrity in between to compare favorably in its own way to the high man on the totem pole, the champagne king—even as the Model T could be compared to the Rolls-Royce. Both have distinction and great quality, and each is superior in its proper setting. Entertaining with beer as the star—well publicized to your guests, presented with imagination, and teamed with a natural food accompaniment—can result in a highly individual and long-remembered event.

The idea is to have every conceivable kind of beer on hand. It will be the greatest thrill your beer-drinking friends will have. Light beer, dark beer, lager and ale . . . Löwenbrau from Munich . . . Heinekens from Holland . . . Tuborg from Denmark . . . Pilsner-Urquel from Czechoslovakia . . . Beamish and Crawford Irish stout, Beamish and Crawford Irish porter, Guinness stout, and Smithwick's Kilkenny from the Emerald Isle . . . Bass and Co.'s pale ale from England . . . 'Alf and 'Alf (nip of Bass ale plus nip of Guinness stout) also from England . . . Queen's ale . . . Whitbread's ale . . . Mackeson stout . . . Isle of Man oyster stout . . . Golden Mead Honey ale . . . and from Scotland McEwan's India pale ale . . . Tennant's Scotch lager . . . Younger's Double Century ale . . . Fix, the light lager from Greece . . . San Miguel, bottled in the Philippines . . . and the San Miguel bottled in Spain . . . Japanese beer . . . the Canadian ales . . . even the nonalcoholic English ginger beer since we're categorizing . . . these, to name a few on the import list. Picture these if you will, lined up in iced champagne buckets or stuck in a tub of ice showing off their fancy labels. The domestics should not be outdone. Serve your favorite brand, *draft*. Order a small keg ahead of time from the brewery.

Don't forget the eye appeal lent by beautiful glasses: tall, thin ones, a collection of German steins, hefty stemmed glasses, old crest glasses, rented, borrowed, or collected for such an occasion.

The food component could be something as simple as a loaf of superb bread, good butter, and a huge bowl of crisp scrubbed white radishes. A better combination of crunching and sipping has never been found.

Or *oysters,* another natural, along with their shellmates, *clams.* These served deliciously fresh and cold on the half shell with lemon wedges and cocktail sauce on the side. (Tips on oysters and clams: Start with the most reliable fish market you know. Order well in advance, if necessary. Then judge the oysters carefully. The ridges on the shell denote the age, at one per year. Those with four or five ridges are considered superior. The shells should be tightly closed. If they gape, they are dead. Run, don't walk, from the fish market to your ice bin or refrigerator, for these are perishable sea jewels. To open oysters or clams: Buy or borrow an oyster knife. Put the point into the hinged back opening of the shell. The idea here is to break the suction, so pry up. When initial opening is made, work open the shell with the fingers. Now with the knife loosen the oyster or clam from the shell.) Use the deeper of the two shells to contain the oyster and the natural juices.

If you like your oysters cooked and hot, how about serving them *Oysters Rockefeller?* For this you follow the above procedure and start at the point where you remove the oysters from their shell. Here follows a recipe for 3 dozen oysters. (Allow 6 oysters per person.)

Into 3 cups commercial sour cream mix $2\frac{1}{2}$ teaspoons finely chopped garlic, and salt and black pepper to taste. Spoon a teaspoon of the sour cream mixture into each oyster shell. Place the oyster on top. Mix 3 boxes frozen chopped spinach as follows: First, thaw the spinach and drain off liquid. Do not cook. Mix with $\frac{3}{4}$ cup Pernod or Kirschwasser and $\frac{3}{4}$ cup grated Parmesan cheese. Spoon this mixture over the oysters until the shells are nicely filled. Sprinkle the top with bread crumbs and some small dabs of butter. Slide under a preheated broiler until piping hot and nicely browned on top. Some enthusiasts of this dish say the oysters are best cooked with the shells placed on a bed of rock salt in the broiling pan.

Maybe you'd prefer some quick-baked clams. Loosen from shell. Chop the meat. Pile back into shell with the natural liquid. Over each sprinkle a little chopped garlic, parsley, chives, and, if you like, Parmesan cheese. Dot with butter. Into the oven for about ten minutes till very hot. Serve with fresh lemon.

Fresh lobsters make a savory combination with beer. See page 152 for a choice of preparations.

Perhaps beer activates your taste buds to thoughts of brown fried shrimp heaped in serving baskets. Then try them tempura or butterfly fashion.

To prepare the shrimp, remove the shells but not the tails from large raw shrimp (allow about 8 shrimps per serving). Use kitchen scissors and split the shrimp down the back to the tail section, being careful not to slit them all the way through. Remove the sandy, black vein by holding them under cold, running water. Press each shrimp out flat. The frying will take about 3 minutes.

To make the batter: Mix 1½ cups flour and 1 teaspoon salt. To this flour mixture add 2 slightly beaten small or medium eggs and 1½ cups water. Blend lightly. Don't overstir as the batter should be slightly lumpy. (This amount of batter will do for about 40 large shrimp.)

Dip the shrimp into the batter, holding them by their tails. Fry them in deep, hot fat (peanut oil is good for this) until golden brown. Don't drop in too many at a time, as it will cool the fat too much (fat should be 375° F.). When brown, skim the shrimp out with one of those large holed spoons, drain on paper toweling and keep warm till serving time.

Dipping sauce: It can be a plain soy sauce or some sour cream zipped up with a little mustard and chopped chutney. Or go all the way and make a *Japanese tempura sauce:*

Start with 2 cups strong beef stock. Add to it 8 tablespoons soy sauce, 8 tablespoons Japanese sweet wine (mirin) or sherry. If you like, add a little fresh-grated ginger or powdered ginger to taste.

A good mayonnaise sauce can be made from: mayonnaise thinned with a little cream, embellished with a pinch of dry mustard, a little sugar, some chopped sweet pickle or pickle relish, minced scallions, minced parsley, and a few drops vinegar (about a teaspoon each of the minced things to a cup of mayonnaise). The rest to taste. Make early and refrigerate overnight, if possible. Stir well before serving.

Beer with sauerkraut, sausages, and ham, and or pig's knuckles.

The thing to remember here: The kraut should be cooked slowly and at length. The length—about 4 hours. And what a difference this slow mellowing makes! For 6 people, buy and wash 2 lbs. sauerkraut (purchased either in bulk form or canned). After the washing, drain and carefully squeeze out as much of the moisture as possible. Salt pork in thin slices is next. Line a heavy kettle all around with this. Then into the center of the kettle place the sauerkraut, 1½ large minced garlic cloves, a good grating of fresh

black pepper, and a good dry white wine to cover (Alsatian is good for this). Into the middle of this toss 1 medium onion that has been stuck with about 5 whole cloves. Put a good tight-fitting cover on the kettle and simmer slowly, slowly, on top of the stove about 4 hours or a little under. Take a look now and then and if you think it is getting a little dry add a bit more wine.

If you will serve pig's knuckles with the kraut, lay them on top of the kraut right at the beginning, and let them share the entire cooking time. Polish or Italian sausages can be laid over the top of the kraut and cooked for the last 40 minutes. Knockwurst or Bauernwurst is faster still: add these for the last 20 minutes of cooking. Cooked ham slices can be heated through in a few minutes on the top of the stove in some of the same white wine you've used to cook the kraut. If a smoked pork loin is what you crave, cook this in the oven. Moderate heat or 350° F. (a good 20 minutes to the pound). Slice thickly and overlay on the kraut when serving, along with any of the other meats. And plain boiled potatoes are good with this: about 25 minutes of cooking time after the water boils, or fork-test for tenderness. Now a selection of mustards, some good rye bread, and you've got it made.

SERVE A SWISS FONDUE BOURGUIGNONNE

One that may well become your favorite and proudest house specialty is this handsomely named dish. It is also handsomely served. It has the advantage of being prepared right on the dining table, and your guests themselves participate. Yet this is not mediocre fare: this is, in fact, one of the highest-style meals you'll ever turn out. It is a particular favorite of my own, and I have never seen a meal so happily admired by both sexes. Blasé gourmets salute its simplicity; peasants are flattered by its sophistication.

The rundown is this: Bite-sized chunks of filet mignon are cooked by the diners in sizzling oil. They season it with a selection of sauces and relishes, a good red wine (part of the necessary taste pattern, perhaps a fruity Swiss Dôle de Sion or a light red Burgundy), a dish of Rosti Potatoes (very authentic Swiss), and a crisp salad (some skip the salad and serve a creamed spinach). Chilled fruit and strong coffee are the perfect follow-up.

The equipment for the Bourguignonne is special. You can't get along without it, but it's worth the investment. It consists of a heavy brass pot with a handle. This fits into the groove of a brass stand under which is an alcohol burner and a metal tray. The forks for the Bourguignonne are two-pronged and very long. Improvisation is not suggested for the equipment. For one thing, boiling oil is boiling oil and the pot that contains it should rest securely in its own special stand to withstand the attack of enthusiastic dippers. The Bourguignonne pot is wide at the bottom and narrows up to a fairly small circumference. For another thing, the authenticity of the equipment adds to the charm of the occasion.

The Fondue Bourguignonne sets can be purchased in New York at Abercrombie and Fitch on Madison Avenue. The smaller size (to accommodate 4 to 5 dippers) is about $25. The larger size (6 to 8), is about $32.50. The special forks are $5 for 4. Many people prefer the smaller sets and use one at each end of a long table, or set up two smaller tables.

The procedure is this: Before each guest is a dinner plate, a dinner fork and a Bourguignonne fork (and any other silver you will need for salad, dessert, etc.), and wine glass. In the middle of the table is the stand upon which the boiling oil will be set. About the oil: You will arrive at your own favorite combination perhaps, but butter and oil in equal parts are generally used. One-third butter, ⅓ olive oil, and ⅓ peanut oil are also a good combination. Be sure the oil and butter are fresh. The Bourguignonne pot is filled to ⅓ with the oil and butter. Start to heat it slowly on top of the stove. When it is sizzling hot, carry it out to the dining table and light the burner under the stand. It is better to start the burner low and it can be turned up a bit when necessary. It should be kept at a gentle sizzle so that the meat will cook quickly.

Have a little serving table set up next to the dining table. On this place your platter of raw beef cubes, sauces, relishes, potatoes, salad, and wine. Pepper mills are very much in order here too.

Let each guest put a few of the beef chunks on his plate, spear one with a long fork, and start it cooking in the hot oil. Just let the forks rest in the oil. It is not necessary to hold them. After ½ minute or so the chunks should be rare. After the first try each diner should be able to arrive at the exact state of doneness he prefers. While the cooking is going on, pass the sauces, relishes, and potatoes, and pour the wine.

As each guest removes his beef from the oil, he should remove it from the long fork with his dinner fork, and immediately put in another piece to cook. Then he embellishes the meat with the sauces and relishes, and eats, drinks, and as you will find with this kind of special meal, becomes very, very merry.

One word of warning: *do not dip the meat in the sauces before putting it in the hot oil, as it will sputter.*

About the planning and preparation for the Bourguignonne party.

Let us start with the meat: It must be top-quality filet mignon, aged, if possible. You should allow ½ lb. meat per person. Order well in advance and have it cut into bite-size chunks from which all the fat has been removed. (You don't want to have to cut the meat before eating it, so the chunks should be of a size that even the ladies can fork comfortably into their mouths.)

All over Switzerland the sauces and relishes vary. Two sauces are sufficient, however. If you prepare a Béarnaise Sauce in advance and chill it, it should be taken out of the refrigerator early and allowed to reach room temperature. Add 1 tablespoon hot water, and give it a good stir to loosen it up. You don't want the sauce to be too stiff when you serve it. The best way to do the Béarnaise, obviously, is shortly before the party so it doesn't have to be refrigerated at all. With a Quick Béarnaise recipe, and provided you are organized with everything else, this is quite possible.

QUICK BEARNAISE SAUCE

Use two small saucepans. In one melt, but do not brown, ¼ pound (or 1 stick) butter. Into the other saucepan toss this combination: 2 tablespoons dry white wine, 2 tablespoons tarragon vinegar, 1 tablespoon water, 1½ teaspoons chopped tarragon, 2 teaspoons chopped shallot or scallion (use a little of the green part too). Boil this combination gently over a flame till the liquid has been reduced by ⅔.

Meanwhile put 3 egg yolks, ½ teaspoon salt, 1½ tablespoons lemon juice, and a pinch of cayenne pepper in an electric blender. Flick the blender on for a few seconds until the eggs are blended. Then, keeping the blender on high speed, slowly add the melted butter and blend for 3 or 4 seconds. Add the mixture in the other saucepan and blend an additional 4 or 5 seconds. This amount should be sufficient for 4–6 people.

FRESH HORSERADISH SAUCE

Try to track down a fresh horseradish. They are often obtainable at Italian vegetable stands. If you can get one, cut off a piece 1½ inches long. Peel it and grate fine. (The balance of the radish can be wrapped in foil and will keep several days in your refrigerator.) If you can't get a fresh radish, buy the freshest in-a-jar you can get. Start with 1½ teaspoons and add more to taste to this combination: ½ pint commercial sour cream, ¾ cup whipped cream, ½ teaspoon salt, 1 tablespoon lemon juice. Add the horseradish and stir till well blended.

The relishes should all be chopped very fine. They can be assembled well ahead. Only the scallions should be chopped shortly before serving. To be considered: chopped parsley, yolks of hard-cooked eggs, whites of hard-cooked eggs, capers, chutney, sweet pickles, olives, scallions, cooked mushrooms, crisp bacon. The relishes are placed in small individual bowls, then the bowls set onto platters. These should not be so large that they can't be conveniently passed around the table. Another attractive way to serve the relishes is to arrange them in neat rows like many-colored ribbons across a long narrow platter.

ROSTI POTATOES

New potatoes are the best for this. Allow 2 good-size potatoes per person, plus a couple more. Peel, cube, and put in cold water, drain, and wash through a couple of times to remove excess starch. Cover with fresh cold water, add ½ teaspoon salt. Bring the water to a good boil and drain it off. Allow the potatoes to cool. Now refrigerate them several hours, overnight, if possible. A good 40 minutes before serving start the browning. Into a heavy frying pan put 3 tablespoons butter, 3 tablespoons fresh cooking oil. Brown the potatoes slowly in the melted fat. Turn from time to time with a spatula till all of the pieces are golden brown. Add a little more salt to taste, pile them into a hot serving dish, and sprinkle with chopped parsley. If you are cooking a very large amount, it is better to use two frying pans so the potatoes all have a chance to brown nicely. Have enough butter and oil so they do not stick to the bottom of the pan. Add a little during the browning if necessary.

A crisp endive salad or romaine is good to follow the Bourguignonne, gently tossed with a French dressing.

A fresh fruit compote, chilled pineapple slices, orange slices with Cointreau and chunks of crystallized ginger, or any favorite fruit dessert happily completes this meal. Plus, of course, a cup of good coffee.

ALL YOU KNEAD TO KNOW: BAKING THE STAFF

The promise was made at the beginning of this book that you wouldn't be instructed in the feminine pastimes of making icings or cookie cutting. But baking bread is a course of another choler. Here is a thoroughly masculine pursuit.

It's a safe bet that the Egyptians—who had either the best press agents in the world or else invented *everything*—baked the first bread about 1550 B.C., which we deduce from the mention of yeast in their medical records. And loaves containing yeast were sealed in the tombs of the Pharaohs.

The first bakers in Austria, Germany, France, Italy, and the Scandinavian countries were honored as leaders. The frequency of the name Baker in our own Anglo-Saxon heritage is proof enough of the importance of living on the fashionable yeast side.

But more than that, making bread is practically an exercise. Civilized man has in many ways lost his manual skills, and given them over to technological substitutes. That's why the experiences of baseball players, bartenders, and even excavation diggers so fascinates men. They stand around for hours marveling at the sure-handedness of a construction worker catching rivets, or a barkeep turning out a precision line of drinks at 5 P.M.

When you bake your own bread, you join the original fraternity again. Kneading dough takes muscle, and it's good therapy. It relaxes both body and mind—and it has atavistic benefits reaching back into the childhood of the race that give you a strong sense of natural "belonging," similar to the experience of swimming in water a mile deep, or climbing to a mountain summit by your own will and muscle.

But, philosophy aside, fresh bread is good eating. How the professional bakers—with notable exceptions—have managed, with all their experience and all their scientific research and all their fabulous equipment, to give us bread that tastes like a blotter, loses its freshness in half a day, has neither flavor nor texture nor any more nutrition than a pile of sawdust is one of the great mysteries of our day. But they have managed, and if only for that reason you owe it to yourself and those you love to reclaim the wonderful aroma of freshly baked bread, the joy of eating it hot, with the butter melting all over it, the knowledge that all this ambrosia is indeed the staff of life.

Never was a more tantalizing invitation given than one that reads something like this: "I'm taking some home-baked bread out of the oven about noon. Are you interested?"

This question uttered any month, in any country, days in advance or on the spur of the moment, will evoke the most wildly enthusiastic affirmation.

So let's get to work. To bake good bread you will need:

A large mixing bowl
A very large wooden board or bowl for kneading
A flour sifter
A measuring cup
A strong mixing spoon
Bread tins for baking (9" x 5" x 3" is the size considered standard)
Scrubbed hands
A strong arm
A "cover-all" apron

The general procedure goes like this: Mix ingredients, allow to rise to double the volume, knead (sometimes the first rising and kneading are reversed, depending on the recipe), punch down the dough, allow to rise a second time, shape into loaves and place in baking tins, allow to rise a third time, then bake.

Approximate time involved:

½ hour for assembling ingredients and mixing
1½ hours for first rising to double volume
From ½ to 1 hour for second rising, depending on recipe
Kneading and punching-down time: approximately 15 minutes
From ½ to 1 hour for third rising
Baking time: 30 to 50 minutes depending on recipe

As you can see, this is no jiffy operation. On the other hand, there is a great deal of "waiting time" involved where the yeast and the oven do the work, so just think what you can accomplish in between.

RECIPE FOR WHITE BREAD

2 packages active dry yeast or compressed yeast
½ cup lukewarm water
2 tablespoons shortening
1 tablespoon salt

1¾ cup lukewarm milk
3 tablespoons sugar
7 cups flour (sifted, unbleached or all-purpose)

Use standard measuring cup. Put into a large mixing bowl the yeast and lukewarm water. Stir to dissolve. Add all the other ingredients, *but only half the flour.* Mix well with a large spoon until mixture is smooth. Now gradually add remaining flour, squeezing dough through the fingers till it is easy to handle. Turn out on lightly floured board and continue to knead dough till it is very smooth and no longer sticks to the board.

The dough must be kneaded until it is light and elastic, so it will rise easily and have a light texture. Kneading the dough will continue to mix all the ingredients and distribute the yeast evenly through the mixture.

When the dough is ready to knead, simply turn it out on a lightly floured board, and gently pat the dough out until it is a slightly flattened ball. Place fingers on edges of dough opposite you. Bring dough up and toward you. Then with the heels and palms of the hands press down and away from you, using an even rolling motion.

When the little blisters of air are evenly distributed under the surface of the dough and it feels smooth and satiny, the dough has been kneaded sufficiently.

Now wash your original mixing bowl and grease it. Place the mass of dough in the bowl and grease the top of the dough as well. Cover the bowl with a damp cloth and allow the dough to rise in a *warm* place (80° to 85° F.) until doubled in bulk (about 1½ hours). Test by punching your finger into the dough. It will leave an indentation when the dough is doubled.

Punch down the dough and allow it to rise a second time (about 30 minutes).

Divide the dough into two portions, and shape into loaves. The shaping is easiest when you follow somewhat the suggestions here:

First flatten the dough with the fists and back of fingers. Form into an oblong shape about 12 inches long by 10 inches wide. Fold the dough in half lengthwise, flattening again with the back of the fingers to press out air. Lengthen the dough a bit by stretching. Fold both ends toward the middle, overlapping them and sealing them well by pressing down firmly with the heel of hand and knuckles. Now start folding the dough toward you . . . three folds, sealing each one with the heel of hand and knuckles. Roll the whole thing back and forth a few times to smooth it, seal the ends by pressing with the hands, even it up lightly between hands and place in greased baking tin (9″ x 5″ x 3″). Place the last-sealed edge downward.

The baking tin will be about ⅔ full. Grease the loaves, cover, and let rise the third and last time. This will take 50 to 60 minutes. Right about here think about preheating your oven. It should be *hot* or 425°.

By last rising the dough should be pretty well spread out in the baking tin, and the center will be nicely rounded. Test it gently with your finger again. An indentation will remain when it's ready to bake. Slide the pans into the center of the hot oven, leaving a little room between them and not touching the sides of the oven so that air can circulate freely. Bake until nicely browned (about 25 to 30 minutes).   2 LOAVES

When you remove the bread from the oven, immediately take out of the pans. Cool on a wire rack or place across the tops of the baking pans. Nope, don't open a window yet. If the bread is in a direct draft, the crust will crack.

Note: If you want an *extra-crisp crust,* do not grease the loaves and do not cover.

If you prefer the crust *very highly glazed,* just before baking, brush the top of the bread with 1 egg yolk that has been mixed with 2 tablespoons water.

Interior color: When the loaf is cut or the roll broken, the color of the interior or crumb may be checked. Color here depends upon the kind of flour, liquid, sweetening, and other ingredients used. If the product has been properly mixed and thoroughly baked, there will be no light and dark streaks. Eggs impart a yellow color, which may vary from light to deep yellow, depending upon the color of the yolk and the amount of egg used in the recipe.

Texture: When the loaf is cut, rub your fingers over the interior. It should feel soft and fine with no crumbliness.

Grain: For the grain to be good, the size and shape of cells or air spaces should be uniform. An even distribution of fine, thin-walled cells, close together with no large air bubbles, is characteristic of the grain of breads made from yeast doughs. Batter yeast breads, however, may have slightly less-uniform cells which are not as close together.

Flavor: A sweet, nutty flavor is characteristic of most well-baked products. The flavor of products varies with the kind and amount of flavoring ingredients added.

Eating quality: Roll a small piece of the bread between your fingers. It should be slightly moist and "give" with slight pressure but return to shape when the pressure is released. A small piece should be tender and tear easily when pulled apart. Test for chewability. The interior should be elastic or springy, soft, and tender.

RECIPE FOR WHOLE-WHEAT BREAD

1 package yeast	2 tablespoons shortening
1 cup lukewarm water	1 tablespoon salt
1 cup milk	6 cups unsifted whole-wheat
¼ cup molasses	flour (or less)

In a large bowl put yeast and lukewarm water. Allow to soften. Heat milk to just under boiling point. Add milk to molasses, shortening and salt. Allow to cool until milk is lukewarm and add to yeast. Gradually add flour, enough to make a soft dough. Mix well and let stand for ten minutes.

Turn dough out on a floured surface and knead for 10 to 15

minutes till it no longer sticks to board. Place dough in a large greased bowl, grease the top, cover with a clean cloth and allow it to rise until double in bulk (about 2½ hours) in a very warm place (80° to 85° F.). Test it with your finger. It will leave an indentation when dough is doubled.

Punch dough down and allow to rise again for 30 minutes.

Cut the dough in half and start to form the loaves (see suggestions earlier for shaping loaves). When about halfway through, cover the dough again and allow it to rest about 15 minutes.

Finish the shaping, and place the loaves in greased baking tins (9″ x 5″ x 3″). Grease the surface of the bread and let rise till the dough has again doubled in bulk (about 1¾ hours). Somewhere along here preheat your oven to 375° F.

Give it the finger test again, and if an indentation remains, the bread is ready to bake. Bake in moderately hot oven (or 375° F.) about 50 minutes till nicely brown. Remove the loaves from baking tins immediately and cool on a rack or across the top edges of the tins.   2 LOAVES

RECIPE FOR OATMEAL BREAD

1 cup rolled oats	½ cup molasses
2 cups boiling water	2½ teaspoons salt
1 package active dry yeast or compressed yeast	2 tablespoons melted butter
½ cup lukewarm water	5 cups sifted, all-purpose flour

This recipe requires no kneading. Prepare the rolled oats ahead by pouring the boiling water over them and let stand about 2 hours. Soften the yeast in lukewarm water and add to the oats along with the molasses, salt, and the melted butter. Gradually stir in the flour and beat the whole until it is well mixed. Allow to rise in a warm place (80° to 85° F.) until doubled in size. Beat the mixture again until it is as smooth as possible.

Grease two 9″ x 5″ x 3″ baking tins and divide the mixture between the two. Allow to rise the second time until doubled in bulk (about 1½ hours). Preheat your oven to 375° F.

When ready to bake, place in moderate oven (375° F.) for from 45 to 50 minutes or until nicely brown and loaves start to pull away from sides of pan. Remove from baking tins and allow to cool on a rack or across the top rim of the tins. Cool well before slicing.   2 LOAVES

Note: Baked bread may be frozen successfully up to 3 months. To freeze: cool first, then wrap, label, and place in freezing compartment.

It will take about 3 hours to thaw (a 1-lb. loaf) at room temperature. While thawing, it should be left in original wrapper.

Set out with your loaves: A great crock of sweet butter. Jars of fine jams, jellies, honey, apple butter. A good cheese or two. A bowl of fresh berries, with heavy cream and powdered sugar. The biggest pot of coffee in the house.

Selah.

THE LOBSTER PLOT

The revered state of Maine may have lost its traditional role as the infallible prognosticator of political tides, but no one will ever replace lobster as the Maine ingredient of one of the world's greatest meals. The tides of taste will never recede from the perfection of their native dish as prepared Down East. We promise that all the craft of generations of rock-ribbed natives, their fires flickering on the shores of thousands of beaches and inlets, is preserved in the sage advice to follow:

All of the lobster is edible except the bony shell structure; the small crop or craw in the head of the lobster; the dark sand vein running down the back of the tail meat. The green is the liver (tomalley) and the white is the fat. Both are highly flavored and should be saved. The red, or "coral," is actually the roe or spawn of the lobster.

CLASSIFICATION OF LOBSTERS

All Maine lobsters are carefully graded according to weight before shipment. In some sections of the country the shellfish are sold by the classification names. The classified weights and names are as follows:

1 lb.—chickens	2 lb.—deuces or 2-pounders
1–1⅛ lb.—heavy chickens	2 lb. to 2¼ lb.—heavy selects
1¼—quarters	2¼–2½ lb.—small jumbos
1½–1¾—selects	Over 2½-approx. 4 lb.—jumbos

BOILED LOBSTER

Place live lobsters in a kettle of briskly boiling salted water. Boil for 15–20 minutes depending upon number and size of lobsters. Boil 5 minutes for the first pound, 3 minutes for each additional pound. Remove from water and place on drainboard or wipe dry. Serve whole lobster either hot or cold with a side dish of melted butter.

LOBSTER STEW

For each person to be served allow approximately ½ lb. live lobster. After lobsters have been boiled 7 or 8 minutes, remove meat immediately, saving also the tomalley and coral in ½ cup butter or margarine. Use a very heavy kettle. Then add the lobster meat, cut into fairly large pieces. Cook all together 10 minutes over low heat. Remove from heat, or push kettle back on stove, and cool slightly. Then add, very slowly, 1 quart rich milk, stirring constantly. Allow the stew to stand 5 or 6 hours before reheating for serving. This is one of the secrets of truly fine flavor.

Note: You do not need salt or pepper when stew is prepared in this manner.

For the perfect lobster stew: Stirring is most important in this masterpiece, otherwise it will curdle. According to experts on fine Maine cookery, the important steps to success in creating the perfect nectar (Lobster Stew) are first the partial cooling before gently adding the milk—a mere trickle at a time; the constant stirring until the stew blossoms a rich salmon under your spoon, and finally, the "aging," since every hour that passes improves the flavor. Two days is set up by masters of Lobster Stew for "aging." But 5 or 6 hours is usually the maximum in home preparation.

LOBSTER SALAD

2 cups cooked lobster meat	Salt and pepper
2 stalks celery, diced	1 tablespoon mayonnaise
1 hard-cooked egg, finely chopped	Lettuce

Mix meat, celery, and egg. Season with salt, pepper, and mayonnaise. Mix thoroughly and garnish with crisp, white leaves of head lettuce. Serve with desired dressing.

BROILED LIVE LOBSTER

For each serving split 1 live lobster. To do this use a sharp-pointed knife. Cross the large claws and hold firmly with the left hand. Make a deep incision with the sharp knife at the mouth end and draw knife quickly through the entire length of body and tail. Open lobster flat. Remove intestinal vein, stomach, and liver. Crack claws.

For 4 servings prepare a dressing of 1½ cups cracker crumbs or cracker meal, ½ teaspoon salt, moistened with 2 tablespoons Worcestershire sauce and 4 tablespoons melted butter. Spread dressing generously in cavity from which liver and stomach have been removed. Cut off 4 of the small claws from each lobster and press into the dressing. Place on buttered broiler and broil 8 to 10 minutes on flesh side, turn and broil 6 to 8 minutes on shell side. Serve with melted butter.

BAKED LOBSTER

For each serving use 1 live lobster. Place lobsters on their backs and with a sharp knife split them open. Remove stomach and back vein, leaving all fat, tomalley, and "juice." For 4 servings have ready a dressing made as follows:

Roll or grind 16 round old-fashioned (soda) crackers into fine crumbs; season with salt and pepper. Mix crumbs with ¼ cup melted butter or margarine, ¼ cup whole milk, then moisten to proper consistency with cooking sherry. Stir fresh crabmeat chunks into the sauce and pack lobsters as full as possible with the dressing.

Pour melted butter over them and sprinkle liberally with grated Parmesan cheese and paprika. Bake in a very hot oven until done and serve immediately.

BAKED LOBSTER DE LUXE

4 lobsters	1 cup stock
½ lb. fresh Maine lobster meat	1 cup small toasted bread cubes
2 tablespoons butter	2 tablespoons sherry
½ cup cream	Bread crumbs
2 egg yolks	

Drop live lobsters into kettle of boiling salted water; boil 10 minutes. Set lobsters to one side, belly up so juice does not run out of shell. For stock, cook celery, parsley, and seasoning in lobster water for 15 minutes; strain. In double boiler melt butter; add cream and yolks of eggs; stir as this thickens; add stock. Cook until the consistency of cream sauce. Remove from fire, add lobster meat and toasted bread cubes, sherry.

Next split your lobsters. Remove intestinal vein, stomach, and liver, cut undershell from tail so meat will show, crack large claws, fill body cavity with dressing—be generous—sprinkle with bread crumbs. Bake in hot oven (500° F.) for 10 minutes; set under broiler to brown crumbs if necessary. Can be fixed, all but cooking in oven, several hours before time to serve. Serve with melted butter.

4 SERVINGS

LOBSTER THERMIDOR

6 cold boiled lobsters, 1¼ lb. each	1 cup white sauce
	1 teaspoon dry mustard
½ cup cooked mushrooms, chopped	Salt and cayenne pepper
	Grated Parmesan cheese

Split lobsters lengthwise. Remove meat and cut in small pieces, add to mushrooms and white sauce, into which have been stirred the mustard, salt, and cayenne. Fill lobster shells with the mixture until well rounded. Sprinkle with cheese and brown under a broiler. Serve hot.

6 SERVINGS

FRIED LOBSTER

Use only the lobster tails, cut in pieces the size of a small egg. Roll lightly in a mixture of flour, salt, and pepper, then dip in beaten egg. Roll again in fine toasted bread or cracker crumbs. (A prepared pancake flour can be used for this final rolling.) Fry in deep fat, like scallops.

To prepare lobsters for this dish: Break tail from body. Cut the last joint from tail, then run a sharp knife around inside the tail shell; the meat will drop from the body end of the tail.

LOBSTER ROLL

Blend 2 cups cooked lobster meat with 1 tablespoon mayonnaise. Add ¼ cup finely diced celery, if desired. Mix well, let stand in refrigerator until ready to use. Split and toast 4 hamburger rolls and spread with melted butter. Fill rolls with lobster and serve.

LOBSTER COCKTAIL SAUCE

Mix ½ teaspoon grated horseradish with 1 tablespoon catsup then add 1 teaspoon lemon juice. For added zip include 3 drops Tabasco sauce.

LUXURIOUS POTTED LOBSTER

2 lobsters, 1½ lbs. each, or 2 lbs.	1 clove garlic, minced
lobster tails	1 teaspoon salt
½ cup butter	¼ teaspoon dried basil
Juice of 1 lemon	⅛ teaspoon tarragon
2 tablespoons tomato paste	¼ cup brandy, warmed
½ cup dry sherry	1 tablespoon minced parsley

Thaw lobsters if frozen and split into halves. Into a large Dutch oven or roasting pan measure butter, lemon juice, tomato paste, and dry sherry. Add minced garlic, salt, and herbs. Bring slowly to just under boiling. Place lobsters, or tails, cut side down (remove thin skin from underside of tails), in this sauce. Pour warmed brandy over top and set aflame. When flame dies, cover and simmer gently 12 to 15 minutes. Sprinkle minced parsley over top. On the plate with each serving serve a little cup of dipping sauce from the pot.   2 TO 4 SERVINGS

A DOWN-EAST CLAMBAKE

You can stage a clambake in your own backyard, on the strand of the nearest body of salt water, or on the actual rock-ribbed coast of Maine. Down-Easters have really made a science of how to succeed in this great cooking adventure. It isn't simple. But if you really have the time, and the helpers, and the yen to put together a colossal feast, here's how you go about it.

There are many ways to arrange a clambake. The variations are due to the materials available and individual fancy. Basically, the processes are the same: To generate sufficient steam to cook thoroughly all foodstuffs within a concentrated space. During the cooking process, there is actually no fire or red coals under the bake. No flame or even red coals come in contact with any part of the bake. The necessary heat is produced by rocks, previously heated by a hot fire. On top of the hot rocks, wet seaweed is placed, which generates the steam. The most popular procedure is as follows:

Dig a shallow, circular hole in the ground from 8 to 10 inches deep. The diameter will depend on the number of persons to be fed. Approximate sizes are suggested as follows:

For 20 persons	3-foot circle
50 persons	5-foot circle
100 persons	7-foot circle
250 persons	9-foot circle
500 persons	Use two 8-foot circles

This hole is next lined with rocks. Some types of rocks will hold the heat better than others; therefore, care should be taken not to use soft rocks that crumble easily or are extremely porous. Flat sandstone, for instance, does not work very well. The harder rocks, especially those having a smooth surface, are preferable. Usually the desirable type is found in round or oval shapes. They should not be less than 6 inches thick. Generally speaking, rocks the size of a football are about right.

Arrange rocks so that the tops are about the same level and as close together as possible. When rocks are all in place, take a small birch tree, pine bough, or any other material available; and brush off all dirt or sand, leaving the rocks as clean as possible. A live green tree branch is suggested as the rocks will have to be swept off clean again later on after the fire has heated the rocks. If an ordinary dry broom is used, it will catch fire very quickly from the very hot rocks. A broom dampened by water, so as not to catch fire as quickly, has been tried; but it only serves to take heat from the rocks. If small live green saplings are available, a broom can be made of them.

For a 7-foot circle, about half a cord of good dry hardwood is sufficient. For a smaller circle, use proportionately less wood. If only softwood is available, it will take a little longer to heat the rocks; and, accordingly, a little more wood will be needed. Sixteen-inch stove-length wood has proven to be about the best size. (Larger sizes take longer to burn.) For an extremely large circle, 4-foot wood can be used. Small kindling wood will, of course, be necessary to start the fire.

Keep the fire going over the entire surface of the circle of rocks. Do not build the fire too high as the purpose is to heat the rocks beneath. Coax fire along and keep it as hot as possible. Expert judgment usually enters into the picture at this point; but, with a fair amount of judgment, the average person can determine when the rocks have reached the right temperature. It is seldom that the rocks will be too hot, though it is possible. A fairly good test is to push aside some of the burning wood from one or two rocks, not too near the edge, and drop about half a teaspoon of water on them. If the rocks are hot enough, the water will immediately sizzle and turn into steam almost instantly or within a fraction of a second.

In order for the rocks to reach this degree of heat, it will probably take 2 hours under ordinary conditions. If the rocks are not hot enough, it will spoil the whole process and they must be reheated. If rocks are too hot, less difficulty will be encountered. The inexperienced will probably not get the rocks hot enough the first time.

When it is decided that the rocks are hot enough, remove all burning wood with a steel rake, hoe or other handy implement, also all remaining coals. At this point it is necessary to work fast as the rocks will start cooling to some extent. Take the green branch and brush off the rocks, removing all the ashes possible. This is done to prevent dirt and ashes from later rising into the food and also to prevent any small unburned particles or remaining coals from creating any further smoke.

Now place on the clean hot rocks a layer of wet seaweed. Down-Easters use the type of seaweed known as rockweed (the kind that lobsters are packed in when shipped). This layer of seaweed should be about 6 inches deep and should cover all the rocks. Care should be taken to cover all rocks around the edges to prevent the canvas cover from burning. As soon as the wet seaweed is placed on the hot rocks, steam will be generated. Work fast so as not to lose any more steam than necessary.

Clams that have been washed clean can now be placed right on top of the seaweed as was done in olden days. A modern and much more convenient method is to place a layer of ½-inch or ¾-inch wire mesh screen on top of the seaweed and then place the clams on the top of this screen. This makes it much easier when the time comes to remove the clams and prevents the clams from getting mixed up in the seaweed.

Spread clams evenly on wire screen or wet seaweed, whichever method is used. A bushel of clams will offer a generous helping for 30 persons; a barrel will suffice for 100 persons.

Do not add any more seaweed. It is not necessary to alternate layers of weed and clams and more weed and then lobsters, etc. Any additional layers will prevent steam from reaching layers above. Place lobsters directly on top of clams. The number of lobsters will depend on the size of bake and the number of persons.

On top of lobsters place any or all the following items, depending on personal taste: sweet corn, frankfurters, sweet potatoes (Irish can be substituted—potatoes should be uniform in size and not too large), and eggs.

Leave the last layer of husk on the corn to keep it nice and clean. The remaining food listed is best if wrapped in cheesecloth bags. It will exclude any dirt and serve to keep items separate. If one does not care to take preliminary efforts to make cheesecloth bags, small quantities of the various items can be carefully placed in a square yard of cheesecloth, the edges being gathered together and tied. To prevent eggs from breaking easily, they should be boiled 2 or 3 minutes beforehand, or just long enough for the whites to become firm. They can then be placed in cheesecloth, the same as the other food, and will be hardboiled when bake is completed.

If chicken is desired, it should be previously parboiled from 20 to 30 minutes, depending on size. Broilers should be cut in half. Larger birds should be quartered. They are then placed in cheesecloth and placed with the other food.

Cover all with a piece of canvas that completely protects the whole thing. Care should be taken to see that as little steam as possible escapes around the edges. Small stones or other weights can be placed on top of the canvas around edges. Make sure the canvas does not touch hot rocks around the edges. Keep stones covered with seaweed or the canvas will scorch or burn.

As soon as seaweed is placed on hot rocks, all food must be placed on the rocks immediately as every minute that goes by means losing the value of the steam being generated.

Many experts agree that no seaweed should be placed on top of the bake. In the olden days when no canvas was available, the bake was covered with seaweed to keep in the steam. This was far from satisfactory as in this method much of the steam escaped. Another reason why no weed should be placed on top is that the juices from the weed, although harmless, are of a rusty brown color due to the chemical composition and often discolor the food being prepared.

After being well covered, the bake can remain for about one hour. This should be a sufficient length of time to cook properly all food contained.

To make sure the bake is ready to uncover, take the edge of the canvas and lift up. If the lobster nearest the edge is done, you are ready. If not, let bake remain covered a while longer. If there is a wind blowing, probably the side in the direction from which the wind is coming will be the coolest edge. Lift up edge at this point for trial to see if your bake is done. If so, you may be sure the rest is done as the hottest part naturally will be in the center.

The *barrel method* of baking clams is convenient and is very popular for small groups. Hot rocks, which have been brought to the required heat, are placed in a large barrel which has soaked overnight in water to absorb as much as possible. Seaweed is placed on top of the rocks, then layers of food, and finally the top covered with damp cloth or burlap bags. If the stones are hot enough, it will take from an hour to an hour and a half for the bake to be done.

If you plan to have your clambake in your back yard, or down at the picnic grounds on the beach or in a nearby glade, the *pot bake* method is probably the best.

This manner of cooking is used primarily in localities where rockweed is not available. The procedure is about the same as at home on the kitchen range. Clams, lobsters, and potatoes are placed in a large kettle or stock pot containing 2 inches or so of water. The pot is placed on a grate over the usual type of campfire. The steam rising through the "bake" does the cooking, which normally takes from an hour to two hours, depending on size. This method can be carried on miles distant from the seashore but lacks the appropriate atmosphere. Without the use of rockweed the flavor is, of course, good but quite different. The use of rockweed in other methods described imparts the true delicious flavor due to the many different chemical sea salts contained.

Among other food items which may be included and served with baked foods are: pickles, potato chips, salt and pepper, sugar, quarts of melted butter, crackers, gallons of coffee, buckets of beer, pints of heavy cream, radishes, cheese, doughnuts. Implements to have on hand for preparing fire and handling foods are: clean heavy canvas gloves, hoe, shovel. Don't forget: picnic plates for lobsters, food trays for clams, cups and spoons for coffee.

ROAST A SUCKLING PIG

This is another adventure which smacks of high doings in old English inns. And it really is the crusher if any among your crowd has cast aspersions—to your best girl, naturally—on the somewhat modest artistry required in your previous cooking efforts of a more basic sort.

Yet this is not too complicated a process. You must first divest yourself of our modern point of view that steaks and chops and loins are inanimate things bought at a butcher's. You have to be realistic about this, and not saddened as a girl I know is, who adores leg of lamb, but almost loses her appetite if the cut is delivered with the tail still adhering. It reminds her of her poodle.

If you suspect that any of your guests are going to be shattered by a sudden recollection of Uncle Waldo, their boss at lunch, or other tender digressions, when you carry in your small triumph, apple in mouth, cranberries in the eye sockets, and a wreath of berries or greens tossed over the head, don't invite them. This repast is for souls with a sense of gourmet historicity, a tribal memory of the grandeur that was Rome, and a thankfulness that they themselves have never appeared on a platter, apple in mouth, regarding the assemblage with twinkling cranberries.

So, to the feast:

First check with your butcher as to the availability of a suckling pig. It will have to be ordered well ahead. German and Chinese butchers are the best for this kind of thing. They not only know where and when to get them, but how to cook them as well, and your culinary cause will be in sympathetic hands. Keep in mind when ordering that the head and feet of the pig will weigh quite a lot, so don't go wild with your guest list. Be sure, too, that you take into consideration the size of your oven.

So now you've brought the little friend home. Clean, wash, scrape, and wipe with a damp cloth. Rub well inside and out with salt, and inside with about 3 tablespoons brandy. Stuff the pig with the following mixture:

½ lb. mushrooms
⅓ cup melted butter
3½ cups crumbs (to be made from soft rolls)
The liver of the pig (which you have parboiled for 4 minutes in salted water, and put through the food chopper)
1 clove of garlic, finely chopped
1¼ lbs. calf liver (which also goes through the food chopper, unless you get the butcher to grind it for you)

½ cup finely chopped onion or scallions
1 cup chopped apples
About 3 tablespoons chopped parsley
Salt and pepper
¼ teaspoon each powdered cloves, nutmeg, thyme, and saffron
2 eggs
½ cup dry white wine

Chop mushrooms fine and dump them into a large saucepan containing melted butter. Put the saucepan over a gentle flame and stir around about 1 minute.

Mix all other stuffing ingredients, except eggs and wine, thoroughly, taste to see if it needs more salt, and add the whole lot to the mushrooms and butter in the saucepan. Cook and continue to stir the stuffing over the gentle flame 6 or 7 minutes.

Remove from the heat. Stir in whole eggs and wine. Allow to cool, then stuff the pig and sew or skewer up the opening.

To place the pig in your roasting pan, first press the forward feet forward, the hindfeet backward, and skewer them so they'll stay in that position. Force the mouth open and insert a small block of wood (small-apple size). Protect the ears from burning by pinning around them two sheets of oiled brown paper. Rub the entire pig with peanut oil or another good fresh cooking oil. The pig should be roasted in an uncovered pan.

Your oven should be preheated to very hot or 550° F. Add 1 cup strong meat stock or bouillon to the roasting pan, and allow the pig to sear at this high heat for 15 minutes.

Reduce the oven heat to slow or 300° F. Now continue to roast the pig until it is very tender, allowing at least 30 minutes to the pound.

Baste the pig every 15 or 20 minutes. Remove the paper from the ears after the pig has cooked for 2½ hours. At this time, brush all over the skin with very thick cream.

When the roast is tender and brown, remove from oven and place it on a hot serving platter. Rub all over with fresh butter till the skin is very shiny.

To garnish: Replace the wood block with a small, shiny red apple. Place cranberries in the eyes, and if you like, put a wreath of parsley and watercress around its neck. This is easily made by tying sprigs of the greens to a circle of wire. The edges of the platter can be decorated with baked apples or spiced crab apples. If you prefer, serve a large bowl of apple sauce on the side.

TO MAKE SUCKLING PIG GRAVY

Mix together three tablespoons flour with a little cold water. Do this gradually so it does not lump. Slowly add to the liquid in the roasting pan, stir, and gradually add a little water and allow to cook for a few minutes till the taste of the raw flour has been removed. To remove excess fat quickly from the gravy, pour it through a cheesecloth that has been wrung out in ice water.

To make this gravy even richer, you can parboil the heart of the suckling pig on top of the stove while the roasting process is going on. When it is tender, chop very fine or put through the food chopper. Add the chopped meat plus a little of the cooking liquid to the gravy and bring to a boil again. Season and serve.

A TOUCH OF GREATNESS:

chef d'oeuvres of famous chefs

Watching the great ones perform is always a help. You serve better after seeing Pancho Gonzales rifle his tremendous shots, and untold numbers of basketball players must have learned as much by watching Bob Cousy on TV as by spending the same amount of time on the court.

If you ever have the good fortune to step into the kitchen at a great restaurant, it usually has two effects which pull in opposite directions. What the chef is doing, and how his staff scurries about to bring everything to perfection at the same precise moment, are fascinating: but you are apt to be overwhelmed by the array of pots and pans, the army of utensils, and the bustling complexities of the scene.

My plan is to bring you the skill without the loss of confidence on your part by brushing against a master at his work. By now you can cook efficiently and comfortably. You've probably already developed a bag of little tricks of your own which mightily improve your favorite dishes. But it's just at this point that you need a few fresh adventures to challenge your skill and enlarge your repertoire.

There are certain hotels, restaurants, and inns where a man feels himself in the presence of a true craft. The atmosphere is courtly, or clublike, or charming in its own particular way, and when you suddenly discover that the food lives up to the place, you know that you've gained a treasure. I haven't tried to be comprehensive in my survey of great recipes by famous chefs, either in exclusivity or geography. That kind of coverage has been done elsewhere. But I did go directly to famous restaurateurs I know personally, who also enjoy prestigious reputations among masculine diners (a far more pesky breed than women, as every headwaiter knows), and with great generosity they selected and developed recipes particularly suited to a man's cooking requirements and his palate—relatively simple preparations mostly (although you must realize that what is "simple" to a world-famous chef might strike an ordinary guy as extraordinarily subtle and complicated), ranging from classic New England dishes to flamboyant Continental masterpieces.

Here they are, with just a word or two to remind you of their place of origin, and the pleasures of dining there as well as sampling their perfections in your own manse.

The lordly *Château Frontenac,* towering over Quebec City like some storied castle, is world-renowned as a symbol of the grand style. Its special recipe brings with it the pine breath and cool beauty of nearby Laurentian streams and waterfalls:

BAKED BROOK TROUT QUEBEÇOISE

3 oz. fresh butter

1 tablespoon chopped green
  onions

¼ lb. salt pork (cut in fine
  julienne strips)

6 brook trout (heads cut off)

12 slices bacon

1 teaspoon lemon juice

¼ teaspoon Worcestershire
  sauce

Salt and pepper

Place butter in open baking pan, add green onions and salt pork, sauté lightly, then place trout, which has been rolled in bacon, into pan. Bake fish in 400° oven, until browned on both sides evenly. Remove trout to a platter. Add in pan: lemon juice, Worcestershire sauce, salt and pepper to taste; bring to a boil and pour over fish. Serve with lemon wedges and steamed potatoes on bouquet of fresh parsley.

The town of Springfield, Vermont, not only has the nicest people on this planet, but it has two personalities. The bustle of Main Street reflects a machine-tool industry which sprang from the minds of America's greatest gunsmiths in Colonial times and has retained their infinitely precise touch to this modern day. Above this is the bucolic quiet of a common-on-a-hillside, and there is no place lovelier. And on this common is *The Hartness House,* named after the Governor whose residence it once was. The Hartness House has everything a traveler may sigh for: traditional dignity and comfortable modernity. An example of this wonderful blend is discovered as you wend your way underground from the main house to what was formerly the Governor's private observatory, sunk into the hillside, and companion to his international reputation as an astronomer. This romantic structure has now been converted to a bar, elegant and modern as any you'll remember from Park Avenue, and the nearby delights of both the Green and the White Mountains are intensified by the cool reminiscence lodged in a perfect martini. The dining room of the Hartness House is, like all the rest of it, the ideal that we all carry in the back of our minds when we go a-traveling. And from the Hartness menu, which host Kingsley Smith has created as carefully as he has created his masterpiece of an inn, we filch:

BROILED JUMBO PANAMA SHRIMP
WITH SEAFOOD DRESSING

1 pkg. Ritz crackers, ground fine	Melted butter
6 oz. chopped shrimp	48 large Panama shrimp,
2 teaspoons garlic powder	cleaned and split
2 teaspoons salt	Lettuce leaves, large
¼ teaspoon pepper	Toast
3 tablespoons Worcestershire	Lemon
sauce	Chopped parsley
Dash Tabasco sauce	

First, be advised that the Panama shrimp are sizable enough to run 8 to 10 to the pound, in contrast to regular shrimp, which run 20 to 26 per pound. In shelling and cleaning and splitting the shrimp, be sure to lift all of the meat clear of the shell *without,* however, breaking the membrane at the tail which holds it. In this way the meat does not adhere to the shell on the bottom, but is cooked evenly throughout. Now mix crackers, chopped shrimp, seasonings, and 12 oz. melted butter to form a loose paste, moist but not fluid. The shrimps are now packed with this dressing, and of course you want it just solid enough to hold in place. Place shrimps on broiler rack and cover each one with lettuce leaves. Broil for 15 minutes. Discard lettuce leaves. Arrange on toast points, pour melted butter over all to taste, season with squeeze of lemon and chopped parsley.   12 SERVINGS

High on another hill, overlooking the Hudson River and the Tappan Zee Bridge, is Westchester's *Tappan Hill Restaurant.* Vying with the view is an equally tremendous menu. Our selection from it is:

VEAL CHOPS AND KIDNEY TRIFOLATI

4 loin veal chops with kidney	Good pinch chopped parsley (the
Salt and pepper (preferably	Italian kind preferred)
pepper from the peppermill)	1 clove garlic, chopped
1 tablespoon flour	6 ounces dry white wine
4 tablespoons butter	

Salt and pepper the chops on both sides and dust with flour; melt butter in sauté pan and brown chops well on both sides, on a low flame, so as not to burn butter; add chopped parsley and chopped clove garlic; cover pan and let cook for several minutes, or until the chops are done. Remove chops to serving platter (preheated); drain fat, if any, from sauté pan and add white wine; let wine come to a boil, stirring the brown juices which will have collected during cooking at the bottom of the pan; a rich, brown gravy will result; pour this over chops and serve while hot.   2 SERVINGS

Those who love New England never pass *The Publick House,* in Sturbridge, Massachusetts, and happily there on its dreaming common since 1771. Here is Chef John Wetteland's mouth-watering memento:

INDIVIDUAL LOBSTER PIE,
TREADWAY INN STYLE

2 tablespoons butter	3 tablespoons butter
¼ cup sherry or ¼ cup water	1 tablespoon flour
with 1 tablespoon lemon juice	¾ cup thin cream
1 cup well-packed lobster meat	2 egg yolks

Note: The Publick House chef does not use flour, but as sauce takes both practice and skill to make, the flour is recommended.

Melt 2 tablespoons butter. Add sherry. Boil 1 minute. Add lobster and let stand.

Melt 3 tablespoons butter in saucepan. Add flour. Stir until it bubbles 1 minute. Remove from heat. Slowly stir in cream and wine drained from lobster. Return to heat and cook, stirring all the time, until the sauce is smooth and thick. Remove from heat.

Beat egg yolks very well. Stir into yolks 4 tablespoons sauce, 1 tablespoon at a time. Add to sauce, mixing well. Heat over hot water either by placing the saucepan with mixture in it in a larger saucepan, ⅓ full of hot water—or heat in top of double boiler. Water should not be allowed to get hot enough to boil. If it does, sauce may curdle or break. Sauce should be stirred constantly while heating. It takes about 3 minutes.

Remove from heat. Add lobster. Turn into small, deep pie plate. Sprinkle with topping. Bake in slow oven 300° F. for 10 minutes.

2 SERVINGS

TOPPING FOR LOBSTER PIE

¼ cup cracker meal   1½ teaspoons Parmesan cheese
¼ teaspoon paprika   2 tablespoons melted butter
1 tablespoon finely crushed
  potato chips

Mix first four ingredients. Add melted butter and blend well.
Sprinkle on lobster pie.

Salisbury, Connecticut, is an unspoiled town, lovely as any in
New England, and yet not far from New York City. One of its
attractions is the *Ragamont Inn*. Its hosts, J. Dean and Eda Ham-
mond, give us some unusual and informal suggestions:
"Here is a dish so simple no recipe is necessary and yet it is very
popular with men at luncheon time or as a late supper tempter.
We list it on the menu as *Grilled Chopped Choice Sirloin with
Horseradish Sauce and Fried Banana*. The Horseradish Sauce can
be as hot or as mild as desired. (See recipe on page 144.) We bread
the half banana slightly before sautéing it to a crisp golden brown.
It is then laid across the top of the sirloin patty with its creamy
horseradish sauce. Served with Lyonnaise potatoes and one's favorite salad bowl, it makes a hearty and tasty meal which could be
prepared outdoors on the charcoal grill after you have fixed the
sauce and readied the banana slices ahead of time.
"Another way of adding excitement and zest to chopped sirloin
(or hamburger!) is to stuff it with wined bleu cheese and serve it
with a wined mushroom sauce or just plain."

Another joyful sight in Salisbury is the *White Hart Inn*. The tap
room is an incomparable spot to be in when the evening chimes
breathe over the village. But ahead is more delight, supplied by
Hotelier John D. Harney, in the form of

WHITE HART SCAMPI

¼ lb. butter   ⅛ fresh lemon
2 cloves garlic, chopped   ½ tablespoon white wine
3 lbs. raw shrimp, peeled and
    deveined

Put butter in large frying pan, add garlic. Heat butter to brown the garlic, then add shrimp. Cook at high heat for 10 minutes or until shrimp is done. Squeeze juice from lemon wedge over pan and add wine. Put in heated casserole and place under hot broiler for 3 or 4 minutes. Garnish with sprig of fresh parsley and serve.   6 SERVINGS

College inns are usually fine places to refresh mind, body, and spirit. Among the best is the *Lord Jeffrey,* in Amherst, Massachusetts, near the beautiful Amherst College campus. Expert at pleasing men, the Lord Jeffrey's innkeeper suggests the classic recipe for:

VICHYSSOISE

4 leeks   1 cup light cream
3 medium-size potatoes   1 cup heavy cream
4 cups strong chicken stock   Chopped chives

Finely slice the white part of the leeks and an inch of the green part. Pare and thinly slice the potatoes. Simmer the leeks and potatoes in chicken stock until very soft, about 40 minutes. The stock should be fat free if the soup is to be served cold; otherwise the fat will rise to the top and look unappetizing. If the soup is to be served hot, it doesn't matter; in fact, you can add 2 tablespoons butter to the stock. When the vegetables are cooked, put them through a coarse strainer or food mill, pushing through all the vegetables possible, then put them through a fine strainer. Better still, put them in an electric blender with the stock; then you won't lose any of the vegetables and the soup will be truly smooth. Blend in light cream with the puréed vegetables and stock and taste for seasoning. Chill for several hours in the refrigerator in a china bowl —a metal bowl will flavor the soup. Before serving, add heavy cream. If the soup is too thick, it can be thinned with milk. Serve in chilled soup bowls and garnish each serving with a few chopped chives.   8 TO 10 SERVINGS

The Blue Spruce Inn, in Roslyn, Long Island, is a touch of country dining only a short distance from Manhattan. Host Carl Werner offers a fine hot appetizer:

RIVER SHRIMP IN DILL

3 lbs. fresh unshelled shrimp	1 bay leaf
2 quarts boiling water	3 peppercorns
1 tablespoon salt	1 teaspoon vinegar
1 clove garlic, peeled, crushed	

Wash shrimp. Put in kettle with the other ingredients. Simmer covered 10 minutes or until done. Allow to stand in liquid 20 minutes. Shell, strain, saving liquor. Serve surrounded with the following sauce:

Thicken 2 cups shrimp liquid with 2 tablespoons flour, stir till smooth. Reduce to half 1 cup dry white wine, add 6 scallions, minced. Add the cream sauce, bring to a boil, stirring. Strain and add 8 tablespoons finely chopped dill, season with salt and dry sherry and serve hot.

The Empire State Club, in the building that towers over the rest of the world, also boasts some high-style dishes. Manager John W. Cremers vouches for the popularity of this one:

BAVARIAN SAUERBRATEN

3 five-lb. pieces bottom round	1½ gallons water
3 medium-size onions	Salt and pepper
1 whole stalk celery	2 cups olive oil
3 medium-size carrots	4 oz. flour
5 cloves garlic, crushed	1 quart bulk tomatoes
¼ bunch parsley, roughly cut	1 quart tomato purée
3 oz. mixed pickling spices	1 gallon beef stock
1½ pints wine vinegar	1 pint sour cream
1½ pints red wine	

Place meat in clay crock, add to it onions, celery, carrots, garlic, parsley, pickling spices, vinegar, wine, and water. Add salt and pepper. Cover and let sit in refrigerator for 3 days.

To cook the sauerbraten, place meat in 450° oven and keep turning until browned. Drain liquid from vegetables (keep liquid). Heat olive oil in large cooking pot and add vegetables. When lightly browned add flour and mix until flour and vegetables have blended. Add liquid, stirring continuously, add tomatoes, tomato purée, and beef stock. Place meat, now browned, in thick liquid and cook in oven at moderate temperature for 3¼ hours, stirring from time to time. When cooked, remove meat, strain sauce and add sour cream. Salt and pepper if necessary.

Serve with red cabbage, Bavarian style, and potato pancakes.

30 SERVINGS

No city in the world can outdo New York either in the quality or the diversity of its restaurants. Those at the very top are incomparable, and so wonderful they are that favineso as well as diplomacy makes it impossible to grade them. Suffice it to say that none surmounts *Chateaubriand* in elegance and offering to the refined palate. One of its most famous is:

COQ AU VIN

½ cup diced salt pork or bacon

2 tablespoons butter

1 three-and-a-half-lb. chicken or 2 two-lb. chickens cut in 8 pieces

Salt and pepper to taste

12 small white peeled onions

12 small mushrooms

2 tablespoons flour

2 or 3 minced shallots or 2 or 3 minced small white onions

1 or 2 minced garlic cloves

2 cups of red Burgundy wine

Parboil salt pork, then sauté it in 2 tablespoons butter till brown, in a large skillet or saucepan. Remove and set aside pork scraps.

Season the chicken with salt and pepper to taste. Brown the chicken in fat in which pork was browned, add the onions and the mushrooms, cover, and cook over low heat till onions are lightly browned, turning occasionally.

Pour ½ the fat in the pan into another saucepan. Blend in the flour, add the minced shallots or onions and the minced garlic. Cook over low heat, stirring constantly till thickened. Remove from heat and gradually add the wine while stirring. Return to heat, add reserved pork, bring to a boil, stirring, and add the whole thing to the chicken.

Cover and simmer till chicken is tender, about ½ hour. To serve, arrange the chicken and vegetables in a deep dish or casserole. Skim fat from gravy and season to taste. Pour over chicken.

4 SERVINGS

Serving many of the same customers in a far different atmosphere is the *Grand Central Terminal Restaurant* on the lower level of the famous station. But, in its own way, it is also superb. As most men already know, there is no better clam or oyster stew to be found in the world than at this haven near the tracks. And here is the magic recipe:

CLAM OR OYSTER STEW

Place a pat of butter in a deep pan, sprinkle a little paprika and celery salt over butter, add ½ teaspoon Worcestershire sauce and 5 oz. clam broth, stir for 8 minutes, till it starts to boil, then add 8 oysters or clams, keep on stirring for about 2 minutes and then add 10 oz. milk, stir until it gets to boiling point. Pour into a bowl, top with a pat of butter and a sprinkle of paprika.

Do not boil, as it will curdle. A double boiler is best for home preparation.

The most talked-about restaurant in New York, and that probably means the world, is *The Four Seasons*. Its walls are decorated by Picasso, and its air, freshened by fountains and pools, suggests some kingly villa in the days when kings waved a hand and the best immediately appeared. Chef Director Albert Stockli has a recipe in keeping with the décor and the tradition in Manhattan that if you haven't been to The Four Seasons, and can drop it unostentatiously but clearly into your cocktail conversation, you've had it. But wait until you have this:

LOBSTER AROMATIC

1 tablespoon chopped shallots
8 oz. butter
2 lbs. fresh boiled lobster meat
1½ oz. Pernod
3 oz. brandy
3 oz. sherry
¼ teaspoon paprika
⅛ teaspoon thyme
¼ teaspoon curry powder

¼ teaspoon ground fennel
⅛ teaspoon cayenne
¾ teaspoon salt
Juice of 1 lemon
1 pint Sauce Américaine
   (See below)
½ pint heavy cream, whipped
   stiff
Cooked white rice

Sauté shallots in butter until a little brown. Remove meat from lobster and add; turn slightly in butter and shallots. Add Pernod, brandy, and sherry and flambé. Mix together paprika, thyme, curry powder, fennel, cayenne, and salt, and when flames have diminished, sprinkle lightly over top and mix with lobster and sauce. Add lemon juice. Blend in Sauce Américaine. Do not stir. Fold in whipped cream a little at a time with a gentle, blending, turning motion. Do not stir and see that mixture does not boil.

Place cooked white rice on serving plate, forming a ring. Spoon lobster meat and part of sauce into center of ring. Spoon remainder of sauce around the rice ring.   4 SERVINGS

SAUCE AMERICAINE

1½ lbs. lobster pieces
½ onion, minced
3 oz. butter
1 bay leaf
4 oz. brandy

1 tablespoon flour
4 tablespoons tomato purée
3 oz. water
5 oz. fish stock

Chop lobster with onion. Place in saucepan. Add butter. Stir over medium-high flame until lobster turns red. Add bay leaf. Add brandy and flambé. Mix in flour, then tomato purée and water. Cover and simmer for 20 minutes. Strain into bowl and add fish stock. Return lobster pieces to the sauce.   1 PINT

If you work at CBS, or on any of the big national magazines put together around Madison Avenue and Fifty-second Street, you'll know that "the place" is, naturally, *Louis and Armand's*. Bigwigs entertain there, and littlewigs watch. Chef Mario de Boca tells us that the dish he is most often asked for is

BREAST OF CHICKEN VALDOSTANA

2 breasts of chicken	1 beaten egg
1 slice prosciutto ham	White sandwich bread crumbs
2 thin slices mozzarella (thickness of 50¢ piece)	(no crust)
	Grated Parmesan cheese
1 oz. white truffles	Butter
Flour	

Bone the 2 breasts of chicken. Remove the skin and pound the breasts as thin as possible. Cut the prosciutto in julienne strips. Place some in the center of each piece of chicken. Place mozzarella over the ham. On each portion add 5 slices white truffles over the mozzarella. Take each side of the chicken and fold toward the center, then take the bottom and top of the chicken and fold toward the center. Press lightly together to form cushion effect. Roll in flour, then dip in beaten egg. Then dip in bread mixture consisting of 3 parts bread crumbs and 1 part grated Parmesan cheese. Now sauté in butter, using heavy skillet if possible. Cook slowly on each side until brown, always over a slow fire. Remove chicken from the skillet. If desired a dash of Marsala or white wine can be added to gravy and poured over the breasts.   2 SERVINGS

Most New York restaurants must, of necessity, be small since Manhattan's life is vertical, and no way has yet been discovered to duplicate the sociability and *joie de vivre* of a fine dining area by putting it in parts piled one on top of the other. The *Restaurant Laurent* is one of New York's most spacious and elegant restaurants, with a bar area that most restaurateurs would envy for dining alone. One of its most popular dishes reflects the opulent Continental atmosphere:

STEAK AU POIVRE MONTPELLIER

Press coarsely ground black pepper or crushed peppercorns into both sides of a 1-inch-thick steak. Sprinkle both sides lightly with coarse salt.

Broil both sides of the steak (slightly rarer than you desire the finished product). Place steak on a warm platter, place platter on a réchaud and put 1 tablespoon Maître d'Hôtel Butter (page 192) over it. Flambé the steak with one ounce of cognac. Remove the steak from the platter to a hot dinner plate. Blend with the drippings remaining on the platter a few drops of Worcestershire sauce and 1 tablespoon sour cream mixed with 1 teaspoon chopped chives. Swirl the platter over the flame for a moment and pour the pan juices over the steak.

Caution should be taken when adding the sour cream to the platter. The platter should be slightly warm and not hot or the sour cream will curdle.

Janssen's, made famous by the founder (he always wanted to see you), is now run in the same grand tradition by his daughter, Mrs. Dorothy Janssen Szcapka, and the sight of the wild game hung by the Lexington Avenue entrance enlivens many a dulled midtown eye. The menu is Hofbrau, in general, and high on it stands

RAHM-SCHNITZEL IMPORTED PFIFFERLINGE

Season and lightly flour a veal cutlet and sauté in butter until golden brown. Remove to serving dish and keep warm. Deglaze the sautoir (heavy frying pan) in which the veal was cooked by pouring in 1 glass white wine. In another pan make a roux (with flour and butter) and add heavy cream to make a cream sauce. Add wine and blend in slowly. Sauté Pfifferlinge (Bavarian mushrooms) in butter with some chopped shallots and a pinch of fresh chopped tarragon. Combine with cream sauce and pour over veal cutlet. Serve with Spaetzle.

The Spaetzle, after being prepared and dropped into boiling water until done, are then lightly sautéed until golden in color. This gives a slightly crusty quality and eliminates the doughiness complained of in other Spaetzle. And here's how to make

SPAETZLE

Flour, milk, eggs
Salt, pepper, and nutmeg, to taste

To each cup of flour add one egg and a small amount of milk; should not be too loose. Mix together (should not be mixed too hard). Press through colander with large holes, into boiling water. Let boil ten minutes. Pour off water; then sauté in butter.

Many restaurants are impressive, others merely beloved. Thanks to the warmheartedness of the family which created it, and their recognition of a famous restaurant's role in a metropolis, *Leone's* qualifies on both counts. Its menu is enormous and noble, but perhaps the noblest Roman of them all is

SLICED STEAK PIZZAIOLA
(as prepared by Chef Pietro Pioli)

Slices of filet mignon—double thickness—are rapidly broiled then sliced thinly crosswise. The Pizzaiola sauce is prepared separately: Minced garlic and a pinch of orégano are sautéed in olive oil until the garlic is golden brown. Canned tomatoes are added to this and simmered until thickened. A few minced anchovies are added to the mixture just before pouring the sauce over the sliced filet.

Another nostalgic and distinctive natural restaurant is Uncle Paul's *Polonaise.* As formal and beautifully toned as a Chopin nocturne, the dining room is the kind of place where you covertly watch to see what your neighbor is eating before *you* order. But you can't miss with

GOLOMBKI
(Stuffed cabbage, Polish style)

Parboil green cabbage for 10 minutes and separate the leaves. Put through a meat grinder 1 lb. beef, 1 lb. veal, and 1 lb. pork. Season with salt and pepper, add ½ lb. cooked rice and mix. Put mixture on cabbage leaves and roll in tubular form. Put in a pan, cover with strong meat stock, and bake about 1½ hours in a slow oven. Serve with sweet-sour sauce made by creaming one boiled potato with about ½ cup of tomato purée and ½ cup sour cream, adding gradually until proper consistency in thickness is achieved.

To many devotees of the theatre, a visit to *Sardi's* restaurant, hard by Shubert Alley, is as much a part of any Broadway evening as two good ones on the aisle. Host Vincent Sardi is one of the most genuinely cordial gentlemen ever to seat you next to Helen Hayes or Vincent Price as if he were favoring *them.* And he is equally generous with culinary secrets. Here is one of his choicest.

SOFT-SHELL CRABS PROVENÇALE

6 soft-shell crabs	2 cloves garlic, finely chopped
¼ cup light cream	1 cup stewed tomatoes
¼ cup flour	2 slices lemon
¼ cup butter	2 boiled potatoes

Wash live crabs thoroughly. Make a cut near the eyes and lift pointed ends on each side of the back shell. Remove sandbags and spongy parts. Turn crabs over and cut out segment or apron at lower part of the shell. Dip crabs in cream and then in flour. Sauté in frying pan with half the butter, turning occasionally until brown on both sides, about 6–8 minutes. In a second frying pan place remaining butter and the chopped garlic and brown lightly. Then add stewed tomatoes and heat through. Pour the tomato mixture over the crabs when they are ready and garnish with slices of lemon. Serve with boiled potatoes.   2 SERVINGS

New Yorkers are pleased to have in their midst certain restaurants where the patron understands in advance that he must come equipped with comforting amounts of time and lucre. In return for this largesse, he enjoys ducal dishes and service, and in the case of the *Forum of the Twelve Caesars,* a décor of such senatorial splendor that he may be difficult for his democratic colleagues to put up with for a while after. But not if he offers them such dishes as the two (they go together, if you're ambitious) following:

CALF LIVER MATIUS

1 medium onion	2 lbs. calf liver
1 clove garlic	2 tablespoons butter or
1 cup white wine	margarine
¼ teaspoon tarragon	⅓ cup applejack or apple
1 cup brown gravy (available in cans)	brandy

Make the sauce first: Chop onion and garlic fine, add to white wine and tarragon and cook until liquid is reduced about half—in other words about ½ cup. Stir in gravy, cook until heated thoroughly.

Cut liver in strips about ½ inch wide and 2 inches long. Heat butter or margarine in a skillet or chafing dish, add liver strips and fry over a medium heat for about 3 minutes, stirring occasionally. Liver should be brown outside but still pink inside. Warm the applejack or apple brandy in a little container, put a match to the liquor and flame. Pour over liver strips. When flame dies out mix liver with the sauce. Delicious with the Forum's Gnocchi.

4–6 SERVINGS

THE FORUM'S GNOCCHI

1 cup water	3 eggs
5 tablespoons butter or	1 teaspoon dry mustard
margarine	1¼ cups grated Gruyère cheese
¾ teaspoon salt	3 tablespoons flour
¼ teaspoon cayenne pepper	1¼ cups milk
1½ cups all-purpose flour	1 egg yolk
	¼ cup cream

Combine water, 2 tablespoons butter or margarine, ½ teaspoon salt and cayenne pepper in a saucepan. Cook until mixture boils, then add flour all at once. Cook, stirring constantly, until mixture pulls away from the sides of the pan and forms a ball of dough. Remove from heat and add eggs, one at a time, beating hard after each addition. Stir in remaining ¼ teaspoon salt, ½ teaspoon mustard and ¼ cup grated cheese. Transfer mixture to a pastry bag with a large plain decorating tube or point in the end. Squeeze dough out of the tube in long pieces (looks like fat spaghetti) into a pan of gently boiling salted water. Cook slowly until dough floats to the surface of the water. Drain and cut into pieces about ½ inch long. Arrange in a shallow baking dish.

Start your oven at broil and make the simple gnocchi sauce: Melt 2 tablespoons butter or margarine in a saucepan. Stir in 3 tablespoons flour smoothly. Then mix in 1 cup milk gradually. Cook, stirring constantly, until mixture bubbles. Stir in ¼ cup grated cheese, remaining ½ teaspoon mustard, cream, and cook slowly for about 5 minutes. Mix the last of the milk (¼ cup) with egg yolk and stir into sauce.

Pour sauce over gnocchi, sprinkling surface with remaining cheese and butter or margarine. Broil until golden on top. Takes about 3 to 5 minutes. Serve hot.

4–6 SERVINGS

The prexy of a great university recently remarked that although he didn't want to say that his school was the best in the business he didn't honestly know of any better one. This is the way Phil Rosen feels about his exclusive *Le Café Chambord,* world famous for its French cuisine. The suggestion of Executive Chef Fernand Desbans —Bouillabaisse—itself symbolizes the Provence region of France and Marseilles. Monsieur Desbans regrets that we do not have Mediterranean rock fish such as *la rascasse* and *le saint pierre* to give this dish the proper Gallic flavor base. But he admits, *voilà,* that with the proper choice of fishes from our home waters something very tempting can be arranged. *Ecoutez:*

BOUILLABAISSE

1½ lbs. red snapper	1 small branch thyme
1½ lbs. sea bass	1 small dessert spoon powdered
1½ lbs. striped bass	saffron
1 lb. halibut	4 oz. vegetable oil (preferably
1 medium onion	olive oil)
1 white of leek	6 oz. white wine
4 ripe tomatoes	Salt and pepper
4 garlic cloves	2 live lobsters about 1½ lbs. each
1 head fennel	1 lb. uncooked shelled shrimp
2 bay leaves	1 lb. mussels in the shell

Skin, clean, and filet the fish. Into a large casserole with wide bottom put chopped onion, chopped leek, peeled tomatoes cut in small pieces, chopped garlic, chopped fennel, bay leaves, thyme, saffron, olive oil, white wine, salt, and pepper. Mix well in casserole.

On top of this mixture lay the fish cut in 3- or 4-inch filets. Cut live lobster in pieces, including the head divided in two, and add shrimp and mussels in shell. Check seasonings. Add additional white wine and boiling water—just enough to cover ingredients.

Put covered casserole on high flame for 15 minutes. (It is important to keep the pot at a fast burn level, so that the ingredients will be properly mixed and married.)

While the pot is on the fire, slice French bread ½ inch thick and toast; rub gently with garlic.

Take fish and shellfish gently out of casserole and arrange in *deep* serving dish. Strain broth over fish and serve while very hot, with above-prepared garlic bread.   6 SERVINGS

. . . and in a somewhat less extensive vein, albeit *élégante,*

VEAL POILLARD

4 veal chops	Enough bread crumbs to cover
Salt and pepper	chops
2 truffles	Grated Parmesan cheese
2 slices ham	Sherry
2 slices Swiss cheese	Brown sauce
1 egg	

Slice veal chops in halves; flatten with a moistened butcher's mallet so as to reduce the meat to half its normal thickness. Season both sides with salt and pepper.

Chop the truffles, ham and Swiss cheese in julienne style. Stuff each veal chop with chopped ingredients and fasten parts together with toothpicks.

Dip the stuffed veal chops into a beaten egg, roll in bread crumbs mixed with grated Parmesan cheese, and fry in clarified butter for five minutes on each side.

Take veal chops out of pan, pour into frying pan 4 oz. sherry and 2 oz. brown sauce (canned will do). Allow mixture to boil for 2 minutes, pour on the veal chops, and serve.   4 SERVINGS

One of the reasons New Yorkers do not have to languish as they hear of the glories of French restaurants in Paris is *The Colony Restaurant,* Gene Cavellero's haunt of the *haut monde.* And he rewards their dedicated loyalty with such treasures as

CHICKEN SAUTE COLONY

Sauté a chicken in butter with 4 oz. raw sliced truffles, then remove the chicken to a dish. To the juices in the pan add ⅓ cup of cream, 3 tablespoons Béchamel Sauce, and reduce. Take from fire and add a little crayfish butter, a few drops lemon juice, a few drops brandy, a little cayenne, and some asparagus tips (cooked). Pour this sauce over the chicken.

Americans love Swedish food almost as much as Swedes themselves do, and New Yorkers and visitors both cherish the genuine board at the *Stockholm Restaurant.* One favorite with all men about town is

SMOTHERED BIFFSTEK

Take a 12-oz. sirloin steak, and flatten it very thin with a meat
hammer. Cut up 2 red or yellow onions very fine and sauté both
steak and onions in hot pan with butter. Serve onions piled high
on top of steak. And with it, stekt potatis: Peel 1½ lbs. boiled
potatoes and slice or cube. Brown 2 tablespoons butter in skillet,
add potatoes, and sprinkle with salt and sugar. Fry until nicely
brown. Sprinkle with parsley and serve.

In a city possibly second only to Rome for fine Italian cooking
(and that possibly open to debate), Manhattan's *Romeo Salta
Restaurant* combines matchless cuisine with a richly intimate atmosphere. Signor Romeo Salta himself has devised the following:

LASAGNE VERDE (Green Noodles)

½ onion, finely chopped	3 tablespoons tomato sauce
2 tablespoons imported olive oil	½ cup water
¼ lb. butter	Salt and pepper
½ lb. chopped beef	1 lb. green noodles
½ cup dry white wine	

Sauté onion in olive oil and butter. Add chopped beef, stirring constantly. When meat is browned, add wine and tomato sauce. Continue to cook over a low flame, gradually add water, a bit at a time;
add salt and pepper to taste. Cook about an hour.

Cook green noodles. Drain; place in large casserole, alternating
layers with sauce. Place in oven for about 15–20 minutes.

Italian cooking being so popular with Americans, our host Romeo
Salta has given us special advice on two very popular additional
preparations men particularly like:

BROILED SCAMPI FOR FOUR

½ onion, finely chopped	Salt and pepper to taste
1 clove garlic, finely chopped	1 cup tomato sauce
1½ teaspoons mustard	16 jumbo shrimp
5 oz. vinegar	Olive oil
1 cup consommé	Bread crumbs

Sauce: Sauté onion and garlic. Add mustard, continue stirring
slowly and add vinegar, consommé, salt, and pepper. Boil for 5

minutes. Add tomato sauce and simmer for another ten minutes over low flame.

Shrimp: Split the back of shrimp and clean. Roll in olive oil, salt, and pepper, then roll in bread crumbs. Broil till brown. They are then ready to dip in sauce. We recommend jumbo shrimp.

SPAGHETTINI WHITE CLAM SAUCE
(ZINGARELLA)

Brown several sections of garlic (we advise not to chop the garlic, so that after giving the flavor the sections may be easily removed) in a casserole containing a base of olive oil about one inch deep heated over a low flame. Add to this fresh clams (about 6 per serving), still within the shells, which have been placed under running water for at least an hour. Season with a dash of orégano and pepper, a few leaves of basil and parsley. Cover and boil for about 10 minutes. Remove from the fire but do not uncover for the time it takes to cook separately the spaghettini. Drain the spaghettini thoroughly before spreading on the sauce.

Many years ago, an unpretentious Italian restaurant, *Del Pezzo's,* located close to the Metropolitan Opera House, won the devotion of those lustiest and most discriminating of food virtuosi, the Italian tenors and baritones and basso profundos of Signor Gatti-Casazza's glittering stable. During the season, if you dropped by to twirl a plateful of spaghetti, your fellow trenchermen would often be Caruso, Amato, Martinelli, or giants of that ilk.

Today, Del Pezzo's, no less beloved by those who cherish fine Italian fare, occupies a regal residence not many blocks away from the old site, but the bravura work in the kitchen still hits all the right notes, such as

ZUPPA DI PESCE

1 lb. whiting	½ cup water
1 lb. striped bass	½ cup white wine
1½ lbs. squid	1 tablespoon chopped parsley
½ lb. medium-size shrimp	½ teaspoon orégano
¼ cup olive oil	Salt and pepper
½ medium-sized onion, finely chopped	1 lb. mussels in shells (washed)
1 clove garlic, minced	1 lb. clams in shells (washed)
1½ cups canned tomatoes	4 toast rounds

Remove skin and wash whiting and bass. Cut each into 4 pieces. Clean squid, cut into small pieces. Shell and clean shrimp. Heat olive oil in large skillet, add onion and garlic, brown lightly. Add tomatoes, bring to boil and simmer 2 to 3 minutes. Add water, wine, parsley, and orégano. Season to taste. Simmer 5 minutes. Add squid, shrimp, mussels, and clams.

Place pieces of whiting and bass around edges of skillet. Cover and simmer 8 to 10 minutes or until fish is tender. Arrange fish and seafood on toast rounds in hot soup plates. Pour unstrained soup over all. Garnish with chopped parsley, if desired.   4 SERVINGS

A wonderful Del Pezzo variant on cooking a chicken is given in

CHICKEN A LA SORRENTINA

1 whole chicken	2 bay leaves
3 oz. olive oil	2 slices prosciutto
1 onion finely chopped	6 oz. chicken broth
2 cloves garlic, finely chopped	6 oz. white wine
¼ lb. fresh mushrooms	Salt and pepper to taste
1 tablespoon butter	Parsley

Brown chicken in olive oil for 10 minutes. Add onion, garlic, and mushrooms, and brown. Strain. Add butter, bay leaves, prosciutto, chicken broth, wine, parsley, salt, and pepper. Put on tight cover. Steam for 15 minutes on a low flame, or until tender.   4 SERVINGS

New York men pride themselves on knowing the great saloons as well as the great restaurants. Tops in their affections (and it has been since well before the turn of the century) is *Billy's Gaslit Bar*.

Robert Sherwood had his favorite corner table there, once upon a time; Marilyn Monroe slips in now and again when she's in town; and the number of celebrities relaxing in the fine old bar often challenges the neighborhood regulars who make it a second home. Billy Condron himself is usually there, heading up a grand gang of bartenders and waiters who all get to be your friends, and good ones, too. The food is simple, by the standards of the others flanking us here, but perfection is its own standard. So, herewith, the secret of Billy's classic

CORNED BEEF AND CABBAGE

4–5 lbs. corned beef	1 clove garlic or 1 whole onion
4 whole cloves	2 stalks celery, sliced
1 bay leaf	1 medium cabbage

Place corned beef in a large, deep kettle. Cover with cold water. Add remaining ingredients except cabbage and heat to boiling. Reduce heat and simmer for 5 minutes. Skim, then continue simmering 3–4 hours, or until tender. Add hot water as needed. Cut cabbage into quarters, remove part of core and arrange on top of corned beef. Cover and cook until cabbage is tender, 10–15 minutes. Serve with horseradish or mustard sauce. Serve with boiled parsley potatoes, mixed fruit salad, and a pitcher of beer.

New York is a city of celebrities. And they get around, or they would cease to be celebrities. And the restaurant with the most autograph hounds baying at its door—sure sign of the genuine quarry—is famous "21." Inside, all is jolly, as the talk at the bar swings from Las Vegas to the safari country, from Miami to the Côte d'Azur, from Hollywood to Paris. Robert Kriendler, a celebrity himself by the process of osmosis, takes all this with friendly calm, and dispenses food that is equally celebrated. Two of the most famous are:

PHEASANT "21"

Take a breast of pheasant and cook in a saucepan with some fresh butter, salt, and pepper. When the meat is browned, remove from saucepan. Add, in same butter where meat is cooked, 1 tablespoon currant jelly. Let the jelly dissolve. Add ½ Delmonico glass of sherry. Let simmer until thick. When thick, add: 10 pitless cherries and the unstrained juice of 1 orange and let it get hot. When very hot, put the breast of pheasant in a serving casserole, and pour the sauce over. Place casserole on the fire and place a cover over it for a few seconds before serving. This dish should be served very hot.

MINCED CHICKEN "21"

1 cup wild rice	¼ pint heavy cream
¼ lb. chicken, dark and white meat, chopped very fine	Salt and pepper

Cook wild rice according to package directions. Place the rice on the bottom of a small "silver dish." Now, place the chicken, mixed with cream, salt, and pepper, on top of that. Spread some Parmesan cheese on top and gratine.

New Yorkers with a yen for seafood get the true New England atmosphere as well in the blue-and-white décor of the *Gloucester House,* with its gleaming copperware adding the Cape Cod note. A marvelous recipe, and easy to prepare, is

CRABMEAT IN BACON

First make a seasoning of: pinch of dry mustard, 1 teaspoon Worcestershire sauce, juice of ½ lemon, few drops of vinegar. Spread this seasoning on very thin slices of Virginia Smithfield bacon. Salt and pepper crabmeat and wrap in the bacon slices, using toothpicks to hold the package together. Cook in oven or under the broiler flame for about 15 minutes, or until bacon is brown and crisp.

Downtown in New York is a Spanish night club, *El Chico,* where the flamenco flares, and the special Iberian dishes have the same triumphant flourishes under Señor Benito Collada's banner. El Chico has pioneered in making popular the food and wines of Spain. Paella Valenciana, normally a dish which takes three and one-half hours to prepare, is served at El Chico in half an hour through methods developed by Señor Collada, and here is how it's done. Two other recipes are included to add to the Spanish atmosphere.

PAELLA VALENCIANA

Take a 3-pound chicken (dressed and disjointed). Sauté until golden brown in olive oil. Place about 3 ounces of this olive oil in casserole. Add 1 medium onion (cut in small pieces), 2 medium sliced green peppers cut as the onion, 2 cloves of garlic chopped very fine. Fry until onion is golden brown. Add 2 or 3 fresh tomatoes, peeled and cut (or canned tomatoes), 5 large cups good chicken broth, and 1 demitasse long-grain rice for each person. Add the sautéed chicken to the rice mixture and stir all together (only once or twice). For each person add 3 clams, 3 slices lobster, 3 shrimp, 1 ounce chopped cured ham. Add a little saffron (chopped very fine) to make rice yellow.

Cook for about 25 minutes. Add some green peas and slices of Spanish pimientos. Add a glass of white wine about 5 minutes before taking off fire. Be sure to let casserole simmer for about 5 minutes after removing from fire.   4 SERVINGS

THE REAL SPANISH OMELET

2 tablespoons olive oil

2 medium raw potatoes, sliced thin

2 small onions, cut fine

½ cup finely chopped parsley

Salt and a little pepper

4 eggs

Fry potatoes in olive oil until brown, add onions, after two or three minutes add the chopped parsley, salt, and pepper. Pour eggs over the ingredients, let settle like a pancake, and then brown and fold as with ordinary omelet.

PISTO MADRILENO

2 cloves garlic

1 large onion, diced

2 small green peppers, cut thin and small

2 or 3 oz. cured ham, diced

2 fresh tomatoes, peeled

2 small summer squash

1 small potato, cut thin and small

1 tablespoon chopped parsley

Salt and a little sugar

6 eggs

First fry the garlic, take it out after two or three minutes, then add the onion and peppers, and three minutes later add ham and all other ingredients except eggs. Cook until tender, but be careful not to burn the ingredients. Add the beaten eggs and keep stirring as you would with scrambled eggs until done.

New Yorkers who like nothing better than to wrap themselves

around a Scandinavian specialty are partial to the handsome *Grips-holm Restaurant,* where the richly cool surroundings seem to add to the savory dishes. One of the most unusual is ours:

BIFF A LA LINDSTROM

1 lb. chopped lean beef	2 tablespoons small diced
2 tablespoons chopped onions	pickled beets
1 tablespoon capers	Salt and pepper to taste
1 whole egg	

Place the chopped beef in a mixing bowl. Sauté the onions and add after permitting to cool. Add the capers, egg, beets, salt, and pepper. Mix all very well. Form three flat patties out of the mixture and fry in butter in pan or chafing dish. Cook rare or well to taste.

3 SERVINGS

Just across the Hudson River from New York is the site of the fatal duel Alexander Hamilton fought with Aaron Burr. Near there, too, in a place happily dubbed the Elysian Fields, the first game of baseball as we know it was played. And, close by these historic grounds, in Union City, New Jersey, is a noble restaurant of the old school, *The Swiss Town House.* The Shader family, experts in all things fine and Swiss, suggests these Alpine adventures:

MINCED VEAL A LA SUISSE (GSCHNETZLETS)

2 oz. butter	1 cup warm water
½ medium onion, chopped	½ teaspoon salt
1 lb. veal, leg or loin, sliced in thin 1-inch strips	1 pinch pepper
	¼ teaspoon paprika
2 medium mushrooms, sliced	½ oz. lemon juice
2 tablespoons flour	¼ teaspoon monosodium
2 oz. dry white wine	glutamate
1 teaspoon beef extract (or bouillon cube)	2 oz. sweet cream

Heat butter in iron skillet; add onion, veal, and mushrooms; sauté over hot flame for 2–3 minutes. Add flour, stir well; add wine, then extract dissolved in water. Allow to simmer for 5 minutes. Add seasonings; then cream. Serve with noodles, macaroni, etc.

ZURICHER LEBER SPIESSLI

½ lb. calf liver   ½ teaspoon salt
½ lb. sliced bacon   ¼ teaspoon pepper
1 teaspoon marjoram leaves

Cut liver in strips measuring 1″ x ½″ x ½″; place one piece of
liver on one end of bacon; season liver; then roll up strip of bacon
with liver and place on a thin skewer. Grill over low heat. Serve
with any green vegetable.

In Philadelphia—the only city in the U.S. where they can erect
a sign reading "This Way to the Shrines" and get away with it—
there is a restaurant which comes close to being a shrine. That is
the old original *Bookbinder's*. Samuel Bookbinder started his eating
place in 1865, and his wife Sarah used to call in the sea captains
from the nearby waterfront, the merchants, and the farmers from
the markets around the corner by ringing a bell which is to this
day right by the door of the restaurant. Woodrow Wilson, Teddy
Roosevelt, Diamond Jim Brady, Henry Taft, McKinley, Charles
Evans Hughes, John Barrymore, J. P. Morgan and the likes of
them—enthusiastic eaters all—never passed by Bookbinder's when
in Philly nor do their modern counterparts. The atmosphere is part
of the lure today: for instance, there's a huge ship's wheel over
the entrance, smack out of a molasses schooner that plied the seas
in the great old days when seafarin' men had steaks for breakfast.
Bookbinder's, however, is most famous for its seafood. And of its
seafood nothing surpasses the deviled crab. So here is your recipe
and procedure for such a noble dish:

DEVILED CRAB

½ green pepper   1 tablespoon Worcestershire
½ large-size onion   sauce
1 stalk of celery   ⅛ lb. butter
¼ pimiento   2 cups milk
1 teaspoon salt   2 lbs. crabmeat
½ teaspoon black pepper   1 egg
1 teaspoon thyme   Milk
                                    Cracker or bread crumbs

Chop vegetables, combine with seasoning and cook in the butter for
20 minutes. Then add 1 cup flour and stir until smooth, like a paste,

for another 20 minutes. After that add the milk, then the crabmeat, and cook until you have a heavy paste. Remove from the fire, make up crab cakes or balls according to size desired. Then mix beaten egg with a little milk. Dip cakes in mixture, then in cracker or bread crumbs, as desired. Drop into deep fat for about 10 or 15 minutes until brown. Place in oven for a few minutes until cakes are good and hot throughout.   6 SERVINGS

The most celebrated restaurant between the East and West Coasts, and Chicago's pride and joy, is, as you no doubt have anticipated, *The Pump Room* at the Ambassador Hotel. We can hardly advise that you make an entrance into your dining room with swords aflame, Pump Room style, but their salad has often caused us to pass by many more ambitious dishes in a hurry to get to such perfection. So here is

LIMESTONE AMBASSADOR

The ingredients should be limestone lettuce from Kentucky, little hearts of artichokes, quartered tomatoes, thin slices of avocado, and slices of hard-boiled egg. The dressing is Roquefort cheese dressing made of: ½ cup Roquefort cheese, 1 soup spoon sweet cream, 1 teaspoon Durkee's dressing, 2 soup spoons salad oil, 1 teaspoon vinegar, salt and pepper to taste, and a dash of Lea & Perrins sauce. Stir until creamy and well mixed, and pour over salad.

Out Chicago way, sooner or later all the bigwigs gather in the magnificent dining room of the *Illinois Athletic Club,* one of the most spacious and noble spots you'll ever see. The bar is incomparable as well, and after a couple of bends of the elbow, here's the dish you'll want, and easy to do at home as well.

I. A. C. EPICUREAN SANDWICH
by Klaus Allseits, Chef

Put 1 slice buttered toast in flameproof casserole dish, then place 1 slice Virginia ham on toast. Add 3–4 slices white meat of turkey and ½ ounce blue cheese on top of ham. Then cover with sautéed mushrooms. Sprinkle with grated Parmesan cheese, mixed with paprika, and bake in oven for 3–5 miuntes.   1 SERVING

It could well be that the original "smoke-filled room" of the American political scene was in the Sheraton *Blackstone Hotel* in Chicago. Because, for all the dignity and beauty of these same rooms, this has long been the meeting place of our most eminent officials, and some less eminent politicians. And then the fur begins to fly, and the golden words assail the air, as both the smoke and the plot thicken. The Blackstone serves in the grand manner, and its menu is a volume. Two truly magnificent recipes are the gift from this famous dining room:

POULET SAUTE A LA MARENGO

A famous chicken dish said to have been served to Napoleon on the battlefield of Marengo in Italy.

1 3-lb. young chicken	6 fresh tomatoes
Salt and pepper	1 clove garlic, crushed
2 oz. butter	9 oz. fresh mushrooms
2 tablespoons olive oil	8 pitted green olives, sliced
2 medium onions	4 eggs
4 oz. dry white wine	Parsley

Disjoint chicken, season with salt and pepper, and sauté in the butter and oil. When slightly colored, add the onions, which are cut in $\frac{1}{2}$-inch dice. When the onions are brown add the wine. Reduce the liquid by $\frac{1}{2}$ and add 4 peeled, seeded, and diced tomatoes and crushed garlic; cover and let cook for 10 minutes. Add the sliced mushrooms and olives; cover and let cook until chicken is tender.

Arrange chicken on serving platter covered with the sauce. Garnish with the remaining 2 tomatoes, which are peeled, cut in half, and sautéed in oil; and four French-fried eggs. Sprinkle entirely with chopped parsley.   4 SERVINGS

LE POMPANO A LA MURAT

Delicious fresh pompano in an adaptation of a Carme specialty named after one of Napoleon's greatest marshals.

Filet four 2-lb. pompanos. Allow two filets per serving. Season with salt and pepper, dip in flour. Sauté in hot oil till golden brown. Place on hot serving platter.

For garnish:

2 large Idaho potatoes	4 oz. butter
Chopped parsley	2 large tomatoes
8 hearts of artichokes	

Peel potatoes, cut in ¼ dice and cook same as French fries, sprinkle with chopped parsley, and place on platter at side of pompano. Take hearts of artichokes, cut in half and sauté a few minutes in 2 oz. butter. Place these on other side of pompano. Take two large tomatoes, cut each in 4 slices and sauté in 2 oz. butter. Place one tomato slice on each filet and squeeze the juice of one lemon over filets.   4 SERVINGS

On the shores of Lake Michigan, in Chicago's handsome Drake Hotel, is a port for fish lovers—the *Cape Cod Room.* From that piscine haven, a simple recipe, but delicious.

BROILED, IMPORTED TURBOT, MAITRE D'HOTEL

Clean and trim the fish. Cut according to desired size. Season the filets with salt and pepper, sprinkle with oil. Broil till golden brown and done. Serve with a slice of Maître d'Hôtel Butter on top.

Maître d'Hôtel Butter: Pound together ¼ cup butter with 1 tbsp. each lemon juice and chopped parsley. Reshape, refrigerate. Cut slices as desired.

Chicago prides itself on its cosmopolitan tastes, and *Jacques* French restaurant is happy justification with its very elegant air and beautifully prepared Gallic dishes. And what better for a Francophile than

FROGS' LEGS PROVENÇALE JACQUES

1 cup butter	3 lbs. frogs' legs
3 tomatoes, peeled and chopped	1 cup heavy cream
1 cup sliced mushrooms	1 cup flour
¼ cup chopped parsley	1 cup olive oil
2 garlic cloves, minced	

First make tomato sauce. Melt butter in skillet, add tomatoes, mushrooms, parsley, and garlic and simmer for 10 minutes. Dip frogs' legs in cream, then in flour. Sauté in oil in another skillet for 10 minutes or until brown. Serve with sauce.   6 SERVINGS

New Orleans, with its mixed cultural heritages, is something of a mecca for Americans interested in food. And usually their first stop—and it has been the same since 1840, when Monsieur Aciatore opened his eating house—is *Antoine's*. The present proprietor and grandson of the founder carries on the tradition of subtle and distinguished preparation of food, and here is one of the recipes dearest to his own heart. It is for a dish related to Eggs Benedict, but in the family's top register:

EGGS SARDOU

2 artichokes

Anchovy paste

2 poached eggs

2 tablespoons chopped cooked ham

Truffles

For sauce:

2 tablespoons tarragon vinegar

1 tablespoon chopped green onion

3 peppercorns

4 egg yolks

1 tablespoon water

½ lb. clarified butter

Juice of ¼ lemon

The eggs are served on artichoke hearts, covered with hollandaise, sprinkled with ham, and topped with sliced truffles.

1. Two artichokes are cooked in boiling water until tender. Petals and choke or flower are removed. Artichoke hearts are foundation for Eggs Sardou.

2. Each artichoke heart is spread with anchovy paste. Poached egg is removed carefully with a skimmer and set on the prepared heart.

3. Aciatore adds lemon juice to hot hollandaise sauce. Butter used in sauce is clarified by melting in a saucepan. After being melted, it is allowed to stand until clear part on top can be skimmed off easily. To make the hollandaise sauce boil tarragon vinegar, chopped green onion, and peppercorns until the mixture is reduced to one tablespoonful when strained. This liquid is added to beaten egg yolks and water and placed over hot water. It is beaten as it cooks over moderate heat until the eggs begin to thicken. Clarified butter is added slowly and the beating continued. Lemon juice is added just before serving. Sauce must be very smooth.

4. Sprinkle each dish with chopped cooked ham, and truffle garnish.

Brennan's is another never-to-be-missed stop in New Orleans. Here you can discover for yourself some of the delights of the fabled cooking to be found in no other part of the country. Owen Brennan happily shares these three:

SHRIMP REMOULADE

On a bed of crisp shredded lettuce leaves, place boiled shrimp (after they have been in icebox for several hours). Over shrimp pour the sauce rémoulade. Sauce: Combine 6 tablespoons vinegar, ½ teaspoon pepper, 4 teaspoons Creole mustard, a little horseradish, celery heart chopped fine, ½ white onion chopped fine, a little parsley chopped fine. Salt well and mix well. Chill in icebox.

CRAYFISH BISQUE

Thoroughly boil about 40 nice-sized crayfish, then drain. Clean the heads, keeping about 30 of the shells. Set the remainder to boiling in a quart of water. Then peel the tails and chop the meat fine, making a paste of it, to which is added 1 cup bread soaked in milk, 1 tablespoon fried onion, and finely chopped parsley, salt, and pepper to taste. Fill the 30 shells with this mixture, set them aside. Start the soup by frying in butter an onion, add some flour for thickening, and ½ cup each of green onions and parsley chopped fine, spray of thyme, and 2 bay leaves. When browned pour in the bouillon made with the remains of the heads, then season with salt and strong pepper; let boil for ½ hour. Add more water if needed. When ready to serve, take each stuffed head, roll in flour and fry in butter until crisp all around, then throw into soup. Let boil for 3 or 4 minutes, serve with very thin slices of toasted bread.

STUFFED FLOUNDER

1 bunch green onions, finely chopped	3 dozen oysters
1 Bermuda onion, finely chopped	1 lb. boiled shrimp, finely chopped
2 cups flour	1 lb. fresh mushrooms, finely chopped
1 cup butter	Salt, cayenne pepper
2 quarts fish stock	6 1-lb. flounders

Make stuffing as follows: Sauté onions in butter, blend flour in thoroughly. Add fish stock and boil for 5 minutes. Scald oysters (do not boil), chop fine, and add with shrimp and mushrooms. Season to taste with salt and cayenne pepper.

Remove backbone from flounders and fill with above stuffing. Broil.

In any gastronome's tour, San Francisco is a major stop. And we stop at three of its most famous restaurants, the first being *Ernie's*. This is a restaurant with the Diamond Jim Brady atmosphere, the lush, plush, flush opulency of the nineties which no amount of functional design can replace in our affections. And Ernie's, as usual, serves us well:

HOBO STEAK

4 lbs. choice sirloin steak	Parmesan cheese
Melted butter	1 package frozen green peas
Salt and freshly ground pepper	6 small white onions, boiled
1 lb. salt	1 can baby carrots
2 ripe tomatoes	1 can small whole potatoes
Bread crumbs	1 box fresh button mushrooms
Parsley	1 bouquet broccoli, boiled in salt
1 head cauliflower, boiled in	water
salt water	

Cut steak from one side almost through, leaving hinge so that it can be flattened out to resemble a butterfly. Tie with string to keep steak's shape during broiling. Brush with melted butter and dust lightly with salt and freshly ground pepper. Broil 4 inches from flame, 10 minutes on each side. Remove steak from broiler and put in roasting pan. Mix 1 lb. salt with enough water to make a thick paste. Cover steak with salt paste, sealing to keep in juices. Roast in preheated 450° oven 10 minutes for rare, 15 minutes for medium rare, 25 minutes for medium, and 45 minutes for well-done. Remove salt crust, brush with melted butter, open steak and place, bone side up, on wooden serving plank.

Halve your tomatoes, cover tops with bread crumbs mixed with finely chopped parsley, dot with butter, salt, and pepper, put in small separate pan, and set aside. (These go in oven last 10 minutes steak is baking.)

Quarter head of boiled cauliflower. Squeeze each quarter gently in clean towel to make a ball. Dust cauliflower balls with Parmesan cheese, put in small separate pan and set aside. (These also go in oven last 10 minutes steak is baking.)

Mix peas with button onions. Glaze baby carrots in butter. Sauté small whole potatoes in butter with mushroom buttons.

With steak at center top of wooden serving plank, you'll find it resembles a steer's head. Put two button mushrooms in position normally suggesting eyes. Place spears of broccoli to form horns. A bit of parsley to decorate top of head. Another mushroom to form nose. Make jardinière of peas with button onions and glazed baby carrots and place to form ruff. Around rim of plank place alternately tomatoes, bouquet of broccoli, cauliflower ball, small whole potatoes and mushroom buttons, continuing until rim is covered. Serve with side bowl of mushroom gravy.   4 SERVINGS

Trader Vic's—ye know it well, ye travelers to Hawaii and New York—is still a mainstay in San Francisco. His menu calls up visions of far lagoons, of smoking volcanoes, and waterfalls hidden away on mountainsides, rushing down gorges in their race to join the booming surf on some distant isle. Thus, a lamb curry:

LAMB CURRY

Use lamb cheeks if possible. If not, ask your butcher for boned-and-trimmed lamb chuck or cubed lean lamb stew meat instead. For 6: trim all fat from 3 lbs. cubed lamb. Dredge with flour. Brown in hot oil in large iron kettle. Add (all finely chopped): 2 large onions, 2 cloves garlic, 6 sprigs parsley, 3 carrots, 2 stalks celery. Slice and add 6 large mushrooms. Cook until limp, slightly brown. Stir in 2 teaspoons curry powder for mild curry, 4 teaspoons for hot curry. Then add ¾ cup dry white wine, 1½ cups beef stock, 1 tablespoon A-1 sauce. Simmer covered until tender—1½ hours for leg meat, up to 2½ hours for the tougher cuts.

The moving finger writes, and having writ, moves on to *Omar Khayyam's Restaurant,* in San Francisco, where host George Mardikian has done wonders with introducing Armenian cooking to bland Western palates. A wonderfully knowledgeable and affable guy, George, naturally, is a master at the classic shish kebab. He yields the science to you in this recipe:

SHISH KEBAB

1 leg of lamb (about 5 or 6 lbs.)	⅓ cup sherry
½ lb. onions, sliced	2 tablespoons oil
1 tablespoon salt	1 teaspoon orégano
½ teaspoon pepper	

Remove all fat and gristle from leg of lamb. Bone it and cut into inch squares. Mix meat with sliced onions and other ingredients. Let mixture stand at least a few hours; overnight preferably.

Remove from marinade, string the meat on skewers and broil on charcoal fire or kitchen broiler.

RICE PILAFF

¼ lb. butter	6 cups of broth (chicken, lamb,
3 cups rice	or beef) or hot water
	Salt and pepper

Melt butter, add dry rice, heat well until butter begins to bubble. Add broth and seasoning. Mix well. Bake in oven for 30 minutes at 400°. Take out of oven, mix well, and bake for 15 minutes more.

Now, let's leave the United States and mosey here and there in other lands to complete the challenge of our great cooking adventures. You know, reading these recipes today—before you've mastered some of the lesser fundamentals in cookery—perhaps you think that you may never get to some of these ambitious and complicated creations. But the day will come, sir; so bide your time. You'll be browsing through here again, and when you look at one of these, a light will suddenly flash on that particular chart where your decisions are made, and you'll proceed as directed. So, let's proceed to these foreign procedures.

There's a little place in London where, in the leisurely way of the British, suspicion is beginning to take hold that the food is beginning to catch on. Or, at least, not to be overoptimistic, within the next few years there will definitely begin to be a feeling of acceptance at *Rule's,* which was founded in Maiden Lane in 1798. Edward VII and Charles Dickens liked the food, and what's good enough for them is good enough for your own guests. Here is the recipe for their famous

STEAK AND KIDNEY PIE

1½ lbs. stewing beef, diced	1 teaspoon salt
4 lamb kidneys, sliced	Freshly ground black pepper
½ pound mushrooms, sliced	2 cups water
1 cup chopped onion	¾ cup butter
¼ cup chopped parsley	3 cups sifted self-rising flour
1 small bay leaf, crumbled	1 cup milk

Put beef, kidneys, mushrooms, onion, parsley, bay leaf, salt, and pepper in a baking dish with water. Cut butter into flour until it resembles a coarse meal. Add the milk and mix lightly to form a soft dough. Turn out on lightly floured board and roll. Cut slits in center of the dough to permit steam to escape. Place on top of baking dish. Bake in a slow oven (325° F.) for 1 hour and 45 minutes.   6 SERVINGS

Now, hopping over the Channel, we stop at a gourmet's dream of a restaurant called the *Hôtel de la Côte d'Or,* the hotel of the golden coast, in Salien, to the southeast of Paris. Here, the magic secret is

LOBSTER THERMIDOR

3 lobsters, 2¼ lbs. each·   ¼ cup prepared mustard
¼ cup olive oil   2 cups heavy cream
1½ teaspoons salt   3 tablespoons flour
Freshly ground black pepper   1 cup milk
¾ cup butter   ½ cup grated Parmesan cheese

Split the lobsters. Brush with oil and sprinkle with 1 teaspoon salt
and pepper. Broil under medium heat for 5 minutes. Remove from
broiler and dot with 6 tablespoons butter. Bake in a hot oven
(400° F.) for 10 minutes. Remove lobster meat from shell and slice
it. Save coral. Brush inside of each shell lightly with mustard.
Meanwhile simmer cream over low heat for 30 minutes, stirring
occasionally. Melt 4 tablespoons butter, stir in flour, add milk
slowly and remaining ½ teaspoon salt, stirring constantly. Cook
until sauce thickens, stirring constantly. Mix in cream and lobster
coral. Return lobster meat to shells and cover with sauce. Sprinkle
with Parmesan cheese and dot with remaining ·butter. Bake in a
hot oven (400° F.) for 10 minutes.   6 SERVINGS

Following all the roads, and discovering that they lead—where
else?—to Rome—we pause at the famous *Passetto,* a restaurant
with a palatial tone guaranteed to make even kings feel regally at
home. And your palatial recipe:

POLLO IN BELLA VISTA

2 two-and-a-half pound   1 garlic clove
  chickens, quartered   2 onions, cut up
1 stalk celery with leaves   1 tablespoon salt
6 peppercorns   3 envelopes gelatine
1 bay leaf, crumbled

Place chicken quarters in a saucepan, just cover with water. Add
celery, peppercorns, bay leaf, garlic, onions, and salt. Bring to a
boil, cover, simmer for 1 hour. Remove the chicken from broth.
Drain it and cool. Chill the chicken for at least 1 hour. Strain the
broth and set aside 1 quart. Soften the gelatine in 1 cup cold water.
Add this to the hot, strained broth and stir until the gelatine is

dissolved. Cool. Chill for ½ hour or until slightly thickened. Spoon very carefully over the chilled chicken to coat it completely. Return to refrigerator and chill for 1 hour.   SERVES 6

In Venice, no dream of romance can ever quite outdo the charms of the *Royal Daniele,* on the San Marco Canal. Competing with the storied view, our eyes on the island church of San Giorgio Maggiore in the foreground, is our special recipe:

ZUPPA DE PESCE DANIELE

1½-lb. lobster, cut up	2 garlic cloves, minced
½ lb. prawns or shrimp	1 bay leaf, crumbled
1 onion, cut up	½ teaspoon thyme
1 stalk celery with leaves	1 teaspoon basil
2 tablespoons vinegar	2 tablespoons chopped parsley
1 tablespoon salt	½ cup dry white wine
2½ lbs. mixed haddock, trout, cod, salmon, red snapper	1½ cups chopped peeled tomatoes
½ lb. squid, cut up	Pinch saffron
¼ cup olive oil	Freshly ground black pepper

Boil lobster and shrimp for 5 minutes in 1 quart water with onion, celery, vinegar, and 2 teaspoons salt. Remove and shell lobster and shrimp. Return shells to the broth with heads and tails of fish and simmer for 20 minutes. Strain and put broth aside. Meanwhile cut up the fish, squid, and lobster meat into bite-size chunks and cut shrimp in half. Sauté in oil with garlic, bay leaf, thyme, basil, and parsley for 5 minutes, stirring constantly. Add fish broth, wine, peeled tomatoes, saffron, remaining 1 teaspoon salt, and pepper. Bring to a boil, reduce heat, cover, and simmer for 20 minutes. Makes about 3 quarts. Serve with slices of bread fried in oil.

The historic *Hotel Krone,* on the rolling Rhine, is known for its wonderful white wines and fish dishes. Combinations being in order, from the Krone comes a fine fish dish, with its companion salad.

SALMON KRONE

1 tablespoon vinegar   6 salmon steaks
1 teaspoon salt   ¾ cup butter, melted

Bring vinegar, salt and 2 quarts water to a boil in a skillet. Add
the salmon steaks, reduce the heat and simmer for 12 minutes.
Drain the steaks and serve with melted butter or hollandaise sauce.
Serves 6. Accompany with salad made with mustard dressing
(below).

MUSTARD SALAD DRESSING

1 teaspoon dry mustard   1 tablespoon dry white wine
1 tablespoon beer   1 medium onion, chopped
1 garlic clove   1 teaspoon chopped dill
1 teaspoon salt   1 teaspoon chopped parsley
Dash white pepper   1 teaspoon chopped borage
½ cup olive oil

Mix dry mustard and beer. Crush garlic clove with salt and pepper.
Rub salad bowl with enough of the olive oil to coat it. Add mustard
and beer mixture and crushed garlic. Add other ingredients. Add
any greens, cleaned and dried. Toss vigorously to coat all leaves.

Now to Bologna we shall go, to visit the *Pappagallo,* in its ancient
and lordly carriage house, part of a fourteenth-century palazzo.
And for your delectation, Latin style, two truly outstanding specialties:

SUPREME DI POLLO ALLA ZURLA

Take 6 small chickens completely dissected and sauté in butter
over a low flame. Add sliced truffles and grated Parmesan cheese
and cook for approximately four minutes.

Wine Sauce: To be cooked in a pan over low heat. Combine
3 pounds leg of lamb, cleaned and cut into small pieces, ¾ pound
pork, also cut into small pieces, 1 medium-sized onion, 2 or 3 cloves,
a sprig of parsley. While cooking add a glass of Marsala and a
glass of white wine. When the liquid has reduced itself, slowly
stir in a half glass of sour cream and a little salt. Serve on toast
with a vegetable.

COTOLETTE ALLA BOLOGNESE

6 veal cutlets, well pounded   Salt and pepper
1 egg, beaten   Parmesan cheese
Bread crumbs   White truffles
Uncooked prosciutto ·   A little lemon

Cover the veal cutlets with bread crumbs soaked in a well-beaten egg and cook over a low flame. When the cutlets are done add the prosciutto, Parmesan cheese, and the truffles and cook until done. Serve with vegetables and potatoes.   6 SERVINGS

Any of these dishes, with the legend of its source behind it, will qualify as your high adventure in entertainment. But there are many other national dishes which also belong in your international repertoire, and so, to complete your worldly knowledge, we straddle the continents again, and check in with the kitchen customs at these many stops in our cook's tour:

BEEF STROGANOFF

Have 1½ lbs. trimmed beef tenderloin sliced ¼ inch thick. Wipe the meat with a damp cloth; and with a sharp knife slice into little strips, ¼ inch wide and 2 inches long. Brown quickly in 5 tablespoons butter in large skillet. Season with salt and pepper, and push meat to one side. Add 1 medium onion, thinly sliced, and 2 cups thinly sliced mushrooms (discard lower half of the mushroom stems). Sauté gently till mushrooms are barely tender and onions are translucent but not brown. Add 1 cup condensed beef broth and a dash of Worcestershire sauce. Heat to the boiling point. Stir in ½ pint commercial sour cream. Stir gently till cream is heated through but do not allow to boil. Add more seasoning if necessary. Serve over hot rice or noodles and sprinkle with a little chopped parsley.   6 SERVINGS

SPANISH PICADILLO WITH BEAN SAUCE

A combination of seasoned chopped beef, fluffy white rice (served separately), sautéed bananas and a black bean sauce.

Start the bean sauce the day before as the beans need soaking overnight. Put 1½ cups black beans in 4 cups water. Bring to a boil and continue to boil for 2 minutes. Turn off the flame, cover the saucepan and let stand overnight. In the morning add ¾ lb. ham hock to the beans and simmer them slowly till tender (about 2 hours). The beans should be covered with water, so add a little more if necessary. Meanwhile in 1½ tablespoons cooking oil, sauté 1 medium chopped onion, and a large clove chopped garlic. When beans are tender, but not mushy, drain only a little of the liquid off if necessary. The beans will be the sauce, so you want the consistency sauce-y. Add the sautéed onion and garlic and salt to taste. Remove the ham hock and reserve.

To make the picadillo, sauté 1 medium-size chopped onion and 1 small green pepper together in 2 tablespoons oil till they begin to brown. Add 2 lbs. lean chopped beef, and brown the meat gently while breaking it up to a crumbled consistency. Add 3 cups stewed tomatoes, 2 tablespoons raisins, 1½ teaspoons capers, a pinch of cayenne pepper, and salt to taste. Cook until the mixture is almost dry. Stir from time to time. If there is a little too much juice from the tomatoes, remove a spoonful or two. Just before serving stir in the chopped white of a hard-cooked egg or two.

Slice 3 fat bananas through lengthwise and sauté them till barely soft in a little butter, turning once. Fried eggs are often served with the picadillo. They are fried in butter over a very low flame in a covered pan till quite firm.

Serve with a mound of fluffy rice (4 cups). Place the sautéed bananas around the rice, and if you are serving fried eggs, place these on top. Arrange the picadillo on a heated platter. Serve all very hot with the black bean sauce. *

CHINESE DUCK

Rub a 6-lb. duck inside and outside with salt, having first thoroughly washed and dried the duck. Inside the cavity place 1 tablespoon grated orange peel, 2 slices fresh ginger, 3 scallions, 8 aniseed and 3 tablespoons sherry. Steam the bird in a covered steamer about 1½ hours till leg meat is tender when tested with a fork. When duck is cooked, remove it to a rack and allow to drain for 30 minutes.

Make a sauce of 4 tablespoons brown sugar, 2 tablespoons honey and ½ cup soy sauce. Blend well and spread over the duck. Rub it well into the skin. Fry the whole duck in deep, hot fat (380° F.) for 6 or 7 minutes until it is the color of light chocolate. Drain. Serve with Chinese sour plum sauce. Little slits can be made all over the carcass of the duck with a very sharp knife. Diners can pick the meat right off the carcass with chopsticks or forks.

4 SERVINGS

MEXICAN CHILI CON CARNE

2 medium onions, chopped
1 clove garlic, minced
2 tablespoons fat
1 lb. ground beef (or leftover cooked meat)
1 teaspoon salt

¼ teaspoon pepper
1 tablespoon or more chili powder
1 can (1 lb., 14 ounces) tomatoes
1 can (1 lb.) kidney beans

Cook onions and garlic in fat about 5 minutes. Remove onions and garlic and set aside. Add meat and stir over low heat until well browned. Add salt, pepper, and chili powder. Return onions and garlic. Add tomatoes and kidney beans, cover, and simmer gently about 30 minutes. Thicken with flour if desired.   4 SERVINGS

SHANGHAI CHOW MEIN

½ lb. pork, diced
¾ lb. veal, diced
½ lb. beef, diced
2 tablespoons fat
⅓ cup soy sauce
1 cup water
1 large bunch celery, in ½-inch slices
1 whole garlic clove
1 small onion, chopped

2 tablespoons cornstarch
¼ cup water
2 five- or 6-oz. cans water chestnuts, drained and sliced
1 No. 2 can (2½ cups) bean sprouts, drained
1 three-oz. can broiled sliced mushrooms
Salt and pepper

Brown meats in hot fat; add soy sauce and 1 cup water; simmer 2 minutes. Add celery, garlic, and onion; simmer 1½ hours; remove garlic clove.

Blend cornstarch and ¼ cup water; stir into meat mixture. Add water chestnuts, bean sprouts, and mushrooms; heat through. Season. Serve over rice or chow-mein noodles.   8 SERVINGS

Chicken Chow Mein: Omit beef and add 2 cups diced cooked chicken; don't brown with other meats.

PERFECT RICE

To make good, easy fluffy rice no matter what brand: Wash the rice in several waters. Swish it around till the water comes out absolutely clear (about 8 washings). Cook the same proportion of rice as water—1 cup rice, 1 cup water. Add ½ teaspoon salt. Cook rice over very high flame till it comes to a boil, then immediately turn the flame down as low as it will go and put a cover over the rice. After 12 minutes take a look to see if all the water has been absorbed—if not, give it a minute or two more. The rice should be perfectly dry. Fluff it up a couple of times with a fork. Leave covered on back of stove till ready to serve. A lump of butter may be put on top of the rice and a light sprinkling of parsley or paprika.

To make an easy version of fried rice, cook as directed above. In another pan, sauté a small chopped onion or 3 scallions. Fry 4 pieces of bacon till crisp, and crumble. Chop 1 tablespoon parsley. Add all to rice, plus ¼ teaspoon soy sauce and ¼ teaspoon dry mustard.

CHOP SUEY

1½ lbs. lean pork (cubes or strips)	Dash of pepper
1 cup sliced mushrooms	1½ cups bouillon, water, or meat stock
3 tablespoons peanut oil	3 tablespoons soy sauce
1 cup sliced onions	1 can bean sprouts
1½ cups sliced celery	¼ cup cornstarch
1 teaspoon ginger	Toasted almonds (optional)
1 teaspoon salt	

Cook pork and mushrooms in hot fat until lightly brown. Add onions, celery, seasonings, and bouillon. Cover and cook until tender, about half an hour. Add soy sauce, well-drained bean sprouts and additional seasonings, if necessary. Thicken with cornstarch mixed to a paste with a little water. Cook slowly for about 10 minutes. Serve on hot rice or fried noodles and sprinkle with almonds.

BAVARIAN-STYLE STEW

2 lbs. beef rump, chuck, round, or stew meat
2 medium onions, sliced
3 tablespoons fat
3 cups hot water
1 bay leaf
3 teaspoons salt
¼ teaspoon black pepper
1½ teaspoons caraway seeds
¼ cup vinegar
1 medium red cabbage
½ cup broken gingersnaps

Cut beef into 2-inch cubes. Brown beef and sliced onions in melted fat in a heavy saucepan or Dutch oven. Add water, bay leaf, salt, pepper, and caraway seeds. Cover tightly and cook slowly for 1½ hours. Add vinegar to stew, place cabbage wedges on top, cover, and cook about 25–30 minutes more or until tender. Meanwhile, soak gingersnaps in ¼ cup warm water. Lift out cabbage and meat; add gingersnaps to liquid and heat to boiling, stirring to make a smooth gravy. Add meat to the gravy, reheat, and serve in cheese noodle ring or on bed of plain boiled noodles. Surround with red cabbage wedges.   6 SERVINGS

SOUTH-OF-THE-BORDER CASSEROLE

1 medium onion, chopped
3 tablespoons oil or bacon drippings
2 fifteen-oz. cans S & W Beans Barbecue
1 sixteen-oz. can whole kernel corn, drained
1 sixteen-oz. can stewed tomatoes, drained
1½ cups grated sharp Cheddar cheese
1 tablespoon cornstarch
1 to 1½ teaspoons chili powder (according to taste)
1 teaspoon salt
¼ teaspoon pepper
8 frankfurters

Cook onion in oil until soft but not browned. Combine with beans, corn, tomatoes, and cheese. Mix cornstarch, chili powder, salt and pepper, and stir into vegetable mixture. Turn into large casserole, top with frankfurters and bake covered at 350° F. for 30 minutes; uncover and bake 15–20 minutes longer.   8 SERVINGS

HAWAIIAN-STYLE SPARERIBS

2 sides spareribs   ¼ cup vinegar
3 tablespoons brown sugar   ½ cup catsup
2 tablespoons cornstarch   1 can (9 oz.) crushed pineapple
½ teaspoon salt   1 tablespoon soy sauce

Cut ribs into serving pieces. Combine sugar, cornstarch, and salt and stir in vinegar, catsup, crushed pineapple and juice, and soy sauce. Cook until slightly thickened, about 5 minutes, stirring constantly. Arrange layer of spareribs in roasting pan. Cover with part of pineapple mixture; add another layer of ribs and top with rest of sauce. Cover pan tightly and bake at 350° F. about 1½–2 hours.
                4 SERVINGS

LAMB OR VEAL CURRY

2 lbs. lamb or veal stew meat,   ⅛ teaspoon curry powder
   cubed   ½ teaspoon ginger
Fat or oil   1 teaspoon sugar
½ cup chopped onions   2 cups boiling water
1 tart apple, chopped   ¼ cup raisins, optional
1½ teaspoons salt

Brown meat in a little hot fat or oil. Add chopped onions, apple, seasonings, and liquid. Cover and cook gently one hour. Thicken, if desired, with a flour-and-water paste. Add raisins and cook 15 minutes longer. Serve over hot boiled rice, and sprinkle, if desired, with shredded coconut, chopped nuts, crumbled bacon, chopped banana, and chutney.   6 SERVINGS

FRENCH BEAN CASSEROLE A L'ORIENT

½ cup (1 stick) butter

½ cup onions, chopped

2 four-oz. cans sliced button
mushrooms, drained

½ cup mushroom liquor

1 five-oz. can water chestnuts,
drained and thinly sliced

¼ cup (½ stick) butter

⅓ cup flour

1 teaspoon salt

½ teaspoon pepper

1 cup milk

2 cups (¾ lb.) shredded
Cheddar cheese

2 teaspoons soy sauce

⅛ teaspoon Tabasco sauce

2 packages frozen French-cut
green beans, thawed

1 No. 300 can French-fried
onions

In ½ cup butter sauté onions, mushrooms, and water chestnuts until tender. Set aside, melt ¼ cup butter, blend in flour, salt, and pepper. Gradually add milk and mushroom liquor; stir until smooth and thickened. Add Cheddar cheese, soy sauce, and Tabasco sauce; stir until cheese melts. In bottom of buttered baking dish (8″ x 6½″ x 2″) layer half of the sautéed vegetables and green beans. Pour half of cheese sauce over. Repeat for second layer and top with remaining sauce. Bake in a preheated 350° oven for 15 minutes. Remove from oven; sprinkle crumbled French-fried onions on top. Return to oven and bake an additional 10 minutes.

8 SERVINGS

FAR EAST TURKEY CHOW MEIN

1 cup diced celery	1 No. 2 can bean sprouts, plus
½ cup diced onion	liquor
1 green pepper, cut in strips	2 cups turkey, cooked and cut in
5 tablespoons butter	medium pieces
¼ cup flour	2 tablespoons pimiento, chopped
1 cup evaporated milk	⅛ teaspoon curry powder
3 tablespoons soy sauce	2 No. 2 cans Chinese noodles

In a 1½-quart saucepan or chafing dish, sauté celery, onion and green pepper in butter. Blend in flour; slowly add evaporated milk, stirring constantly. Cook until sauce is smooth and thickened. Add remaining ingredients, except Chinese noodles, and cook until heated through. Serve over warmed Chinese noodles.

And—since the last shall be first—let us end your wanderings on a high Peruvian note. This unusual specialty may be served as a first course, or as an hors d'oeuvre, and it is called

SEVICHE

Use a deep casserole and mix contents well.

Cut raw halibut or haddock in thin pieces about 1 by 1½ inches in size. Add several thin slices of Bermuda onion and 1 jar of hot peppers, also sliced thin. Leave pepper seeds in, if you like the dish well spiced. Add a good deal of salt—possibly as much as 2 to 3 tablespoons. Mix and cover with lemon juice. Put in ice box for 24 hours.

Note: The seviche gets hotter each day if it is left in the icebox. The above recipe is sufficient for a small family over a period of about ten days.

outdoor cookery

YOU MAY FIRE
WHEN READY, GRIDLEY

Playing with fire is a man's job.

Even in this day of subtle matriarchal pressures, the man is usually permitted full control of the outdoor grill. It is his natural domain, an atavistic throwback to the days when he dragged his kill into the cave and broiled it over the fire at the entrance while the wife and kiddies were assigned the less glamorous jobs of chewing on the sinews to make thread, or assembling a claw necklace.

So it behooves you to do this well.

There's a great deal more to outdoor cooking than sticking a piece of meat in the fire until it turns black. Perhaps another reason why men excel as outdoor chefs is the challenge of each meal—

211

conditions are never quite the same. Wind direction and velocity vary, the fire itself is capricious, fuels do not act as the book says, the very temperature itself—including humidity—sets up a variance in cooking time and other factors. So the chef proceeds like the master of a sailing vessel. He has his mechanical aids, like the skipper, but in the last analysis his trip to safe port relies on judgment, the nice juxtaposition of experience, conjecture, observation, and firm decision that come out all in one piece of successful action.

We are going to explore some of the deepest currents as well as the smallest eddies in the exploration of our craft.

Not everyone is lucky enough to have an outdoor cooking area immediately available at all times. So we must of necessity be considering picnics, trail cookery, and beach *chef d'oeuvres* as well as the great popular sport of preparing the meal in the back yard or on the terrace.

Not having any obligations to the good people who make gadgets and ridiculous clothing for outdoor workers, we beg you to take it easy on too much grill work, just as you would on your car. But just the same there are certain basic implements you'll need, for safety in many cases as well as perfection, so decide to go in for these as a first step.

IMPLEMENTS

The worst idea is to try and work with any old thing you may have around the house. You just wind up with plastic implements that explode or melt near a fire, others with painted areas which blister and peel off in the heat, and ordinary working gloves that play you dirt and release a finger tip into the coals at the very moment that you need absolute protection. So, get:

Asbestos gloves
Several long metal serving forks for turning meats
Spatula
Long-handled tongs for placing coals
Metal dishes or small trays to hold meats and other supplies
Several metal cups with large handles
Syringe-type baster, with metal or glass (not plastic) shaft
Large carving knife
Small carving knife

Set of skewers with double tines to prevent slippage
Aluminum foil

Wear a baseball cap, or your favorite fishing hat, while you're cooking. Saves your hair from catching sparks, cinders, or ash, and developing a fine patina of animal fats and coal dust. And—don't be proud—wear an apron: the pockets are good to keep matches and other gadgets in, and your slacks will be protected.

Presuming that you already have a complement of good service implements in your kitchen, don't give in to the impulse to simply move them outdoors. Silverware does badly, and good china breaks easily. Buy a set of good plastic plates, large salt and pepper containers, and as many wooden-handled forks, knives, and spoons as you may need. They're in for fairly rugged treatment, ranging from getting stepped on as some satyr chases a nymph over your plate to being dropped in the fire or a stream.

GRILLS

There are all kinds of barbecue grills on the market. Almost all of them are fun, and have their purpose. Whichever you choose, keep these things in mind: *you're* going to do the cooking; the cost of the unit isn't going to help you very much once you've launched your meal. So here are a few ruminations on the subject: (See page 221 for pictures of grills.)

For most purposes, the well-known portable grill is the best. Don't get the biggest and the fanciest at first. But don't get one so tiny, either, that your heat and your working area both turn out to be insufficient. Be sure that the grill you select has a mechanism for controlling the distance between the food and the fire. Check the rods on the top of the grill—they should be close together so that you won't lose a chop or a 'burger entirely in case it acts up and turns sideways. It is preferable, but not entirely necessary, to have some way of ventilating your fire.

The grill with wheels is the favorite, enabling you to move your base of operations into the shade, or out of the rain, or a little more to windward, as conditions dictate. This type will run from a foot to three feet in diameter. Pick a medium size to start with. And heft it before you buy it. Heavy-gauge metal lasts the longest, of course, but the best of equipment gets rough treatment and prob-

ably you'll want to replace it with new and shiny gear every season
or so. The weight is important because you're going to have to
clean this thing. After you're through using it, it will be full of
ashes and unburnt coals and "fill" that you may have been using
for ventilation (we'll get into this next, on fuels), and you're going
to have to hose or wipe it down. Also, you'll be moving it back
into the garage or into the house from time to time and you don't
want a monster you can't manage. There are even occasions when
—wheels or no—it may be necessary to pick the whole thing up,
with the glowing coals in its maw as well, and move it. You'll be
glad then to have picked a middleweight. These braziers look about
like this and the best of them have a bit of height to them, so that
you're not kneeling or bending all of the time. They come up to
waist high, but a bit under that will do as well.

Many chefs prefer a permanent fireplace, built outdoors in the
patio or near the house, which can be the center of the cooking
ceremony. These can be very wonderful indeed, especially if you
take the trouble in building them to include Dutch ovens, and
various cooking levels on which to place your grill. They are excellent for large menus, and you can build up a great and enduring
fire in them. Drawbacks include the point that they soon get quite
blackened and unsightly, and try as you will to prevent it, become
coated with fat drippings and other splashes from the food which
draw flies and in time get quite odoriferous. In addition, everyone
else is tempted to burn leaves, rubbish, and practically everything
in your pet fireplace, and it winds up being a not too pleasant
catch-all instead of the bright and clean fire unit you desire. Of
course, you can clean it: that is, if washing fireplaces is your idea
of a pleasant way to start out having guests. However, if you don't
mind keeping things up to date, and swabbing down each time
after you've used it, the best fireplace can function as well as your
grandmother's old stove in the farmhouse kitchen. There are a
number of books on the market which have complete instructions
on how to build any number of fireplace designs.

The type of grill shaped like a tea table is sensible, if you expect
to do your cooking on the same spot—driveway or terrace, perhaps
—most of the time. It offers a little more cooking space than the
brazier, in exchange for the loss of mobility. The fire pan is usually

adjustable. Ventilation is superior on this model. After you know what conditions you'll be cooking under, and have learned your techniques pretty thoroughly, perhaps this is the one you'll settle for.

A good hand grill is a must. You put your steak, chops, fish, or whatnot in it—and have absolute control for flopping, moving, etc. This grill requires cuts of meat which are uniform in depth, and chops must be cut level, with top and bottom parallel, to fit into it snugly, and get equal exposure to the heat. Obviously, your guests must also want their meat done about the same for this type —you can't work it rare, well-done, or medium, without a lot of pulling in and out. But it's a great help in handling the food. Best way is to use it right on top of the rods of your main grill, like a frying pan.

The little hibachi is a wonderful side-kick device for broiling hors d'oeuvres and other tidbits to keep your guests happy with their refreshments while the main course is on your larger grill. These Oriental cookers come in all sizes, but since they're made of cast iron, the smaller ones are easiest to handle. Very compact to take along on beach picnics. One standard feature: excellent damper for fire control.

Also on the small side, and best reserved for picnic use, is the little folding grill. This is the kind to take along on hikes in your pack basket, or to lie flat in the back of your car. Best for fairly simple meals, obviously, since there's no heat control.

In a spit barbecue unit, the spit is motor-driven, and, of course, this opens up a world of dishes—roasts, fowl, game, and kebabs— which human patience and muscle can hardly endure to turn out on the plain grill.

New on the market, and absolutely ingenious, is an all-kebab motor-driven spit grill. The skewers revolve and deposit their juices in the drop pan, below, for basting. The price makes this something of a luxury, but after you've been won over to the kebab, bub, you'll save your pennies for this one.

In the case of both motor-driven spits, an outdoor electrical outlet is pretty much of a necessity. Be sure to use heavy-duty outdoor wire. A combination of plugs and indoor extensions is risky business outdoors—wet grass, a spilled drink, a few drops of rain, or just a bug with a bit of dew on his mandibles can blow out your fuse at the least, or burn down your house at the most. Some spits are battery-powered. You takes your choice on this, but don't get mad at us if your spit slows to a dribble.

FUELS

Without any doubt, charcoal is the best under any circumstances, unless you're packing it on your back deep into the woods. Lump charcoal smells a little more charcoaly than briquets, but the latter burn more slowly, work up a hotter and steadier fire, and don't spit quite as many sparks at you. The briquets come in bags of all weights up to 20 pounds, and store handily. The small 1- and 2-pound self-starting charcoal boxes with a wick in them are as clever as all get-out in concept, but they don't always start and they don't always provide enough heat for serious cooking. They're best, in my opinion, for standby or emergency use. One advantage is cleanliness. No matter how hard you work at it, when you're handling charcoal, you'll be lucky if all you do is smudge your hands. The little boxes, therefore, are nice for roadside picnicking, etc., or for moments when you want a fast little spot of heat for minor preparations.

If you're using the brazier type of grill, you'll do well to encourage ventilation at the bottom of the bowl by first putting in it a bed of gravel, pebbles, cinders, or prepared "filler" and then placing your charcoal on top of this under layer. It also will serve to hold the heat and back up your charcoal when the time comes for your cooking.

There are innumerable starters on the market, ranging from sprays to sticks. The best thing to do here is to experiment. The most effective trick I ever saw was to soak several pieces of charcoal in alcohol overnight before cooking, and thus have a long-burning torch at the bottom of your fire. Most of the squirt fuels do this to a lesser degree. They have a bad habit of giving you a fine flash while *they* burn, but affecting the charcoal very little. You begin to think you're going to have to cook on lighter fluid alone. Milk cartons, of course, being soaked in paraffin, are great torches. Some people cut a hole in them and stuff them full of briquets, and a couple of these bombs get things going right nicely. Best gadget on the market by far is an electrical coil you simply insert into the charcoal. Plug in and in ten minutes everything's blazing happily.

If your outlet is handy, don't miss out on one of these. But don't let your wife use it as a hair curler, no matter how much it may resemble one. This one's got *resistance* and her hair hasn't.

Don't use wood unless you have to, simply because you'll be working too hard to build up your bed of coals, and to maintain it. Avoid resinous woods—pine, spruce, and anything coniferous—for cooking, but use these to start your fire if possible, adding birch bark or birch wood if you can find it. After your fire is on its way, switch to hardwoods like oak, maple, etc., for slower burning and better coals. Obviously, never use green wood or rotten wood. If it's raining, and you still need a fire, look for dead branches on trees still standing. And, as a last resort, split fair-sized and large pieces of wet wood in two or in quarters to get at the dry wood inside.

Comes the time when your charcoal or wood-ash fire just won't get going, don't resort to blowing on it with your face close to the coals. You may lose your hair and eyebrows in a perhaps welcome, but suddenly unfriendly, flicker of flame. Also you may get a faceful of ashes. A fan made out of newspaper is helpful, but unless you wave it with great caution, you're going to blow ashes all over everything, and perhaps on the waiting food. The best gadget to have is just a length of light rubber hose—two feet or a yard will do, with the hole only a half inch or so in diameter. You blow through this at a safe distance from the fire, and direct the nozzle right to the charcoal where it needs it most. It always works, and you don't even have to pop your eyes out of your head. Sometimes just a sheet or two of a newspaper, spread out over the entire bed of charcoal, will confine the heat for a moment or two, driving up the total temperature, so that when the paper bursts into flame you've got a truly merry glow underneath. Twists of paper, easy to light, and burning for a longer period, may also coax a glow into your coals. But the little coil of hose (a device thought up twenty years ago, when we were often cooking out at temperatures well below zero, and building our fire in caves dug into the snow) never has been known to fail.

HEAT: ITS CARE AND TREATMENT

This is the area in which the chef has to draw his most important conclusions from his own experience, and then stick to them.

There are a great many authorities on heat control, and before you're through you're going to think you've heard from most of them. There are the slow-heat boys, and the hot-flash boys, and never the twain shall meat. But list you:

Generally speaking, your main problem is to have maximum heat that will be steady and maintain its temperature. Obviously, then, you must wait out a period in your charcoal fire when the blue flames are licking up and you think that's going to be just about right. No: wait until the coals are all red and glowing, but then don't wait any longer, because gray ash will begin to settle on them and your heat quotient will go down.

When you're cooking steaks, lamb, or hamburgers, it's a good idea to set your charcoals a little deeper in the middle of your grill pan. These meats must (in my opinion) be broiled quickly and in considerable heat in order to preserve their juices and wonderfully fresh flavor, not to mention the additive of the charcoal taste and odor. If your hot center is just right, you're on your way. If it's too hot, you place the meat at some distance from it, moving it in from the outer edges in order to increase your heat—a trick that eliminates cranking your grill pan, or twisting other gadgets, to control your heat by distance established vertically.

Most other foods, however, require less heat over a longer time. You'll be surprised, if you haven't had the experience already, how long it takes foods to cook thoroughly over a fire which seems satanic even at some distance.

For steady heat, it's often a good idea to arrange your charcoals in patterns which give off an even glow on all parts of your roast. Thus: spaced an inch apart, or in a rotary pattern.

Trim your meat well before cooking. Extra fat will start a merry blaze that actually doesn't harm your food any but often blackens the outside while the meat is still raw inside, and often spoils the timing of your whole meal by practically blowing the main course out of a cannon right onto the table, before anyone is really ready for it.

Always let meat stand for a while at room temperature before putting on the fire. Otherwise it may stick when suddenly applied to the hot metal.

Sear steaks and chops over a hot fire immediately. This prevents loss of juices, which may happen if you apply the heat too slowly. They'll be ready for turning when the juices appear on the top surface.

After turning, cook less thoroughly. Here is the stretch wherein you determine whether the meat is rare, medium rare, medium, or well-done. There probably isn't a cookbook in existence, except this one, which will suggest that you cut open a beautiful piece of meat to see what's doing inside, because that way you obviously lose delicious juices, mutilate the appearance of your fine cut, and vary the taste pattern around the cut portions.

But . . . don't overlook the many factors in outdoor cooking. The humidity—reduces the heat of your fire. The temperature—affects it up or down. The wind—increases your heat with every puff. The thickness of the meat—may vary from what you asked at the butcher's.

So . . . even though your sense of timing may be correct, and your parallelogram of forces well worked out, you still run the risk, particularly with a large steak, of passing by the point of no return in the matter of rareness. And permit me to point out that no soul is more damned, no reputation more sullied, no future more besmirched, than that of the host who responds to the cry of *"Make mine rare!"* with a slice or two of well-done. So, until you really know with the sure instinct of the homing pigeon, with the infallible sense of the great Canada goose heading for a mountain tarn on which to rest and refresh his flock, with the patient perfection of a fullback on the football Giants waiting those precious seconds before he lights on out on the "draw" play—swallow your pride and take a look inside, anyway.

If your fire is blazing up out of control and you've used your distance factor as much as the grill will permit to get away from the center of heat, you can use a sprinkle of water to tone down your blaze. A water pistol or one of the syringe-type roasting basters will do the job very neatly. Not too much water, though. A few drops puts an amazing damper on the spirits of a high fire.

To gauge the degree of your fire, the classic method is to hold your hand over the coals at about the same distance the food will be. If you must withdraw your hand in two seconds, that's a high heat; 6 seconds, medium; 10 seconds, low. (Unguentine is also recommended.)

Keep a supply of wooden toothpicks or small metal skewers on hand to stick into the tail parts of steaks, chops, or any kind of meat with a loose-flying section that might dangle into the coals and simply burn instead of cooking. Skewering these loose ends to the main section of meat helps keep the juices in as well.

MEATS AND VEGETABLES FOR OUTDOOR COOKING

For the most part, you will want to buy the same cuts for steaks, chops, and roasts, as you would for cooking indoors in your kitchen. However, there are certain advance precautions which should be taken for outdoor cookery. In general, order the meat cut thicker than usual—a minimum of $1\frac{1}{2}$ inches thick, and preferably about 2 inches for steaks and chops. Remember to buy enough for "come-back" helpings. The general rule is to allow $\frac{1}{4}$ to $\frac{1}{2}$ pound of boneless cuts or ground beef per serving. Allow $\frac{1}{2}$ to 1 lb. or more per serving of meat with bone in it. When you order your hamburger, ask the butcher to mix in some of the fat with the lean meat when he grinds it—prevents your meat from drying up in the intense heat over the coals.

If you plan to cook your food over a motor-driven spit, there are special boning and binding instructions for your butcher which should be followed so that at no point will your roast collapse. Explain your plan of action to him—a good butcher will prepare the meat right.

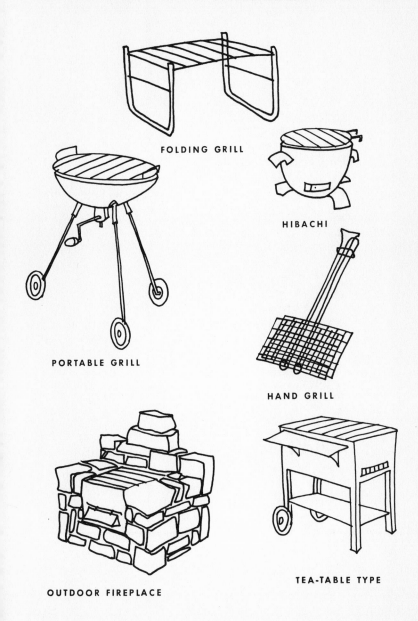

FOLDING GRILL

HIBACHI

PORTABLE GRILL

HAND GRILL

OUTDOOR FIREPLACE

TEA-TABLE TYPE

AND ANOTHER WORD

Cooking outdoors is the greatest fun of all, without doubt. But never when it is done in a hurry. Plan your affair so that there are agreeable things to do, pleasant places to relax, while the cooking is in progress. And then relax in such a communicable way that others catch the mood from you. Nature itself is never in too much of a hurry, and on this occasion you are as close to her as you are apt to get in this mechanical age. Set an elastic timetable. Smile at small accidents and reluctant fires. And your disposition—not to mention your digestion—will be all the better for it.

For the outdoor grill, choose meats which you would fry or broil at home. Club sirloin, T-bone, and cubed steaks; ground beef patties, frankfurters, ham slices, lamb steaks, sliced liver sausage, summer sausage, bologna, and sliced canned luncheon meat all are good choices.

Choose vegetables which require little preparation. Wrap potatoes, corn on the cob, or sweet potatoes in aluminum foil and place on the back of the fireplace or in hot coals to roast.

A good idea to enhance your outdoor cooking is to marinate your meat in advance. Even 1 or 2 hours in a marinade improves both flavor and tenderness of meat. If possible, place meat in its flavor bath overnight in refrigerator. Start with equal parts of olive or salad oil and claret or Burgundy—say ½ cup each. Then adventure with flavors, adding 2 tablespoons each catsup and soy sauce, 1 teaspoon curry powder, freshly-ground black pepper, finely-minced onion; garlic, if desired. When soy sauce is used, omit salt. Meat should be turned several times while in the marinade; baste with the liquid during broiling.

Notes: Tomato sauce may replace catsup. Added seasonings are Accent, Tabasco, prepared or dry mustard, celery salt or seed, Worcestershire. Sear meat quickly before starting to broil; never pierce meat with a fork before or during broiling. Small tongs are handy to turn meat sections.

Another way to step up your meat flavor (if you're not—as I am —a let's-have-it-right-off-the-hoof-and-no-nonsense-to-spoil-it-man) is to experiment until you've discovered the barbecue sauce of all time. There are many, and because in some parts of the country this is considered to be such a fine art, we'll include a number.

Let's start with the simplest, not strictly barbecue sauces, but at least taste addenda. Here's how they'd work out for steak:

BUTTER-BROILED STEAK

Four small steaks about ½ inch thick. Spread one of the following butters generously on top side of steaks. Broil butter side up for 3-5 minutes (depending on how well done the meat is desired). Salt. Turn steaks, butter other side and salt well. Broil 3-5 minutes or until browned. Serve garnished with parsley.

Provolone Butter: Blend together ¼ cup (½ stick) softened butter, 1 teaspoon chopped onion, ½ teaspoon Worcestershire sauce, and 2 tablespoons grated Provolone cheese.

Garlic Butter: Blend together ¼ cup (½ stick) softened butter, ½ garlic clove minced, and 1 tablespoon prepared mustard.

Parmesan Butter: Blend together ¼ cup (½ stick) softened butter, 2 teaspoons orégano flakes, and 2 tablespoons grated Parmesan cheese.

Basil Butter: Blend together ¼ cup (½ stick) softened butter, 1 teaspoon grated onion and ½ teaspoon basil.

Chili Butter: Blend together ¼ cup (½ stick) softened butter, 2 teaspoons grated onion, and 1 teaspoon chili powder.

I am a great admirer of Lea & Perrins Worcestershire sauce and use it in everything from Bloody Marys to barbecue sauces. L. & P. has made a science of this thing, and why not give them the credit for some superb taste discoveries? Here's their proudest:

TEXAS BARBECUE SAUCE

2 cups water	1 cup cider vinegar
½ teaspoon black pepper	1 5-oz. bottle Worcestershire
4 tablespoons brown sugar	sauce
1 teaspoon garlic salt or	Juice of 4 lemons
2 cloves garlic, chopped fine	4 tablespoons butter
2 teaspoons salt	

Bring water to boil in a large 2-quart kettle, add pepper, simmer 5 minutes. Add brown sugar, stir until dissolved, add garlic salt or chopped garlic, salt, vinegar, and stir. Add ½ the bottle of Worcestershire, simmer for a few minutes, add lemon juice and stir.

Then add balance of the Worcestershire and stir while heating. Add butter as sauce heats just before use.

In making up this sauce it is easier to make it in a larger quantity than you need for a single barbecue. By omitting the butter, it will keep for weeks in the refrigerator. When ready to use, heat slowly with the butter. Omit butter when barbecuing pork.

The secret of a good barbecue is to use plenty of sauce so it will be absorbed while the meat is cooking.

Four other L. & P. barbecue sauces follow: one made with catsup, one with tomato juice, one with lemon, one with wine. Each has its own characteristic flavor.

CATSUP BARBECUE SAUCE

2 medium onions, chopped	1 bouillon cube dissolved in 1
4 tablespoons fat	cup water
½ clove garlic, mashed	2 tablespoons Worcestershire
½ cup catsup	sauce

Cook onions in fat until golden, add rest of ingredients. Simmer for 30 minutes. Use as a basting for turkey broilers, chicken, short ribs, hamburger.　　　　　　　　　　　　　　　　　1 PINT

TOMATO JUICE BARBECUE SAUCE

2 teaspoons salt	4½ teaspoons Worcestershire
¼ teaspoon pepper	sauce
1½ cups tomato juice	½ to ¾ cup vinegar
¼ teaspoon cayenne pepper	1 teaspoon sugar
¼ teaspoon dry mustard	3 cloves garlic, minced
1 bay leaf	2 tablespoons butter or salad oil

Simmer all ingredients together for 10 minutes. Use as a basting for chicken, chops, turkey, etc.　　　　　　　　　　　　2½ CUPS

LEMON BARBECUE SAUCE

1 clove garlic	2 tablespoons grated onion
½ teaspoon salt	½ teaspoon black pepper
¼ cup salad or olive oil	1 teaspoon Worcestershire sauce
½ cup lemon juice	

Mash garlic with salt in bowl, stir in remaining ingredients. Chill 24 hours. Especially nice as basting for chicken.

WINE BARBECUE SAUCE

¼ cup salad oil
½ cup red or white wine
1 clove garlic, mashed
1 teaspoon grated onion

½ teaspoon salt
1 tablespoon Worcestershire
   sauce
½ teaspoon black pepper

Mix oil and wine, add rest of ingredients, chill several hours. Pour over poultry or meat, let chill 3 hours. Baste again with sauce during cooking. Use red wine for steaks or lamb; white wine for chicken or veal.   ¾ CUP

BARBECUE SAUCE ROYALE

¼ cup vinegar
¾ cup water
2 tablespoons sugar
3 tablespoons Lipton's onion
   soup mix
½ teaspoon pepper

1 teaspoon salt
⅛ teaspoon cayenne pepper
1 tablespoon prepared mustard
1 thick lemon slice
¼ cup butter
½ cup catsup

Combine all ingredients except catsup. Simmer 10 minutes. Stir in catsup and heat. Serve with steak, chicken, hamburgers, or hot dogs.
APPROXIMATELY 1 PINT

And, since while we're about this barbecue sauce bit we might as well wrap it up, here are three other eminently tasty variants:

BARBECUE #1

1 tablespoon fat
¼ cup chopped onion
1 tablespoon sugar
1 teaspoon dry mustard

1 tablespoon Worcestershire
   sauce
½ cup catsup
2 tablespoons vinegar
¼ cup water

Cook onion in hot fat until soft. Add rest of ingredients and simmer.

BARBECUE #2

1 onion, chopped	2 tablespoons vinegar
2 tablespoons salad oil	1 tablespoon mustard
½ cup catsup	¼ teaspoon white pepper
½ cup water	1 teaspoon celery salt
2 teaspoons Worcestershire	Dash of cayenne
sauce	

Cook onion in oil for 5 minutes. Add remaining ingredients and boil 10 minutes.

HERB SAUCE FOR LAMB

1 small onion	12 fresh mint leaves
2 cloves garlic	¼ cup vinegar
1 teaspoon dried rosemary	½ cup water

Chop onion and garlic fine and add rosemary and mint leaves which have been crushed. Add vinegar and water and let mixture stand overnight. When ready to barbecue, brush steaks or chops thoroughly with the sauce. As the meat cooks, baste occasionally.

Thus ready for the big show under the skies, here are your further considerations:

The Grill: When the fire has burned down to a good bed of coals, lay the food to be grilled—steaks, chops, bacon, split frankfurters, fish, or halved small chickens—across the grill just as though it were the oven broiling rack. It's best to rub the grill first with a piece of beef suet or with a small cloth moistened with melted fat. Turning, salting, and basting the meat are matters of personal preference. Most barbecue cooks prefer to turn the meat only once or twice during broiling and to salt at the end of cooking. Avoid puncturing the meat with a fork when turning. It's more satisfactory to turn with cooking tongs or a couple of pancake turners.

The Flat Plate: Any of the meats listed above can be cooked on the flat plate. The procedure is to rub the hot plate lightly with suet or oil, then pan broil the meat on the hot surface exactly as you'd cook it on a skillet.

The Spit: The barbecue spit provides a good way of roasting chickens (halves or whole) and compact solid roasts of meat such as rolled beef roasts, boned pork shoulder or boned legs of lamb. For these the spit is run through the center of the meat so that in turning no one side of the roast will be thinner and therefore more quickly cooked than another. The spit is slowly revolved over the coals and the distance from the spit to the hot coals usually is 15 inches. Often the meat is basted during cooking with barbecue sauce, applied with swabs. The time required for cooking meat in this manner is in general about the same length of time required to cook a similar cut in an oven at moderate temperature.

Your first thought, naturally, will be for

STEAKS

Steak de luxe is from 2 to 3 inches thick, charcoaled on the outside, pink and tender inside, served sliced with the grain.

If this is out of the question (and except for that very special barbecue it often is) have your steak at least 1 inch thick. Allow from ½-1 lb. per serving. Grill a 1-inch steak about 6 minutes on each side if you like it medium. For rare, grill 5 minutes; well done, 7 minutes.

A 2-inch steak takes much longer: 18 minutes each side for medium, 16 for rare, 20 for well done.

Grilled Cube Steak: Soak cube steaks in Texas Barbecue Sauce at least 15 minutes. Grill 15 to 20 minutes over glowing coals. Serve, if desired, with toasted buns, with additional Texas Barbecue Sauce.

Minute Steaks: Sauté minute steaks (¼ inch thick) in a little hot fat in a skillet about 1 to 2 minutes on each side. Remove from pan, add 1 teaspoon butter and 1 teaspoon Lea & Perrins Worcestershire sauce to pan drippings, stir while heating, pour over steaks.

London Broil: Trim 1½ lbs. flank steak of excess fat and membrane and score on both sides. Let stand 8 to 24 hours in 1½ cups Texas Barbecue Sauce, turning occasionally. Remove from sauce, grill over hot coals or broil until brown but still rare (about 5 minutes on each side). Season with butter, salt, and pepper. Cut into very thin slantwise slices to serve.   ABOUT 4-5 SERVINGS

And then . . .

BARBECUED CHICKEN

Grilled: Cut a 2- to 2½-pound ready-to-cook broiler into serving pieces. Let stand in any of the barbecue sauces 8 to 24 hours, or as long as possible. Grill over hot coals slowly—about 25 minutes or until tender, turning often. Baste frequently with additional barbecue sauce.

Broiled: Heat broiler 10 minutes. Fix chicken as for grilling, place on broiler pan, cut side down. Broil slowly, turning and basting often until tender and brown (30 to 45 minutes).   4-5 SERVINGS

BARBECUED TURKEY BROILERS

Grill or broil as for chicken (above) using 3- to 6-pound ready-to-cook turkey broilers.

BARBECUED LAMB

This method of cooking lamb provides delicious small "lamb roasts" for the guests. Select a split loin of lamb. Have the meat man divide the split loin into about six chops, cutting through the bone but not completely separating the cuts. Rub the meat lightly with a cut clove of garlic, then roast on the grill over glowing coals. Turn as frequently as necessary for even cooking and baste with a favorite barbecue sauce. Ordinarily 40-45 minutes should be long enough to allow for the roasting. Then with a sharp knife divide into chops and allow one for each serving. A half rack of lamb also may be barbecued in this way.

You may want to cook several different kinds of meats for the picnic grill and multiply the fun. You might offer a choice of frankfurters wrapped in bacon, ground beef patties and barbecued bologna slices.

PICNIC GRILL

Picnic Patties: Season each pound of ground beef with 1 teaspoon salt and ⅛ teaspoon pepper. For extra-juicy hamburgers, add ¼ cup cold water per pound of meat.

Shape patties before leaving home and wrap in waxed paper. For easy separation, place a square of waxed paper between each patty. Fry on a hot greased grill.

Barberpole Franks: Wrap each frankfurter with a strip of bacon and fasten with toothpicks. (This can be done before leaving home.) Fry on a hot greased grill, turning to cook bacon on all sides.

Barbecued Bologna: Slice bologna ¼ to ½ inch thick and brown on hot greased grill. While slices brown, spoon barbecue sauce over them.

Complete the menu with buns, olives, and pickles, crisp celery and carrot sticks, a salad if you wish, coffee, milk, and fresh cherry pie.

And, more variations on the barbecue theme:

FRANKS

Simmer frankfurters 7 minutes, but do not prick.

Grill frankfurters over hot coals until brown.

Broil whole or split lengthwise 2 or 3 inches from broiler heat for 6-7 minutes. Serve in toasted buttered buns topped with Texas or other barbecue sauce or Mustard Sauce.

Pan fry gently until brown in frying pan in butter. Remove frankfurters, add 1 to 2 teaspoons Lea & Perrins Worcestershire sauce, heat, and pour over frankfurters in toasted buttered buns. Pass Catsup Barbecue Sauce.

Bake frankfurters in shallow covered pan in Texas Barbecue Sauce, in moderate oven (350° F.) for 20 minutes. Baste often during baking.

In foil: Wrap individual franks with 2 tablespoons of any barbecue sauce in foil. Heat on hot coals 10 minutes.

HAMBURGERS

1 lb. chuck beef, ground (80 per cent lean, 20 per cent fat)	2 to 3 tablespoons minced onion
1 teaspoon salt	2 teaspoons Worcestershire sauce

Add a dash of cold water and lightly mix all ingredients; shape gently into 4-6 patties. Grill over hot coals 4-5 minutes on each side. Patties may be pan fried in hot fat in a frying pan, or they may be broiled in a kitchen broiler, placing them 1½ inches from heat. Broil 4 to 5 minutes on each side. Brush with Texas Barbecue Sauce once or twice on each side during cooking. Serve cooked hamburgers in split toasted buns or between slices of toasted bread with Texas Barbecue Sauce.

Zesty additions: Spread toasted buns with softened butter to which Worcestershire sauce has been added (¼ cup butter and 1 teaspoon Worcestershire make enough for 6 buns). Top hamburgers with minced onion or onion rings, sweet pickle relish, or cheese slices.

For extra flavor, sprinkle grilled or broiled hamburgers with grated Parmesan cheese just after broiling. Serve in toasted buttered buns.

CHEESE HAMBURGER DE LUXE

¼ cup (½ stick) butter
¼ cup flour
2 cups milk
1⅔ cups shredded Cheddar cheese
½ teaspoon salt
Dash cayenne pepper
1 teaspoon Worcestershire sauce

4 slices toast
4 slices Swiss cheese
4 hamburgers, cooked
4 slices bacon, fried till crisp
4 slices sweet onion
4 slices tomato
Sliced pimiento olives

In a saucepan, melt butter and blend in flour until smooth. Add milk gradually and cook, stirring constantly, until thickened. Add Cheddar cheese, salt, cayenne pepper, and Worcestershire sauce; stir until blended. Top each slice of toast with Swiss cheese, hamburger, bacon, onion and tomato. Pour hot cheese sauce over sandwich and garnish with sliced olives.   4 SERVINGS

SPARERIBS

Grilled: Cut 4 lbs. spareribs into 3- to 4-rib portions. Simmer in 2 cups water until almost tender (about 1 hour) or pressure cook in 1 cup water at 15 lbs. pressure 20 minutes according to manufacturer's directions. Dip each piece in Texas Barbecue Sauce, and grill over hot coals, turning often to brown well. Brush with more Texas Barbecue Sauce frequently during grilling.

Baked: Place 3 or 4 pounds cut-up spareribs, meaty side up, in shallow roasting pan. Add 1 lemon and 1 large onion, thinly sliced. Roast in very hot oven (450° F.) 30 minutes. Pour off fat. Then add 1½ cups Texas Barbecue Sauce, and continue baking, basting often, in moderate oven (350° F.) 1 hour or until brown.

3-4 SERVINGS

SHORT RIBS

Grilled: Cut meat from bones of 3 lbs. beef short ribs cut in serving pieces. Let stand in 1½ cups Texas Barbecue Sauce 2 or 3 hours; then grill over hot coals, turning often to brown. Brush often during grilling with Texas Barbecue Sauce.

Braised: Brush 3 lbs. beef short ribs cut in chunks with Texas Barbecue Sauce. Brown well in 2 tablespoons fat in large heavy frying pan or Dutch oven. Add 1 clove garlic, minced, and ½ cup minced onion and cook until onion is golden. Add 1½ to 2 cups Texas Barbecue Sauce, cover, and simmer 1 hour or until tender.

FISH STEAKS

Choose ¾-inch-thick salmon, halibut, or swordfish steaks cut in serving-size pieces. Let stand in Texas Barbecue Sauce or Lemon Barbecue Sauce 1 hour. Grill close to hot coals about 3 minutes on each side or until golden brown.   3 LBS. MAKES 8 SERVINGS

LAMB STEAK

Choose cut (from leg) 1 to 1½ inches thick and cook same as beefsteak.

LAMB OR PORK CHOPS

Choose cuts 1 to 1½ inches thick and cook same as steak. Be sure when cooking pork chops that you cook over a low fire, and test inside before final browning over fast fire, to make sure meat is well done.

A nice accompaniment to any outdoor food is:

CHUCK-WAGON BEANS

3 one-lb. cans (6 cups) baked beans in pork and molasses sauce	¼ cup brown sugar
	1 teaspoon dry mustard
	1 teaspoon salt
1 eight-oz. can seasoned tomato sauce	4 drops Tabasco
	6 slices bacon or ¼ lb. salt pork cut in cubes
1 cup finely chopped onion	
½ cup catsup	

In 2-quart casserole combine beans, tomato sauce, onion, catsup, brown sugar, and seasonings. Bury bacon in beans. Bake uncovered in slow oven (300° F.) 3½-4 hours. Toward end of cooking time, bring bacon to top.   6 SERVINGS

KEBABS

If you're willing to stray from the traditional steak-and-chops outline over the coals, one of your very best explorations is the kebab area.

The kebab is actually the result of skewering and then broiling various kinds of vegetables interspersed with meat. Here's one, for example:

LAMB KEBAB

Cut into 1½-inch cubes about 2 lbs. lamb shoulder or boned leg of lamb meat and marinate for 2-3 hours in ½ cup each lemon juice, red wine, and olive oil, to which you've added a dash of salt and pepper, and a pinch each of basil and tarragon. (Use rosemary if you prefer or another favorite herb.) Turn meat in marinade occasionally.

Thread on special barbecuing skewers chunks of lamb alternating with your choice of canned whole onions, canned potatoes, pitted ripe olives, stuffed green olives, squares of bacon, gherkins, canned pineapple chunks, canned peach halves, mushrooms, and/or small red tomatoes. Keep the proportion of meat high—thus: meat, onion, meat, mushroom, meat, tomato, etc. Baste with the marinade or butter while broiling over low heat. Should take about 10 minutes.

Veal kebabs can be made the same way. Ditto pork kebabs, in which case also skewer thick slices of tart apples. If you decide on ham kebabs, by all means use the pineapple chunks.

Other machinations in which to marinate:

French dressing with 1 clove of garlic added.

½ cup wine vinegar, 1 teaspoon curry powder.

Mix 1 cup salad oil, ¾ cup soy sauce, ½ cup lemon juice, ¼ cup each Worcestershire sauce and prepared mustard, 1-2 teaspoons coarsely cracked pepper and 2 minced cloves of garlic. This is called California marinade.

Beef Kebabs—You can cut up a sirloin steak into chunks, and make terrific kebabs out of it, alternating on the skewer with mushrooms, onions, and small tomatoes. If you want to use a cheaper meat, get about 3 lbs. lean beef round or chuck, and marinate in California sauce, above, for at least 24 hours.

MEAT-CHEESE KEBABS

1½ lbs. ground beef	½ cup milk
¾ cup uncooked rolled oats	¼ teaspoon garlic salt
3 tablespoons minced onion	2 teaspoons Worcestershire
1½ teaspoons salt	sauce
¼ teaspoon pepper	½ pound sharp American
1 teaspoon monosodium	cheese cut into 16 squares
glutamate	8 buttered hot dog buns

Combine all the ingredients except the cheese and buns and mix well; chill. Shape meat mixture into 16 meat balls, each one around a square of cheese. Thread meat balls onto skewers, sealing meat closely around skewer; chill, if possible. Broil 4-5 inches from glowing coals, turning as needed to brown and cook evenly, 8-10 minutes.   MAKES 8 SERVINGS

Note to neophytes: It isn't as spectacular a gesture as skewering all your ingredients together, but you may find—at least, at first— that you'll have things more under control if you do the meat on one skewer and the vegetables, etc. on the other. Their timing can be a little different, and until you're sure of how to average off these differences in one operation, experiment with the separate-skewer method and observe the comparative speeds.

GAME COOKERY

There's a lot of shooting still going on in this country, but not very much eating going on as a result of it. One reason is some people are strangely distressed when they find themselves cracking their fillings on birdshot, in spite of the romance of the situation. And also—whether or not this is a sign of our national physical deterioration, as some claim—our palates have become accustomed to the comparative blandness of barnyard poultry, and some of the game birds seem a touch gamey, at that.

However, you may be faced with the necessity of preparing a dish from the quarry proudly produced by a friend, so you might as well be prepared. If he is crazy enough to come up with a bear, even though the meat is not unpleasant (a bit like mutton the last time

I ate one, shot in the Vermont woods), skip the whole thing, and lose your friend, if you must, rather than go through trying to butcher the beast.

Even enthusiastic hunters confess to the fact that much game cookery consists of trying to tone down the flavor of the flesh and disguise it. Venison, however, has its own flavor, and it is pleasant enough. It has a delicate texture, and a wild taste, not too strong.

But it's not beef. For example, the fat is not palatable in any sense, and the meat must be trimmed clear of it before you can start cooking. You (with the help of a pig) supply your own, usually dry salt pork.

If you're sure your venison has been hung for at least two weeks, which can be arranged through your butcher, you'll then be ready for

VENISON STEAK

After the fat is trimmed off, rub the meat with garlic and brush with olive oil or butter. Sprinkle with salt and pepper. Venison should be cooked rare but well browned. Place 3 inches over the coals and give it about 4-5 minutes for each side of a 1-inch-thick steak. Finish it off by pouring over it about ⅛ cup melted butter and ⅛ cup lemon juice, and giving it a last blast over high flame. A butter sauce of ¼ cup butter and ½ tablespoon finely chopped parsley creamed together will add to the serving, with salt and pepper to taste.

If you're not sure how you or your guests will go for venison straight off the hoof, as it were, in the steaks, you might try

VENISON CASSEROLE

4 lbs. trimmed tenderloin, cut in 1-inch cubes	1 lb. ham, sliced
	2 cups small onions
¼ cup flour, pinch of sage, pinch of orégano, salt, and pepper	4 cups diced potatoes
	2 cups sour cream
	½ pound sliced mushrooms
5 tablespoons butter	½ cup red wine

Shake cubes in a bag with the flour seasoned with the sage, orégano, salt, and pepper. Sauté in butter for about 20 minutes or until well browned. Line a 3-quart greased casserole with the ham slices, add successive layers of venison, potatoes, and onions. Bake, covered, in a moderate oven (350° F.) for 50 minutes. Then add the sour cream, mushrooms, and wine. Bake for another half hour.

SERVES 7-10

It is more difficult to pick wild ducks and geese out of the sky than to select your tame varieties. Also, since they run to a somewhat fishy taste, they should always be cleaned promptly after shooting, stuffed with ½ lemon and a peeled onion for 24 hours before cooking.

ROAST WILD GOOSE OR DUCK

Remove the stuffing. Rub the inside of the bird with salt, pepper, and powdered sage, and stuff with slices of apple and a few onion slices. Truss (see directions for roast turkey, page 112), rub exterior with salt and pepper, cover breast with two slices fat salt pork, cut very thin. Roast in a slow oven (300° F.) until tender, at least 2 hours for goose and about 1¼ for duck. Baste frequently.

Here again, a casserole may come to your aid:

WILD DUCK CASSEROLE

2 ducks	⅓ cup carrots, cut in strips
1 lemon	1 cup cubed potatoes
2 medium onions peeled	1 cup shredded lettuce
2 tablespoons olive oil	1 cup tomatoes
1 minced garlic clove	Pinch of orégano
4 thin slices bacon, cut in	2 cups boiling water
narrow strips	Salt and pepper
12 small onions	

Stuff ducks as before, let stand 24 hours. Remove stuffing, split ducks. Brown in olive oil, with garlic added. Broil bacon. Put ducks and bacon in well-buttered 3-quart casserole and add other ingredients. Salt and pepper to taste. Cover dish, and bake in slow oven (300° F.) until tender, for about an hour.   4 SERVINGS

Here are some contrasting methods for the smaller game birds—grouse (which is about the same as partridge, for our purposes), pheasant, and quail.

ROAST PHEASANT

1 plump young pheasant, 2-3 lbs.	Few celery leaves
(dressed weight)	1 slice lemon
Salt and pepper	4 slices bacon
1 bay leaf	Melted butter
1 clove garlic, crushed	

Sprinkle the pheasant inside and out with salt and pepper. Place the bay leaf, garlic, celery leaves, and lemon in the cavity. Tie legs together with string; turn wings under. Cover breast with bacon and cheesecloth soaked in melted butter. Place pheasant breast up in baking pan. Roast in preheated moderate oven (350° F.) for 30 minutes per pound, or until the pheasant is tender, basting frequently with melted butter. Remove the cheesecloth and string.

2 SERVINGS

QUAIL IN SOUR CREAM

1 quail, disjointed
Flour
Salt and pepper
Cooking fat

Butter
2 cups sour cream
2-3 oz. dry white wine

Both pheasant and quail meat are dry. This recipe counteracts the dryness and complements the natural flavor of the game.

Shake the quail pieces in a paper bag containing the flour, salt, and pepper. Shake off excess flour and seasoning and brown the pieces in a heavy frying pan, using cooking fat to which butter has been added.

Pour sour cream over the sautéed quail and add the wine. Cover the frying pan and cook over low heat, turning the pieces several times until the meat is tender.

PHEASANT IN CREAM

1 large pheasant, cut in serving
 pieces
1-1½ cups cream

Pinch of sage
Salt and pepper

Cover pheasant with water. Place over low heat and simmer for 15 minutes. Remove to buttered casserole, cover with cream and add seasonings. Place in a slow oven (250° F.) and bake, covered, until meat is tender, about 2½ hours.   4 SERVINGS

ROAST GROUSE

Chop about ½ cup each onion and cabbage. Mix together and add 1 beaten egg and enough evaporated milk to make a moist stuffing for the grouse. It will generate steam that will permeate the meat and make it tender and juicy. Stuff bird, then rub exterior liberally with butter. Place breast up in shallow roasting pan and cover with 3 slices bacon. Roast in a moderate oven (350° F.) until tender, about 1 hour. Remove bacon strips 15 minutes before it is done, add ½ cup white wine or cognac, and baste several times before removing from oven.   3 SERVINGS

ROAST QUAIL

Rub each quail (1 to a person) with salt and melted butter, roll in flour, and surround with thinly cut trimmings of fat salt pork. Wrap in fresh grape leaves for flavor, if they are available. Otherwise, baste often with 2 tablespoons butter, melted in ¼ cup hot water. Chop boiled chicken livers (1 to a person), season with salt, pepper, and onion juice, moisten with melted butter, and dust with one teaspoon chopped parsley. Spread mixture on as many pieces of toast as you have quail, arrange a bird on each, and garnish with parsley.

Having admitted to eating porcupine, it would be cavalier to look down on squirrel and rabbit eaters, even though Dan'l Boone and his trick of shooting the branch *under* the squirrel to stun him and leave the meat untouched are now well behind us.

But if you're really for it, out in the woods, and eating what you can get, let's turn to

FRIED SQUIRREL

Clean and quarter each squirrel. Soak in cold salted water, with just a little vinegar in it, for 30 minutes. Dry, dust with flour seasoned with salt and pepper. Fry in bacon fat until a deep brown and nearly tender, about 30 to 45 minutes. Add white wine or hard cider barely to cover. Simmer over low heat until liquid has been absorbed. Add butter to the frying pan and sauté squirrel until crisp. Serve very hot.

RABBIT WITH SPLIT PEAS

1 lb. split peas	Salt and pepper
1 teaspoon salt	2 rabbits, cut in serving pieces
3 medium onions, diced	3 tablespoons olive or vegetable
1/4 lb. mushrooms, sliced	oil
1 teaspoon sweet basil	2 cloves garlic, mashed
Pinch of thyme	3 tablespoons butter, melted

Soak peas overnight in cold water to cover. Drain. Now cover with 2 quarts fresh water, add salt, and boil for 15 minutes. Drain again. Put into a buttered casserole. Mix in onions, mushrooms, basil, and thyme. Season to taste with salt and pepper. Rub rabbit pieces with oil and garlic and put on broiler rack 2 inches under heat. Broil for 15 minutes, turning often and basting with balance of oil combined with butter. Bury rabbit pieces in the peas. Bake in a moderate oven (350° F.) for 1½ hours.   4-6 SERVINGS

HASENPFEFFER

Carefully wash and dry a 2½- to 3-lb. dressed rabbit. Cut into serving portions. Place in a deep crock and cover with equal parts cider vinegar and water (about three cups each). Add 1 medium onion, thinly sliced, 1/3 cup sugar, 2 bay leaves, 4 whole cloves, 6 whole peppercorns, 1 teaspoon tarragon, 2 teaspoons salt. Marinate 36-48 hours (no longer or it gets tough).

Remove the rabbit pieces from the marinade and allow to drain for ½ hour or more. Brown the pieces in hot butter and oil—half and half in a deep, heavy skillet. Slowly add 1 cup of the marinade liquid, cover and simmer over very low heat about 1 hour or until very tender. Remove the Hasenpfeffer to a hot platter. Add 1 cup commercial sour cream to the sauce. Stir until very hot but don't boil. Correct seasoning and pour over the rabbit pieces.

ON THE TRAIL

We also include herewith a number of recipes which are useful and valuable for camping out when you are depending on your back for transportation or have canoe or car to bring along a camp stove.

A great many experienced hands in the outdoors will settle for camp stoves. They have gas, liquid, or canned heat, and, of course, you must cook over them only with pan or pot. Lots of good food can be prepared thus, and much time is saved with this type of equipment.

But you lose the thrill of actually cooking your food over an open fire, and the wonderful flavor that belongs incomparably to cooking outdoors and especially in the deep woods, within sight of a lake or stream.

Here are a few hints from experienced woodsmen which will make your trail cooking simpler and more enjoyable. And, of course, don't forget to see the special one-pot recipes, which—to use a nauseatingly overworked phrase—are literally a source for that abused term "a meal in itself."

Before you set out on your trip, work out a complete menu for every day, and for every meal.

Start off with meat meals on your first or second day (if the weather isn't too hot, and you stand a chance of cooling your meat over the first night), and then shift to prepared foods and pick-ups.

Prepared foods will include soups, which should be a staple of your menu, fruit drinks (you'll be surprised how much better than water they taste at mealtime in the big woods), milk, eggs, and other dishes which come in powdered, dehydrated form. Carry plenty of dehydrated fruits.

Permit yourself a few, but not too many, canned luxuries. They're heavy to carry, and don't always pay their way. Corned beef hash is a real treat for a hungry trail crew. Certain stews are just as welcome.

Chocolate candy is one of the most satisfying and reviving light foods for trail work. Take a good supply along, not forgetting to keep it cool as often as circumstances permit. Best plan is a number of small units, separately packaged, so that you don't lose your hoard in one exposure to heat.

Before you hit the trail, melt a large block of paraffin into a mold approximating the size of a candy box. Drop as many large strike-anywhere matches into this as the liquid paraffin will hold. Allow to solidify. Now you have a completely waterproof stock of matches that will burn like candles—you can even drop this paraffin package into a stream and the matches will survive to light for you. (This is my own invention, and capitalists are invited to invest and to go halfies.)

When the weather turns forbidding, stop on the trail and stuff a few twigs or bits of birch bark into your pack while they're still dry; these are to start your fire. If you're feeling strong enough, pick up a couple of sizable cuts of wood as well—it will mean a good fire even in the rain, if you're this farsighted.

The kind of collapsible small grill pictured earlier in this chapter is perfect for the trail. Set it up between a collar of good-sized rocks for protection from the wind and heat reflection, and you're all set. Set a couple of flat rocks near the fire, with one end practically in it, and you'll have a fine table on which to keep food warm while you're completing other dishes.

Always carry one deep pan either with a long handle or with a pail handle for suspension over the fire. This is going to be "home" for all the one-dish recipes you'll find a few pages from here. It is also your washtub and general carryall. Don't forget a sizable, but light, coffeepot. Carry a nest of light frying pans. Tin cups will do for soup, fruit, water, coffee, and candle holders.

Always carry a lightweight axe rather than a hatchet. The latter is O.K. for small jobs, and small scouts, and you might as well have one along, too. But for any kind of a chopping job, you'll thank your inspiration and trouble in bringing a man-sized axe.

Check the terrain of your trip in advance, and try to plan a number of pick-up meals, based on the probability of picking up fresh meat at crossroads general stores, eggs from farmers in the back country, or fish and small game from the countryside. The latter are more problematical than the first, so always have some emergency ration—cornmeal and oatmeal are light to carry, easy to prepare—in case you miss out with bait and bullet.

You'll find that a "reflector" oven, which cooks by reflected heat directly from your open fire, is a really luxurious item in the woods. Fresh biscuits or bread, with a raisin or two perched on top, are the equivalent of strawberry shortcake after you've been on the trail for more than a few days.

Don't forget the advice previously advanced in the matter of woods for cooking. The coniferous trees—spruce, pine, cedar, etc.— are excellent to start with, and don't overlook the cones themselves as fine kindling. But don't cook over this wood; it's resinous and burns too quickly to give you any kind of dependable heat. Oak, maple, birch, and other hardwoods are best for your serious cooking heat. Build your fire with logs as thick as you have on the three sides away from you, forming a space in which to put your kindling. These logs will contain your coals, and also burn in turn to maintain a steady heat. If your fire is slowing down, sometimes candle drippings will help it along in strategic spots better than kindling.

The Dartmouth Outing Club has numbered many fine cooks among its members, and they run a course each year up in Hanover to pass on the secrets of trail cooking to new undergraduates. This is no gourmet fare, but it often seems like it to envious non-DOC skiers or mountain climbers who come upon the Hanoverians dining sumptuously, at least by comparison with the usual hardtack and cold-water diet of such hardy souls.

Here are a few to tear out and tuck into your pack just as you leave for the big woods:

STEW

Allow several hours over open fire for this. Cut 2 lbs. shoulder of lamb or bottom round in chunks about 1½ inch on a side. Cover with water and cook 2 to 3 hours, adding a little hot water as it boils away.

Cook separate from meat 2 carrots sliced, 2 onions sliced, 5 medium spuds sliced thin and added after other vegetables have been cooking ½ hour.

When meat and vegetables are tender, add latter to meat with a little of the vegetable water, and season.

Thicken if necessary with paste of flour and cold water.

6 SERVINGS

MEAT LOAF

1½ lbs. bottom round ham-
burger
2 eggs, beaten and mixed with
meat
Small onion chopped

¾ cup bread crumbs or
shredded wheat
Little pepper, salt, nutmeg
Enough milk to moisten well
Salt pork or bacon

Mix all ingredients except salt pork or bacon. Press mixture into a deep pan (bread tin), cover with thin strips of salt pork or bacon, cover with boiling water and bake moderately for 1 hour.

6 SERVINGS

CAPE COD TURKEY

Shred and soak salt codfish overnight or bring to boil and drain off water. Boil codfish and add enough spuds after 15 minutes. Cook together about 45 minutes till both fish and spuds seem tender. Mash and mix spuds with fish and serve with little cubes of fried salt pork.

CORNED BEEF SLUM

3 slices of bacon, chopped up
1 small onion, chopped
¼ green pepper, minced
2 tablespoons butter

1 can corned beef, chopped
1 small can tomatoes (15 or
20 oz.)
⅛ lb. soda crackers

Fry bacon with chopped onion and pepper, add butter, then corned beef and tomatoes. Cook 25-30 minutes and add crackers. Serve as soon as crackers become soft.   6 SERVINGS

BULLY BEEF

In a saucepan—cover canned roast beef with water and bring to boil, remove meat, and thicken the broth with flour and cold-water paste. Season well, add chopped onion browned in fry pan with butter, return meat, pulled into medium-size chunks, to gravy and reheat. Serve with spuds, rice, or macaroni.

SALMON OR TUNA

For each can of fish make the following cream sauce: Wet 1 tablespoon flour with milk and stir till smooth. Add this to 1 cup boiling milk and 1 tablespoon butter. Cook slowly. Season with salt and pepper (a few pieces of onion are allowable).

When you add a can of peas to this creamed fish, you create a "wiggle" (famed throughout the Appalachian Mountain Club Huts).

MACARONI, CAMP STYLE

1 eight-oz. pkg. macaroni	3 tablespoons Worcestershire
2 cups grated Cheddar cheese	sauce
(½ lb.)	Salt and pepper to taste
¼ cup chili sauce	¾ cup hot melted butter

Cook macaroni in boiling salted water (3 quarts water, 1 tablespoon salt) until tender (9 to 12 minutes). Drain and spread out on a large hot platter. Sprinkle with cheese, chili sauce, Worcestershire. Add salt and pepper to taste. Pour over the hot melted butter and toss with 2 forks until sauce is creamy. Serve at once.

And a last word on your outdoor cookery. You will be sure, of course, that your coals are doused with water and/or sand, if you must dump them and leave the spot. If they are to be left in the grill basket near your home or campsite, keep it away from the sides of buildings or inflammable substances and away from the path of someone who might stumble over the red-hot contraption late at night (it might be *you*).

If you have any pots and pans to wash, you can speed things up or eliminate harder scrubbing later on by boiling up some water in them, before you douse your fire, or just rinsing them with the water before the food gets a chance to set.

If you are bedding down in the woods, either in a three-sided leanto or a tent, here's a trick that was passed on to me by an old tracker from the Michigan big woods. Take a five-gallon tin of maple syrup or some sweetened liquid, puncture the tin full of holes, enough to make a watering-can pattern in either the top or the bottom, and then just slowly pour this in a circle around your campsite, keeping the magic ring about twenty feet on all sides from where you plan to sleep and store your food and clothes. (You'll probably want to hang both the clothes you have worn and your food supplies in a pack, suspended by a wire, from the branch of a tree, to protect them from ants and small animals: but even this won't keep them away from porcupines. The prickly ones like a nice sweat-soaked belt almost as much as a pound of butter to chew on, and I've seen them climb onto tables and stumps to take flying leaps for clothes and foodstuffs even when suspended in mid-air. A porky will even sample your belt and socks while you're still in them, perhaps sleeping in your clothes. I've had it happen, and it's a strange sensation to awaken with a 30-pound pin cushion sitting on your chest and nibbling at your midsection.)

At any rate, the outer circle of syrup will distract beasties large and small and protect you far more effectively than a barb-wire fence.

Meanwhile, keep your wood and your feet dry.

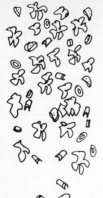

CHAPTER

supporting cast:

ALSO APPEARING TONIGHT

You have noted by now a certain high-minded courage (sometimes called pig-headedness) in the offerings of this book. It has been deliberately selective, and the author is prepared to have the finger of scorn pointed at him for certain unforgivable omissions, *unforgivable* in this case meaning that the finger pointer cooks a dish I don't particularly relish.

Recommendations in this chapter on sauces, desserts, and the like have followed the same capricious pattern, but always with the policy that what's here is good in a certain special way for men, both in the preparing and eating. The usual practice is to try out a number of them and then settle on an inner circle of favorites. You'll find many ideas here which are not ordinarily encountered, and many of them, especially in the dessert line, will probably be among your most stolen possessions.

I do not think that the masculine type of meal should go in for the groaning board bit, consisting of an endless parade of side dishes and extras. Let the board groan from the heft of the main dish and a nice assortment of wines, and then let the added attractions win their Oscars for the best supporting role—simple and memorable.

Every good man needs a few reliable sidekicks.

Here are yours:

SALADS

Men traditionally refer to salads as rabbit food, and tend to be somewhat suspicious of the entire *genre*. This is owing in some degree to the fact that salads have been used by very many estimable ladies as a catch-all—something just a faltering step this side of the garbage pail, a grab bag of leftovers artfully concealed under a carapace of mayonnaise and errant fruit juices, throbbing hopefully in front of the horrified recipient.

Restaurants have also contributed a nudge or two toward sending this perfectly wonderful kind of food into a shadowy never-never land. Their collections of greens often suggest a gathering from the weeds and grasses behind the owner's house, festooned with various bits of colored paper, and wetted down with a dribble of discouraged cheese juice or a fiery liquid which turns out to be vinegar, although evidently distilled from pulverized snake's tongues.

Thus, our man, intending to have a sensible dinner, becomes discouraged at the idea of any innovation. He gives the whole idea up, and settles for a huge steak, a pile of French fries and fried onions, washed down with a couple of steins of beer.

I won't state that salads will keep your waistline down, since we decided when we went into this book that men who eat and exercise moderately are not apt to get too gross, and a book on the joys of eating has no sense in dwelling on the nonexistent pleasures of noneating.

But salads will help. They are admittedly filling. But that's not the point. They can also be delicious. There's something about a properly prepared salad that's clean and fresh in its taste as in its looks. And eating it will give you the same sense of virtue as drinking a glass of pure water—and a lot more flavor and vitamins.

And thus you'll be less inclined to fill up those yawning inner cavities with the really weight-lifting stuff.

So now, here's to it. You'll find some old favorites in our collection, and a few new ideas too:

You can take nearly anything, doctor it up, and provided it's served with a very good salad, you have a meal. Of course, if your entrée flies gourmet colors, a good salad only solidifies your master status.

What makes a good salad? T.L.C. (tender, loving care). Care, that is, in shopping for the ingredients, washing and storing them, in the tossing, and in the dressing. The big plus is imagination. Here are a few tips on that score:

When shopping for salad greens, think further than the head of iceberg lettuce. Certain markets specialize in unusual greens, and these are the ones you're after. Among the lettuces generally available are romaine, chicory, Belgian endive, escarole, and Boston. In the spring, field lettuce is in good supply; so are Bibb lettuce, limestone and tender dandelion greens. Later on you might strike up a friendship with a hard-working grow-your-own type and fall happily into the possession of some rare curly and red types. Chinese cabbage (long, crisp stalks) is becoming much better known, and some is even occasionally seen in supermarkets. The tender leaves of raw spinach are delicious all by themselves or in other greens' company. Watercress is always fine to have on hand. A few sprigs of this on a dinner plate do a great job when no salad is on hand. Parsley . . . always. Here is an herb always available, and I don't know of a green salad it doesn't enhance. Speaking of herbs, many vegetable markets have them fresh over the spring and summer, especially the better-known ones like tarragon, dill, basil, mint, and chives. Herb plants in the window aren't a bad idea either. With a little care, you have them around for weeks of happy clipping. Greenhouses are the main sources for these.

"Wash thoroughly, drain, and store in a cold place." Every cookbook tells you that. Here is a little elaboration. Lettuces keep better if the head is not torn apart when washing. Tear off the tough outside leaves and do your best to wash out all the sand. Hold it under a good strong spigot running cold water, then swish it up and down a few times in a pan of water. Turn the lettuce upside down in a colander and allow it to drain. This seems to take forever, so help it along a bit by shaking the colander up and down. If you are going to use the greens the same day, you can tear the leaves apart and let them drain on paper towels. If you have a back yard, you can do as the French do and pile the greens into one of those wire baskets with handles (available in gourmet shops); then take the basket out of doors and swing it round and round in a great arc till all the water flies out. *Quelle* sport.

The greens keep nicely for days if you wrap them loosely in a clean linen towel. This helps to absorb the extra moisture and keep them crisp. As for fresh herbs, don't wash them till just before using, and then swish out the moisture on a paper towel. Store them in a jar in the refrigerator, with the stems in about an inch of water (except for parsley—give that the lettuce treatment).

Experiment with different oils and vinegars. The Italians take great pride in their olive oil, and it is inspected and graded by the Italian government. Try to find one that has been *packed* in Italy as well as prepared there as it is reputed to travel better in those sealed cans and insures you against adulteration from grower to your salad bowl. One fine Italian restaurateur favors the olive oil of the Lucca district. Virgin olive oil means the first press, and this is the best quality. The French olive oil is proclaimed by some to be finer and lighter. The best test is your own. Buy small containers if possible and arrive at your own choice. I happen to have a great enthusiasm for olive oil, but if you prefer another kind of oil, that's okay, too.

Besides the good old cider vinegar, there are herb vinegars (especially tarragon), garlic vinegar, and wine vinegar. If you don't have any vinegar in the house, fresh lemon juice is a good substitute, and with some a preference.

A good way to do a green salad is in front of your guests and as a separate course either before or after the main course. For this you will need a large tray or serving table on which you have assembled the largest possible salad bowl (even for two people this is the answer, as it makes a cinch of the tossing) and the washed and crisped greens (left whole, if possible, up to this point). They can be brought in on a clean linen towel. It takes only an extra minute or two to break them into the salad bowl, and the effect is impressive—like vegetables straight out of the garden . . . only washed. Besides the greens that will go into your salad bowl, have on hand a pepper mill and salt shaker, a little granulated sugar (a pinch of this makes for a smoother dressing), dry mustard (also a pinch), some jars of dried herbs and a mortar to give them a grind (again just a pinch—perhaps tarragon or dill and a little parsley), or a few sprigs of fresh herbs and scissors to clip them, bottles of vinegar and oil (or a prepared dressing that has everything in it).

After the greens are in the bowl, sprinkle the dry ingredients into a little clear spot. Mix them together with a touch of the vinegar, then continue with the proportion of oil to vinegar that you like. The standard proportion is 3 of oil to 1 vinegar. I find 4-to-1 or even 5-to-1 is more to my liking. In any case, add only enough dressing to coat all of the leaves (you can always add a bit more, but you can't siphon it out very well). There should be no residue of dressing in the bottom of the bowl when you have finished the tossing. And don't go about the tossing as if you were attacking a cement mixer. Any good maître d' will tell you that gently-but-thoroughly is the best approach. At this point if you *really* want to seem knowledgeable, retreat to the refrigerator just long enough to pick up the salad plates, which you have chilled, chilled, chilled.

So, let's try out some of the green:

Probably the most popular salad today with men is

CHEF'S SALAD

Break 1 medium head lettuce and 1 romaine lettuce into 2-inch lengths. Add the leaves from ½ bunch watercress, 4 chopped scallions, ½ cup sliced celery, 1 cup Swiss cheese which you have cut into thin strips, 1 cup cold cooked meat cut into thin strips (the meat can be ham, beef, chicken, or veal). Season and toss with French dressing. Overlay more strips of the meat and cheese on top of the salad, plus olive slices and sliced hard-cooked eggs.

CAESAR SALAD

Salt

1 cut clove garlic

3 heads of romaine or other greens, washed and crisped

5 anchovy filets, reduced to a paste

Olive oil

Fresh ground or cracked pepper

Worcestershire sauce

4 tablespoons grated Parmesan cheese

1 2-minute coddled egg

1 fresh lemon

A bowl of fresh croutons

Very special, this. It is definitely a made-at-the-table salad, not to be mixed in advance. Ordinary lettuce is too bland. A more flavorsome green like romaine is suggested or a combination of romaine and endive or escarole.

Rub a generous amount of salt over a large wooden salad bowl. Rub the bowl with the cut garlic clove. Carefully break the salad greens into the bowl. Add the anchovies and about 4 tablespoons olive oil. Toss this all together gently. Add pepper to taste (and more salt if you need it), a few drops of the Worcestershire sauce, the Parmesan cheese, and right in the center break the coddled egg. Directly over the egg, squeeze the juice of the 1 lemon. Toss the salad a second time, gently but thoroughly. Drop the warm croutons over the salad. Toss lightly once more before serving.

4 LARGE OR 6 MEDIUM SERVINGS

One of my favorite salads is still the one I mentioned in Chapter 2, in describing my TV appearance. The salad is:

CHICKEN SALAD JOMAR

Boil 1 large roasting chicken, cut up, until tender. When cold, remove meat and cut in fairly large pieces. Add sections from 2 oranges and 2 sliced bananas; season with salt. Make a sauce of ½ cup whipped heavy cream, ½ cup mayonnaise, 1 tablespoon catsup, 1 teaspoon each of Worcestershire sauce and A-1 sauce, juice of ¼ lemon, sparking this with a generous splash of cognac and an equally enthusiastic dash of Cointreau. Mix well, pour over chicken and fruit, mixing with care so orange sections will not be crushed.

6 SERVINGS

AVOCADO AND LITCHI NUT SALAD

Remove the tough outside leaves from a couple of heads of romaine. Break them up and add several sprigs of watercress. Toss together with French dressing and place on individual salad plates. Cut an avocado or two into thick rings. Sprinkle with lemon juice and arrange on top of the greens. In the center of the avocado slices place several preserved litchi nuts that have been well chilled and drained. Dribble a little more French dressing over the top and sprinkle with some finely chopped parsley and chopped radishes.

AVOCADOS QUEEN ELIZABETH

This is one of the favorite recipes on board the *Queen Elizabeth*.
Take a ripe avocado, split it lengthwise. With a spoon, cut out little balls of the pulp till it has all been removed from the skin. Be careful not to break the skin of the avocado as you do this. Sprinkle the pulp immediately with lemon juice to keep it from turning dark. Toss a generous portion of cooked crabmeat in with the avocado, and mix the two gently together with Russian dressing. Spoon back into the avocado shells and serve with wedges of fresh lemon. This, surrounded by some tomato wedges and asparagus spears, is a very good main luncheon or supper dish.

CHILLED CUCUMBER SALAD

Peel 4 large cucumbers and slice them paper thin. Put in a bowl and sprinkle them generously with salt. Let them stand for a half hour or more, and drain off all the liquid. Pour over them ¼ cup wine or tarragon vinegar, ½ cup olive oil, ½ teaspoon sugar, 1 teaspoon chopped chives or scallions. Mix and allow to chill and marinate at least an hour. Before serving, drain again, mix in 2 tablespoons sour cream (optional). Sprinkle the top with finely chopped parsley and coarse cracked pepper. The cucumbers can be served in place of another salad, or they can be heaped into the center of a serving platter and surrounded by tomato wedges over which herbs and French dressing have been sprinkled.

HOT POTATO SALAD

New potatoes are the best to use for hot potato salad. Allow 1 good medium potato per person, plus a couple more. Cook the potatoes whole in their jackets till barely tender. This will take about 40 minutes. Pierce with a fork and quickly peel off the skins and cut the potatoes into slices. Dribble over them a very little French dressing, cover, and keep warm till you add the hot dressing. Start the dressing while the potatoes are cooking. It will take about 10 minutes to make. For 6 people mix together ½ cup olive oil and ½ cup wine vinegar. Pour it into a saucepan and add 1½ teaspoons salt, 3 tablespoons sugar, a good grating of fresh pepper, and the yolks of 2 eggs. Place the saucepan over very low heat, and stir constantly until smooth and thickened. Pour the hot sauce over the warmed potatoes. Toss. Slice a small onion into thin rings. Dip the rings in paprika, and place them on top of the potatoes. Keep warm till serving time.

SHRIMP SALAD

Cut cooked, cleaned shrimp into large pieces. Squeeze a little fresh lemon juice over them. To the shrimp add ⅓ as much chopped celery. Mix with enough mayonnaise to hold the mixture together. Sprinkle in a few capers and a few wedges of hard-cooked egg and toss lightly. Serve on a crisp lettuce leaf with wedges of lemon. Surround with tomato wedges.

LOBSTER OR CRABMEAT SALAD

Same recipe as for the shrimp salad, but eliminate the capers and eggs.

LENTIL SALAD

Drain a can or two of lentils. Add a few chopped onions and some chopped parsley. Add salt and pepper to taste, and mix with French dressing. Place a few thin onion rings on top of the salad. Serve very well chilled on a crisp lettuce leaf.

WALDORF SALAD

Peel 6 large apples and cut into cubes. Sprinkle them with lemon juice so they won't turn brown. Add 1 cup chopped celery, 1 teaspoon salt, ½ cup broken walnut meats, and ½ cup red grapes that have been washed and split and had their seeds removed. Mix with mayonnaise dressing and chill.

PINWHEEL FRUIT SALAD

Over some crisp chicory arrange slices of fresh oranges, grapefruit, and avocado in a circle pinwheel fashion. Sprinkle the avocado slices with lemon juice, and pour French dressing over all.

MELON-BALL SALAD

Combine cantaloupe and honey dew melon balls, either frozen or fresh. Toss them together with French dressing. Put a lettuce leaf on a salad plate with a mound of cream cheese in the center. Over the cheese dribble some mayonnaise that has been thinned with cream. Spoon the melon balls around the cheese. Sprinkle fresh mint over the whole thing.

SPRING SALAD

1 cup shredded cabbage	½ cup diced cucumber
1 cup diced tomatoes (remove seeds)	½ cup sliced radishes
1 cup grated carrot	2 tablespoons chopped chives or scallions
1 cup chopped celery	2 tablespoons chopped parsley

Toss all together with a mayonnaise dressing that you have thinned with heavy cream, seasoned with salt, pepper, mustard, and paprika; or toss with a zippy French dressing.   6 SERVINGS

TAKE-YOUR-CHOICE SALAD

In a large platter or bowl arrange separate sections of thick tomato slices, Bermuda onion rings, green pepper slices, white radishes, and iceberg lettuce wedges. Serve with a pepper mill and a bottle of good French dressing.

CRISP CABBAGE SALAD

Shave 1 medium head green or red cabbage (or a mixture) as thin as possible. Add to the cabbage 1 tablespoon chopped sweet pickle, 1 teaspoon celery seed, 1 teaspoon each sugar, salt, pepper, ½ teaspoon dry mustard, and mayonnaise and sour cream (half and half). Add enough dressing to mix the cabbage thoroughly, but don't make it soupy.

STUFFED TOMATO SALAD

Just as there are several ways to stuff a chicken, there are several ways to stuff a tomato. We give you a couple.

Peel the tomato and leave whole. The peeling can be done quickly by tossing the tomato into rapidly boiling water. Leave it there only a few seconds, then spear with a fork, take a sharp knife and strip down the thin outside skin. If you don't know how to boil water, spear the tomato with a fork and hold it for a couple of seconds over a hot flame. The skin will pop, and you can skin it right off.

Cut a thin slice off the top of the tomato. Scoop out the center so just the outside flesh remains. Sprinkle with salt inside and out. Invert on a plate and chill. Meanwhile, combine these ingredients (for 4 tomatoes): 1½ cups boiled, cubed potatoes, 1 teaspoon grated onion, ¼ cup chopped celery tops, 2 tablespoons chopped parsley, salt and pepper to taste, enough mayonnaise to hold the mixture together, and a couple of teaspoons cooked peas. Fill the tomatoes and place each on a crisp lettuce leaf. Serve with extra mayonnaise that has been thinned with heavy cream.

HERBED-CHEESE TOMATOES

Prepare the tomato for stuffing as in the recipe above. Sprinkle well with salt and fill with this mixture: cottage cheese, plus salt, pepper, chopped chives, chopped dill, chopped parsley, a ½ teaspoon of each to 1 cup cheese. Mix all together. Fill tomatoes, and dribble a little thinned mayonnaise over all. Serve surrounded by thin cucumber slices and sprigs of watercress.

CHICKEN SALAD

1 twelve-oz. can (or 2 cups cooked) white-meat chicken	½ cup sour cream
	Salt and pepper
1 cup diced celery	

Combine chicken, celery, and sour cream (use mayonnaise or prepared dressing if you wish). Mix well. Season with salt and pepper. Serve on lettuce. If desired, garnish with asparagus tips and tomato wedges.

OCEAN SALAD

1 thirteen-oz. can (2 cups) tuna	¾ cup mayonnaise or salad
1 six-oz. can (1 cup) lobster	dressing
2 five-and-three-quarter-oz. cans	Watercress
(2 cups) shrimp	Lemon wedges
2 cups diced celery	

Drain tuna, lobster, and shrimp. Flake tuna and lobster. Hold out 12 whole shrimp for garnish. Combine remaining shrimp, tuna, lobster, celery, and mayonnaise or salad dressing. Add 12 shrimps on top, arranging in spokes. Serve on watercress; garnish with lemon.   8 SERVINGS

WILTED LETTUCE SALAD

1 medium-size head lettuce	1 tablespoon sugar (rounded)
1 onion, chopped fine	4 slices bacon
½ teaspoon salt, dash of pepper	¼ cup vinegar
Small clove finely cut garlic	
(optional)	

The loose-leaf head lettuce is preferred, but any kind will do. Break it rather fine. Add salt, pepper, sugar, garlic. Fry bacon (cut into small thin pieces) until crisp. Add vinegar. Let come to a boil, pour over lettuce. Mix thoroughly and serve while warm.

6 SERVINGS

SALAD DRESSINGS

Here are some of the better known, and a basic springboard to mixing your own.

FRENCH DRESSING

1 cup olive oil or salad oil	½ teaspoon dry mustard
¼ cup vinegar	½ teaspoon paprika
1 teaspoon salt	1 tablespoon grated lemon rind
½ teaspoon sugar	(optional)

Put all ingredients in a glass jar with a tight cover. Shake well to blend. Store in refrigerator, and shake well before each use.

ZIPPY FRENCH DRESSING

To each ½ cup of the French dressing add ½ teaspoon grated onion, 1 tablespoon sugar, and 1 whole garlic clove. Let the garlic marinate in the dressing for an hour or more before serving.

SOUR CREAM DRESSING

To 1 pint cultured sour cream add ½ teaspoon dry mustard, 2½ tablespoons fresh lemon juice, 2 tablespoons chopped chives, and salt and pepper to taste.

VINAIGRETTE DRESSING

Mix together 4 tablespoons oil to 1 of vinegar. Add salt and pepper to taste, and ¼ teaspoon each dry mustard, chopped parsley, tarragon, chives, and chervil. Some hard-cooked egg whites, finely chopped, can be added just before serving.

HOME-MADE MAYONNAISE

With a rotary beater, blend together in a warm bowl (that you have rinsed with hot water and dried well) 2 egg yolks, ½ teaspoon salt, ½ teaspoon dry mustard, ⅛ teaspoon white pepper, ½ teaspoon confectioner's sugar, and 1 teaspoon vinegar or lemon juice.

When these ingredients are well mixed, begin to add the olive oil. You will need 1 cup in all. It should be added very slowly, drop by drop, and the beating must never stop. After about the first ¼ cup of the oil has been added, pour in another ½ teaspoon vinegar or lemon juice. The rest of the oil can be poured a little faster now, but it should never exceed a thin trickle, and the beating should never stop. When the mayonnaise is thick and well blended, add another ½ teaspoon vinegar or lemon juice.

If you use an electric beater, set it on medium speed. If you want to achieve the texture of home-made mayonnaise with the store-bought stuff, you can come close by adding half thickened or lightly whipped cream.

GREEN MAYONNAISE

A half and half combination of mayonnaise and mixed herbs. The fresh herbs in season are what you want for this. Suggested are fresh raw spinach, tarragon, chives, parsley, and watercress, all chopped to nearly a paste and blended with the mayonnaise.

This is an especially good dressing for seafood and cold poached chicken. Chill a couple of hours before serving.

RUSSIAN DRESSING

To 1 cup mayonnaise add ½ cup chili sauce, 1 tablespoon lemon juice, and a few drops of onion juice.

CURRY DRESSING

Very good with meats or fish. Stir in ½ teaspoon (or more) curry powder to ½ cup French dressing.

GARLIC FRENCH DRESSING

Make a fine paste of 1 clove crushed garlic (or put the clove through a garlic press). Mix with ¾ cup French dressing.

ROQUEFORT DRESSING

Roquefort cheese can be crumbled or mashed for this dressing. If you prefer to mash it, blend it slowly with French dressing. Use half as much cheese as dressing. Add a few drops of Worcestershire sauce.

SAUCES

No cover-ups here. A good sauce should be a simpatico embellishment for a food that is already good in itself.

HOLLANDAISE SAUCE

2 egg yolks	½ cup butter or margarine
¼ teaspoon salt	⅛ teaspoon paprika
1 tablespoon lemon juice	

Put egg yolks and salt in electric blender. Cover and mix until well blended. Scrape the ingredients down from the sides of the container with a rubber spatula. Add the remaining ingredients, cover, and process until thick and smooth. Pour into the top of a double boiler and heat over boiling water. Serve on vegetables. Note: Should the sauce separate when heated, beat in two tablespoons boiling water, a drop at a time.   1 CUP

GARLIC BUTTER SAUCE

This is very good over pasta, steamed artichoke bottoms. Melt ¼ lb. butter. Add 1 clove minced garlic, ¼ teaspoon dried tarragon, ¼ teaspoon dried thyme, ½ teaspoon dry mustard, 1 tablespoon fresh lemon juice, celery salt to taste.

ROSSEBERRY SAUCE

Good over cold sliced meats. Mix 2 tablespoons dry mustard together with 2 tablespoons wine vinegar. Add 1 cup wine vinegar gradually. Take out some of the vinegar and make a paste with 1½ teaspoons powdered sugar. Add 4 tablespoons fresh grated horseradish to the paste. Beat it all together with the vinegar. Add salt to taste and a sprinkling of chopped parsley.

REMOULADE SAUCE

Perfect over shrimp or crabmeat. Mix together: 1 cup mayonnaise, 1 tablespoon chopped parsley, 1 minced garlic clove, 2 hard-cooked eggs, finely chopped, 4 tablespoons fresh lemon juice, 1 tablespoon capers, 1 teaspoon dry mustard, ¾ teaspoon chopped chives, pinch cayenne pepper, 1 teaspoon chopped fresh dill or ½ teaspoon dried dill, salt to taste. Blend and allow to chill together at least 2 hours before serving.

DILL SAUCE

Good over cold vegetables and seafood. Combine 1 cup olive oil, 4 tablespoons lemon juice, ¾ teaspoon dry mustard, 1½ tablespoons fresh chopped dill or 2 tablespoons dried dill weed, ½ clove minced garlic, and salt to taste. Combine ingredients and chill overnight in refrigerator.

MUSTARD SAUCE

Blend together in the top of a double boiler: 2 teaspoons prepared mustard, 1 scant teaspoon sugar, 2 tablespoons flour, and a pinch of salt. Add ¾ cup fresh or bottled clam broth, and 2 tablespoons wine vinegar. Cook and stir over hot water till the sauce is smooth and thick. Serve hot or cold with fish.

MARCHANDS DE VIN SAUCE

Combine 4 oz. each of chopped mushrooms, ham, and consommé. Add ½ bunch shallots chopped fine and 1 onion chopped fine. Thicken with a little flour and add 4 oz. red wine. Cook for ½ hour or so, after seasoning to taste.

BASIC CREOLE SAUCE

Cook ¼ cup each minced onions and green pepper in 2 tablespoons shortening until soft. Add 1 (8 oz.) can tomato sauce, 1 teaspoon salt, 2 tablespoons red wine vinegar, ¼ teaspoon Worcestershire sauce and ⅛ teaspoon orégano. Simmer 10 minutes. Use as is for a dipping sauce for jumbo shrimp at cocktail time, or add 1 (4½ oz.) can deveined shrimp to the sauce and serve over omelets, poached eggs on toasted English muffins, rice mounds, spaghetti.

MORNAY SAUCE

A rich cheese sauce for eggs, vegetables, or fish. Melt 2 tablespoons butter in a saucepan, blend in 2 tablespoons flour and make a paste. Add 1 cup hot chicken stock (or strong consommé) all at once, stirring constantly. Add 1 cup warm cream all at once and continue to stir. Stir in 1 cup grated Swiss or Parmesan cheese. Add a dash of cayenne pepper and salt to taste. The sauce should be smooth and thick.

SAUCE DIABLE
(as served at Ernie's Restaurant in San Francisco)

½ cup vinegar
Crushed black pepper (2 turns of mill)
1 cup chopped shallots
Thyme and bay leaf
½ cup white wine

1 tablespoon mustard
2 cups brown gravy
1 tablespoon Worcestershire sauce
2 tablespoons butter

Combine vinegar with crushed black pepper, shallots, thyme, and bay leaf. Add white wine with mustard and reduce to ½. Pour in gravy, cook for approximately 15 minutes and then strain. Add butter and Worcestershire sauce.   4 SERVINGS

VARIATIONS ON A VEGETABLE THEME

TOMATOES

HERB BROILED

Wash and halve tomatoes. Sprinkle with salt and freshly ground pepper, a little sugar, chopped fresh or dried basil, chopped onion, chopped parsley. Top with bread crumbs and dots of butter. Place tomato halves in an oven-proof dish. Bake in a hot oven for 15 minutes (till cooked but still firm). Place dish under the broiler the last couple of minutes to brown.

PAN-FRIED TOMATOES PROVENÇALE

Choose a couple of pounds of ripe, firm tomatoes of small to medium size. Wash and slice in half horizontally. Heat 4 tablespoons oil in a frying pan. Place tomatoes cut side down in pan and sauté for five minutes. Before the cooking is complete, prick the skin on upper sides with a fork. Turn the tomatoes over. Sprinkle over 1 clove finely minced garlic and 2 tablespoons chopped parsley that have been mixed together. Sprinkle with salt and freshly ground pepper and continue cooking the tomatoes over a low flame till they are golden brown and soft.

Peas

PETITS POIS FRANÇAIS

Use 1 package frozen peas or 1½ lbs. fresh peas. If you use them fresh, they will require about 30 minutes of cooking after shelling. If you use the frozen peas, add no water, and do not defrost. Place peas in a saucepan and over the peas throw 3 chopped scallions (the white part plus part of the green) or three small white onions, 4 lettuce leaves, which you have washed and shredded, salt, pepper, ½ teaspoon sugar, and a good lump of butter. Cover and cook slowly about 8 minutes till peas are tender but still retain their crisp texture.   SERVES 3 TO 4

CHINESE SNOW PEAS

Chinese vegetable markets are the source for these. Cook the whole pod of the snow peas, having first washed them and pulled off the little strings around the edges. After washing, you need add no more water to the cooking pot. Add a good lump of butter (the Chinese use a little peanut oil), salt and pepper to taste. Cook about 5 minutes or less, depending on the amount. The pods should be very green and crisp in texture. Wonderful prepared just that simply.

Lima Beans

PUREED LIMAS

Cook a box of frozen baby lima beans according to directions on the box. Push the beans through a coarse sieve. Add a lump of butter, salt and pepper to taste, a grating of nutmeg, and 4 tablespoons warm cream. Blend well and serve very hot.

LIMAS BONNE FEMME

In a saucepan put 2 tablespoons butter. Sauté 3 tablespoons chopped onion in the butter until it is transparent. Add ¼ cup slivered cooked ham, and 2 shredded lettuce leaves. Add 1 box frozen lima beans and cook according to directions on the box. When tender add salt and pepper to taste, and 1 tablespoon chopped parsley.

Corn

BROWNED CORN

Buy fresh or frozen corn on the cob. Half cook it in boiling water. Cut it off the cob and brown the kernels slowly in a generous amount of butter in a heavy frying pan. Salt and pepper to taste.

CORN PUDDING

Buy 6 fresh or frozen ears of corn on the cob. Grate the corn off the cobs into a bowl. (If you use frozen corn, defrost it first.) Add to corn yolks of 3 eggs slightly beaten, 1 pint milk, 3 tablespoons melted butter, 1 teaspoon sugar, 1 teaspoon salt, and 2 grated saltine crackers. Mix these ingredients together. Beat 3 egg whites till stiff, and fold in with the corn mixture. Bake in hot oven till set (about 25 minutes).

Potatoes

Potatoes are, in this streamlined day of every man looking like a young man, almost banished from the menu. And, in general, I approve of that in home cookery, since you can have them nicely prepared when you dine out, and working them over in your own kitchen is often scarcely worth the trouble. Furthermore, you can buy French fries and potato puffs in the frozen state which are well-nigh perfect. However, if you have a yen for the old kitchen variety, here are several ways to prepare them:

GERMAN FRIED

Wash your spuds, peel, slice very thin. Let them soak ½ hour in cold water, drain and dry. Next, heat fat in frying pan, put the potato slices in, sprinkle with salt, and cook slowly until crisply brown. One medium-sized potato will do for one person.

FRENCH FRIES

Wash and pare small potatoes, cut in eighths lengthwise in the shape you know so well. Soak an hour in cold water. Then boil them for a couple of minutes in salt water to shorten your frying time. Fry in deep fat, then remove and drain on brown paper when they are only slightly browned. Then heat up fat to high degree, return potatoes to fat, and, using frying basket, whisk them about actively until they are really crisp and brown. Drain again on brown paper, salt, and serve.

POTATOES WITH ONION AND BACON

Heat in the bottom of a heavy frying pan 5 tablespoons chicken fat or bacon fat. Slice 4 medium potatoes and 4 medium onions very thin and toss them into the pan. Salt and pepper. Cut 3 slices bacon in very thin shreds and place over the potatoes. Cover the pan and cook over a medium flame about 15 minutes, till just soft. Shake the pan from time to time. Arrange the potatoes on a serving dish and sprinkle with paprika. Overlay with slices of crisply fried bacon.   6 SERVINGS

BAKED POTATOES

Idaho potatoes are best for baking. Scrub the skins and rub with a little oil. Bake about an hour in a medium oven. Prick the skins a few times with a fork. When done, the potatoes should be tender all the way through when fork-tested. Cut a small cross on top of the potato and push all around the skin till the potato is broken up inside. Put a lump of butter on top of the cut section, and sprinkle with paprika. Serve with plenty of extra butter, salt, and pepper.

GRATED POTATO BALLS

Grate raw potatoes. Mix with a little grated onion. Squeeze out the moisture, and form into small balls. Cook in half oil, half butter to cover until they are brown. Season with salt and pepper and sprinkle with chopped parsley.

CARROTS

GLAZED CARROTS

Cut raw carrots into strips the thickness of a little finger. Cook in boiling water about 15 minutes, till barely tender. (If you use canned carrots, Le Seuer, available in supermarkets, is a very good brand.)

Make a glaze by melting together in a heavy large pan 6 tablespoons brown sugar (or part honey) and 2 tablespoons butter. Add the cooked carrots and simmer over very low heat till glazed. These are ideally served on a bed of fresh mint, with grated fresh lime peel sprinkled over the carrots.

CREAM-SAUCED CARROTS

Over hot cooked carrots pour this sauce: 2 egg yolks mixed with
½ cup heavy warm cream. Add salt and pepper to taste, 1 teaspoon
sugar, a few drops lemon juice and 1 teaspoon chopped parsley.
Stir sauce over low heat till thickened and pour over carrots.

Cabbage

CARAWAY CABBAGE

Shred fresh cabbage and cover with water in a saucepan. Cook till
tender and drain. Season with salt and pepper, a light sprinkling
of caraway seeds and a big dollop of sour cream.

Mushrooms

BROILED MUSHROOMS

Buy large firm white mushrooms. Remove the stems. Wipe the
caps and soak them in cold water and lemon juice for 5 minutes.
Drain and dry the caps. Season with salt and pepper and dribble
on a little olive oil. Broil them for about 6 minutes under a low
flame. When serving pour over them some melted butter and
lemon juice. Sprinkle with chopped parsley.

MUSHROOMS IN CREAM

Slice mushrooms and sauté in butter over a low flame (or use
canned mushrooms which have been well drained). When the
mushroom slices are very hot in the butter (they should not
brown), add a few tablespoons heavy cream, salt, pepper, and some
slivered almonds. Simmer together a few minutes and add a light
sprinkling of parsley.

Onions

BRAISED SCALLIONS

Wash scallions. Cut off long roots and some of the green, leaving
about 6 inches of the scallion intact. Put in a saucepan and barely
cover with water. Cover and cook a very short time till just tender.
Drain and season with butter, salt, pepper, and a sprinkling of
chopped chives.

FRENCH-FRIED ONION RINGS

Peel and slice onions in thin rings. Put some flour and salt in a paper bag. Add a few onion rings at a time and shake them up and down till they are coated. Drop the rings in deep, hot fat and cook until brown. Drain on absorbent paper.

BROCCOLI

BROCCOLI WITH CAPERS

Cook frozen broccoli according to directions on box. Drain and remove broccoli from pan and in the pan put ¼ cup olive oil and 1 clove garlic, minced. Sauté these together until warm, add salt, pepper, and 1 teaspoon capers. Put the broccoli back in the pan and stir around till the stalks are coated.

BEETS

BEETS TARRAGON

Start with cooked baby beets, canned or fresh. To 24 add 1 table-spoon butter, 1 teaspoon sugar, salt and pepper, and 2 tablespoons tarragon vinegar. Shake over the fire till piping hot. Prepare smooth paste with 3 tablespoons flour and a little water and mix with beets. Add another tablespoon butter, 3 big spoons of commercial sour cream, and 1 teaspoon dried tarragon. Stir together lightly and serve.

SPINACH

SPINACH GARNI

Cook frozen chopped spinach according to directions on box. Stir in 4 tablespoons heavy cream, salt, pepper to taste, a grating of nutmeg. Serve very hot with crisp crumbled bacon or chopped hard-cooked eggs sprinkled over the top.

SQUASH

BAKED ACORN SQUASH

Put a whole small acorn squash in a medium oven. When it is tender to the fork- test (about 1 hour) remove from oven, split, scoop out seeds, sprinkle with salt, pepper, butter, and nutmeg.

LAST RESORTS: GIVING THEM THEIR JUST DESSERTS

There is no better way to top off a good meal than with a bowl of fresh fruit, a fine cheese or two—one bland, another more authoritative—and one of the coffee delights such as brûlot or royale, which you've already learned to make. Zabaglione, also described in the coffee section, is a delight, although it takes a bit of practice to attain perfection.

Otherwise, desserts should be a production, if at all. Pastries and cakes you can buy at your local bakery. I would avoid the grocer in this department, since his wares seem all to have been cut from the same sponge. There are good frozen pies on the market, particularly by Farmhouse Pies (Connecticut Pie Baking Corp.), and they come from the oven fresh and fragrant. Puddings, in my opinion, are for invalids and mamma's boys and the less said about them the better.

WATERMELON MAGNIFIQUE

Your dessert, if you have one at all, should have a flair to it. Witness the masterpiece of my friend Ladislas Farago. Like most Hungarians, he is a wizard around food. And this is wizardry:

Halve a good-sized watermelon lengthwise and scoop out the insides. Cut the fruit in chunks, add other fresh fruits and steep overnight in Cointreau and kirsch, pouring on the liqueurs with a heavy hand. At time of serving, coat the bottom of the hollowed watermelon with pistachio ice cream; follow this with a layer of the fruit, over this a layer of lemon or lime ice; then more fruit, over this a layer of orange ice; then another layer of fruit. In a final magnificent gesture, pour over all a split of champagne.

Almost as terrific is

MELON SURPRISE

Pare a ripe honeydew melon not too sparingly—so that no hard peel is left on. Now cut a quarter section out of the melon lengthwise and scoop out the seeds. From the bottom of this melon container cut a thin slice to prevent the melon from rolling. Set the melon on an ovenproof plate, fill the cavity with sliced fresh peaches and sprinkle them lightly with 1 pony chartreuse and 1 pony kirsch. Other fruits may be substituted as a stuffing or a mixture of fruits may be used, varying the liqueur flavors with the fruit chosen, but always retaining the pony of kirsch. Replace the cut-off quarter on the melon and refrigerate for at least 4 hours to chill thoroughly. When ready to serve, beat 4 egg whites till stiff, flavor with one tablespoon sugar, and add a scant ½ pony of the liqueur used for flavoring the fruit filling. Cover the melon top and sides with this meringue and bake quickly in hot oven (450° F.) until delicately brown. Serve immediately.

CREPES SUZETTE

Your other beau geste is Crêpes Suzette. You can buy the crêpes in jars if you wish from a specialty store. Or if you're particular on this point, try this recipe:

3 tablespoons sifted flour	½ teaspoon sugar
1 whole egg	¼ teaspoon salt
1 egg yolk	2 tablespoons clarified butter
1 cup milk	

Mix flour, egg, and egg yolk with a wire whisk. Add milk, sugar, salt. Mix.

To clarify butter, melt it in a small container, skim off foam, pour off and reserve fat and discard sediment in bottom of container.

Heat a four-inch skillet and brush with clarified butter. Pour in one tablespoon batter and tilt pan immediately so batter will spread over entire bottom of pan. Cook crêpe quickly on both sides. Repeat till all crêpes are cooked. This will make 12 to 16. If you plan to serve the crêpes later, wrap in waxed paper to keep them moist.

And here is your procedure in the spectacular preparation of the dish in your chafing dish:

Your advance preparations are as follows: Cream ¾ cup soft butter with ¾ cup extra-fine sugar. Add the grated rind of 1 lemon and ⅔ cup orange juice. Mix well.

For 4 servings:

1½ cups of the butter mixture	2 teaspoons fine sugar
4 ozs. Curaçao	½ teaspoon lemon juice
8 crêpes	4 ozs. warm cognac

Dissolve butter mixture in skillet of chafing dish. Add Curaçao and four crêpes. Fold crêpes in half, then quarters. Push to side of pan and repeat with remaining four crêpes. Simmer fifteen minutes. Sprinkle with sugar and lemon juice. Add cognac, light, and serve while blazing.

Not quite so spectacular, perhaps, but fully as successful, can be some of these other, less ambitious ideas.

POIRES AU FOUR AU SAUTERNE

Peel and core 6 large, fresh pears. Combine ⅓ generous cup seedless chopped raisins, ⅓ cup brown sugar, and 1 teaspoon grated lemon rind, and moisten with a little sauterne. Spoon a portion of this mixture into each pear, arrange pears in a buttered casserole, and pour around them 1 scant cup sauterne. Cover and bake for about 40 minutes in a moderate oven (375° F.). Just before serving, pour some brandy into a soup ladle, add 2 lumps sugar, and set aflame, letting the flaming liquor drop over the hot pears. Serve immediately with petits fours.

FRESH PEARS PACIFICA

6 fresh Bosc or Anjou pears	Sour cream
¼ cup fresh lime juice	Slivered almonds toasted
¼ cup honey	(3-4 oz.)
¾ cup rum	

Cut unpeeled pears in half lengthwise. Scoop out center with a melon cutter. Place cut side up in shallow casserole. Fill hollows with a blend of lime juice, honey, and rum. Broil in preheated oven about 15 minutes, basting occasionally. Serve hot with topping of chilled sour cream and slivered almonds.

FRESH PEARS IN CURAÇAO

Peel ripe pears and slice them thin into serving bowl. Sprinkle with sugar or honey, freshly squeezed orange juice, juice of ½ lemon, and ½ cup Curaçao. Serve very cold.

APRICOTS FLAMBE

In a chafing dish heat apricots from a No. 2½ can. The apricots, approximately 18 halves, should first be drained of their juice and pricked with a fork. Pricking the fruit insures that the sauce penetrates and flavors each piece. Sprinkle the hot, pricked apricots with ½ tablespoon powdered sugar and add 3 tablespoons orange juice,

½ teaspoon apricot brandy, and a tablespoon Cointreau. Heat again.

Heat separately ¼ cup mellow, high-quality brandy. Pour it over the hot fruit. Ignite and spoon the flaming sauce over the fruit. Serve over a quart of vanilla ice cream.

CHEESE AND STRAWBERRIES

Use half cream cheese and half cottage cheese and put through a sieve. Moisten with heavy cream, beating until well mixed. The cheese should be firm enough to pack. Wet squares of cheesecloth in ice-cold water and place in heart-shaped wicker basket or other mold. Pack the cheese mixture in; set to chill for two hours or longer. To unmold, set on platter, remove basket, strip off cheesecloth. Serve with red and white Bar le Duc (currant preserves) or fresh strawberries, sugar, and cream, or wild strawberry preserves.

FRUIT COMPOTE

1 can black cherries with juice
1 box dried apricots
1 can peaches, drained
Juice and grated rind of
  1 orange
Juice and grated rind of 1 lemon
½ cup brown sugar (taste later
  and if not sweet enough, add
  ¼ cup more)

Place all above ingredients in large baking dish and bake in a moderate oven for 1½-2 hours. Cook way down until caramelized. Serve cold, or better, reheated, with sour cream or unsweetened fresh cream.

BROILED GRAPEFRUIT

Cut and core grapefruit. Sprinkle generously with brown sugar, fill center with sherry, and broil until top is slightly browned.

And here's a good one to make in your electric blender:

RASPBERRY MOUSSE

Put 3 packages frozen raspberries in the blender. Then put 1 pkg. unflavored gelatine into the raspberry purée, warming it slightly so that the gelatine permeates. Add 3 beaten egg whites, ½ pint

whipped cream, a little sugar and a little lemon juice to taste. Pour
into a mold and store in the icebox until jelled.

And finally, if you're yearning for an old favorite which never
disappoints:

BAKED APPLES

Ingredients: Cooking apples (1 to a serving); Calvados (or apple
cider), 1 tablespoon per apple as well as 1 tablespoon white sugar, 1
teaspoon butter, grating of nutmeg, lemon rind, squeeze of lemon,
sprinkling of cinnamon.

Wash and core apples, dry, and rub skin lightly with butter.
Place in buttered baking dish and fill each cavity with butter, sugar,
seasonings, and liqueur. Place in 350° F. oven and cover for first
half hour. Finish baking uncovered and, if necessary, baste with
a mixture of hot water and lemon juice with a little of the liqueur
added. An hour's cooking time should suffice, but apples vary and
they may be considered done when easily pierced with a fork and
nicely glazed. Serve with thick cream.

whirligigs

GIVE YOUR BLENDER
A WHIRL

Your blender is really one of the great ways to give your menus a new twist. This whiz kid in your kitchen is ready to do a lot of small miracles for you that Aunt Jemima's elbow couldn't take.

The two makes you can rely on without any doubt are the Waring Blendor and the Osterizer. There are others, and undoubtedly good ones. But there's a motor in this thing, steel blades, and a lot of minute adjustments: you know the score in lawnmowers, outboards, and automobiles, and this is much the same. These two won't leave you stranded, and they'll serve you over an extended life. They've been around for a long time.

First, take some advice from a cold-timer:

1. Don't toss ice cubes fresh from the refrigerator into your blender. It is not a cement mixer: it is a precision-built, beautifully

tooled machine. Crack your ice first either in an ice crusher (cast your eye on those new electric crushers, by the way) or by the old hammer-and-turkish-towel routine. This advice goes for other ingredients. A whole carrot or orange or potato might please a horse, an ostrich, or an Irishman, but your blender would rather you'd dice it first into pieces no bigger than—well, no bigger than dice.

2. It isn't sensible to whip cream in your blender unless it's part of a recipe. It *will* whip cream, but those joules and volts are too sadistic to be satisfied with just whipping. The poor old cream turns into butter before you know it, and you have to reach for the toaster instead of the brandy. A terrible fate.

Egg whites, too, are a notorious flop if you expect to whip them into stiff peaks in a blender. Egg whites, like Tyrolean peasants, need lots of *air* to stand up in those lovely white peaks and so require the services of a beater—mechanical or man-muscled.

3. If you would become a master blender, you must first perfect your timing. Each make of blender varies as to the shape of the ingredient container and the power of the motor, so you will have to run your own second tests to meet the temperament of your machine. A few seconds can make the difference between a chopped or a completely blended result—so time your recipe to the consistency you prefer. Five seconds to three minutes is the blending time on any recipe, so here's a chance to use your stop watch for something besides clocking the dogs.

4. In the interests of self-preservation and unless you are immune to dry-cleaning bills, you should never have your blender more than three-quarters full, and it's a good idea to hold the blender top on when you start the motor. You must allow for recipes foaming or fluffing up in volume.

The point to remember is that here is a whole new dimension in cooking. You'll want to experiment with your blender in contrast to some of the more traditional methods and make up your mind which you prefer. You can really do some terrific things with this little round-towner.

Let's warm up first with a

FROZEN DAIQUIRI

4 ounces Bacardi rum
2 level teaspoons granulated
   sugar
2 teaspoons grapefruit juice

2 teaspoons maraschino (a cordial made from wild cherries
   grown in Dalmatia)
Juice of 1 medium lime
3 cups finely cracked ice

It is extremely important not to alter this order of ingredients. Chill your cocktail glasses by pouring in cracked ice and a little water. Now you're ready to freeze-spin your Daiquiri. Hold onto the top of the blender and turn to high speed. Blend ingredients for about 20 seconds, watching carefully the while. This Daiquiri for 2 when perfect should be the consistency of lightly frozen sherbet.

And now we can get along to so many things that there's no sense in stinting on the number:

CLAMATO COCKTAIL

2 old-fashioned glasses clam
   juice (bottled or fresh)
1 old-fashioned glass tomato
   catsup
Juice of 1 medium lemon

2 dashes Lea & Perrins Worcestershire
Couple of shakes of salt
1 cup cracked ice

Start with all ingredients well chilled. Blend this mixture thoroughly at low speed about 1 minute.   4 SERVINGS

CHILLED AVOCADO SOUP

1 large ripe avocado, peeled and
   diced
2 cups rich chicken broth (1
   medium can equals 2 cups)

3 teaspoons lemon juice
⅛ teaspoon garlic salt
½ teaspoon table salt
½ teaspoon ground nutmeg

Blend at high speed for about 1 minute. Chill thoroughly. Just before serving, float one tablespoon heavy cream on top and sprinkle with nutmeg.

CHILLED FRESH TOMATO SOUP

4 medium-size tomatoes (sliced in 6 sections)
1½ cups chicken broth
1 teaspoon lemon juice
2 leaves fresh basil (or ¼ teaspoon dried basil)
1 small rosette fresh parsley (or ¼ teaspoon dried parsley)

2 small tender celery leaves (or ¼ teaspoon dried celery flakes)
1 level teaspoon sugar
½ teaspoon garlic salt
1 level teaspoon salt
¼ teaspoon freshly ground pepper

Blend all ingredients for about 2 minutes, then strain to remove tomato seeds. Chill thoroughly and top with a thin slice of lemon and finely chopped parsley.

FRUIT SOUP
(Based on the famous Swedish Fruktsoppa)

1 raw apple, peeled and diced
10 cooked, pitted prunes
6 pitted whole apricots (you can buy these in cans)
½ cup prune juice

½ cup apricot juice
Juice of ¼ lemon
Peel of ¼ lemon (just the yellow part, thinly sliced)
1 cup finely cracked ice

Blend this soup for about 2 minutes and serve very cold.

FRESH BLUEBERRY PANCAKES

1 cup sifted flour, less 2 tablespoons
½ teaspoon salt
½ teaspoon soda
¾ teaspoon baking powder

½ cup fresh blueberries
1 egg
1 cup buttermilk
1 tablespoon butter, melted

Sift the flour, salt, soda, and baking powder into a bowl. Add the blueberries. Put remaining ingredients into the glass container. Cover and run until thoroughly blended.

Add the processed ingredients to the flour. Mix just enough to dampen the dry ingredients (leave lumpy). Drop by tablespoonfuls onto a lightly greased griddle, and bake until brown. Turn only once. Serve at once with butter.   6-8 PANCAKES

GERMAN PANCAKES

3 eggs, separated
1 tablespoon sugar
½ teaspoon salt

½ cup sifted all-purpose flour
1 cup milk
1 tablespoon soft shortening

Beat egg whites with a rotary beater until stiff. Put the egg yolks, sugar, salt, flour, milk, and shortening in the glass container. Cover and mix at high speed until perfectly smooth. Gradually fold the processed mixture into the egg whites. Bake 1 pancake at a time. Pour about 1½ cups batter into a hot, lightly greased 10-inch skillet. Bake over moderate heat until brown. Turn and brown other side. Sprinkle with confectioner's sugar. Roll, cut into pieces. Serve warm.   2 LARGE PANCAKES

SOUR MILK GRIDDLE CAKES

1 egg	¼ teaspoon salt
1 tablespoon sugar	½ teaspoon baking powder
1 cup sour milk or buttermilk	½ teaspoon soda
1 cup flour	1 tablespoon melted shortening
¼ cup cornmeal	or salad oil

Put the egg, sugar, and milk in the glass container. Cover and mix at low speed until well blended. Add remaining ingredients and run at high speed until smooth. Bake on an ungreased griddle until nicely browned. Serve with butter and syrup.   6 CAKES

APPLE FLAPJACKS

1 cup milk	2 teaspoons melted butter
1 apple, quartered	⅛ teaspoon cinnamon
1 egg	¾ cup sifted flour
2 teaspoons sugar	1 teaspoon baking powder

Put the milk, apple, egg, sugar, butter, and cinnamon in the glass container. Cover and run at low speed until the apple is grated. Add the flour and baking powder. Mix at high speed until blended. Pour from the corner of the container onto a hot, well-greased griddle. Bake until brown on both sides. Serve hot with pork sausage.   8-10 CAKES

DEVILED EGGS

6 hard-cooked eggs	¼ teaspoon dry mustard
2 teaspoons sugar	4 teaspoons vinegar
¼ teaspoon salt	1 tablespoon butter

Cut eggs in half. Remove yolks. Put yolks in the glass container with seasonings. Cover, and start at low speed. Stop and, with a rubber spatula, push the ingredients down into the processing well.

Cover, and run at high speed until smooth. Put the blended mixture into the egg whites. Sprinkle with paprika.   6 SERVINGS

EGGS VIENNA

2 four-ounce cans Vienna-style
  sausages
6 eggs
6 tablespoons milk
1 tablespoon soy sauce
1/4 teaspoon salt

1/8 teaspoon pepper
1/4-inch slice onion
3 tablespoons butter
1 No. 2 can bean sprouts,
  drained

Drain contents of 1 can of the sausages. Cut into thin strips. Put the contents of the second can into a saucepan and heat. Put the eggs, milk, soy sauce, salt, pepper, and onion into the glass container. Cover, and run at low speed until the onion is liquefied and thoroughly blended.

Melt the butter in a skillet. Pour in the egg mixture, cut-up sausages, and bean sprouts. Cook slowly. Lift the mixture from the sides and bottom of the skillet as it thickens, letting the uncooked egg mixture go to the bottom. Cook until creamy and moist. Serve on a hot platter, garnished with hot whole sausages.   6 SERVINGS

OMELETS

To make the omelets below, place all ingredients except the eggs in glass container of the blender. Cover container and turn on blender. Run until ingredients are coarsely chopped, about 3-10 seconds. Turn off blender. Add eggs and blend just until mixed, about 1 second. Pour into 9-inch frying pan in which 3 tablespoons butter have been melted. Cook over moderate heat, lifting edges gently with a spatula to let uncooked portion run underneath. Fold and serve at once.   MAKES 3 OR 4 SERVINGS

Cheese:
1/3 cup water
1 cup diced process American
  cheese

5 eggs

Chicken:
1/3 cup milk
1/4 teaspoon celery salt

1 cup coarsely diced cooked
  chicken
5 eggs

Ham:

⅓ cup water   5 eggs
1 cup coarsely diced cooked
    ham (or use same amount
    diced mushrooms, or shrimp)

STUFFED TROUT

3- to 4-lb. whole trout, cleaned   1 teaspoon poultry seasoning
    and boned   Dash white pepper
1 teaspoon salt   ¼ cup melted butter
½ large lemon   1 cup cut-up celery
White bread slices   1 medium onion, cut up
3-oz. can mushrooms, drained

Rub the inside of the trout with salt. Sprinkle with juice from ½ lemon. Break 1 slice bread into the glass container. Cover and run at high speed until finely crumbed. Empty into a measuring cup. Repeat the process until 2 cups crumbs are obtained. Put into a mixing bowl. Add mushrooms, seasonings, and butter. Put the celery and onion into the glass container. Cover and chop coarsely at low speed. Use a rubber spatula to move the ingredients from the sides of the container down to the processing blades.

Add the celery and onions to the mixture in the bowl. Mix well. Fill the trout. Fasten together with toothpicks, or sew with string. Lay on aluminum foil in a baking dish. Bake at 425° F. for 30 minutes, covered. Uncover, and bake 15 minutes more. Baste with melted butter if desired.   6 SERVINGS

BLENDER HOLLANDAISE SAUCE

Heat ½ cup butter to bubbling. Into electric blender put 2 egg yolks, 2 tablespoons lemon juice, ¼ teaspoon salt and a pinch of cayenne. Flick motor quickly on and off twice at high speed. Turn motor on high; add butter gradually.   4 SERVINGS

Delicious over broccoli and asparagus, and the great topper for Eggs Benedict.

TARTAR SAUCE

1 cup mayonnaise

4 or 5 sprigs watercress

2 sprigs parsley

4 ripe olives, pitted

½ medium-sized dill pickle, cubed

1 hard-cooked egg, quartered

Put the mayonnaise into the container. Add the watercress and parsley. Cover and run until the greens are finely chopped. Stop the blender, scrape the ingredients from sides of container with a rubber spatula. Add olives, pickle, and hard-cooked egg. Process until well chopped and blended. Serve with fish or seafood.　　1¼ CUPS

BEARNAISE SAUCE

2 egg yolks

1 tablespoon tarragon vinegar

½ teaspoon salt

2 tablespoons cream

Dash cayenne pepper

½ cup butter, melted

2 tablespoons fresh tarragon leaves or 2 teaspoons dried

½ bud garlic

Place all ingredients in glass container. Blend thoroughly—about 1 minute. Place in top of double boiler and cook over hot, not boiling water, beating constantly with a wire whisk, until sauce achieves the thickness you like.

BARBECUE SAUCE I

1 cup diced onions

¼ cup melted butter

1 teaspoon dry mustard

1 tablespoon Worcestershire sauce

¼ cup lemon juice

Small piece of outer peel of lemon

½ cup chili sauce or 1 chili pepper

¼ cup brown sugar

1 teaspoon salt

6 peppercorns

Tabasco sauce if desired "hotter"

Put all ingredients into glass container. Blend thoroughly. Place in saucepan and heat until bubbly. Serve with meat or chicken or use to baste during roasting.

BARBECUE SAUCE II

¼ cup lemon juice   ½ teaspoon salt
¼ cup salad oil   ¼ teaspoon ginger
½ teaspoon Kitchen Bouquet   ¾ cup drained cooked apricots

Place all ingredients in glass container. Cover and run until contents are thoroughly blended (about 30 seconds). Use over spareribs, roast pork, duckling or chicken. Makes 1½ cups sauce.

BLENDER WELSH RABBIT

4 slices white bread   ½ teaspoon Worcestershire
1 cup hot milk   sauce
1 cup Cheddar cheese, cubed   1 tablespoon butter
½ teaspoon dry mustard   ¼ teaspoon salt
                                           Dash of pepper

Break one slice bread into the glass container. Cover and run until crumbed. Add milk, cheese, mustard, Worcestershire, butter, and seasonings. Cover and mix for 2 or 3 seconds. Process until smooth. Break the remaining bread into pieces. Add one or two pieces at a time through feeder cap opening. Add enough of the bread to gain the consistency you prefer. Serve on crisp toast. Keep hot over boiling water if necessary.   4 SERVINGS

BAKED BEANS

1-lb. can baked beans in tomato   1 tablespoon chili sauce or
   sauce   catsup
¼ cup sour cream   ¼ cup cubed Cheddar cheese
¼-inch slice onion

Put the beans in a greased casserole. Put the remaining ingredients in the container. Cover and start at low speed. Turn to high speed and blend until smooth. Add to beans in casserole. Bake at 350° F. for 25 minutes.   6 SERVINGS

BLENDER BORSHT, BORSCH, BORSCHT

(I never did arrive at one spelling—there are so many authoritative voices on the subject—but you'll find this recipe filled with taste surprises.)

To start off with, I have borrowed an idea from the Chinese, whose marvelous cookery often includes rice flour for those very smooth sauces and soups. For this Blender Borscht, we use Minute Rice to get our thickness and smoothness. This will give you 4 generous cups.

1½ tablespoons Minute Rice

2 cups beef broth (2 teaspoons Bovril, a strong beef extract made in England, plus 2 cups boiling water, or pour water over beef bouillon cubes)

½ cup chopped, cooked red cabbage (canned, or fresh cabbage boiled for 5 minutes)

1 medium onion, cooked

1 cup cooked diced beets

2 chopped garlic-flavored frankfurters (Kosher franks are good)

½ teaspoon salt

½ teaspoon lemon juice

Cover rice with boiling water in blender and allow to stand for 10 minutes. Blend with other ingredients about 2 minutes until perfectly smooth. Chill thoroughly and top with a generous blob of processed sour cream.

CHEESE SOUP

2½ cups raw celery cut in 1-inch pieces

2 cups water

¼ cup butter

2 tablespoons flour

1½ teaspoons salt

½ cup light cream

2 cups American cheese, cubed (about ½ pound)

Put 1 cup water in container, add the celery, cover, and process at high speed until celery is completely liquefied. Pour into a saucepan. Put other cup water and the remaining ingredients into the glass container. Cover and run until smooth. Add to celery mixture and cook over low heat until smooth. Add more water if a thinner soup is desired.   8 SERVINGS

SPAGHETTI SAUCE

½ cup sliced onions	1 can tomato paste
1 small clove garlic	1 teaspoon salt
¼ cup olive oil	⅛ teaspoon pepper
1 lb. ground beef	½ lb. mushrooms
1 No. 2½ can tomatoes	

Put the onions and garlic in the container. Cover and run until coarsely chopped. Sauté in 2 tablespoons of the olive oil until slightly brown. Add the meat and cook 10 minutes. Put the cooked mixture in the container. Add tomatoes, tomato paste, and seasonings. Cover and blend until smooth. Stop once or twice and push the ingredients down to the processing blades with a rubber spatula. Pour the mixture into a covered saucepan and simmer for 2 hours. Sauté the mushrooms in remaining olive oil until lightly browned. Add to the cooked mixture and heat for 10-15 minutes before serving. Serve on freshly cooked spaghetti.   6 SERVINGS

AVOCADO DRESSING

½ cup orange juice	2 teaspoons mayonnaise
½ lemon, peeled	1 avocado, cubed
⅓ teaspoon salt	

Put orange juice, lemon, salt, and mayonnaise in container and blend until smooth. Add avocado and run until smooth. Serve on lettuce and tomato salad.   ABOUT 1½ CUPS

THOUSAND ISLAND DRESSING

1-inch square of green pepper	2 hard-cooked eggs, quartered
8 stuffed olives	1 sprig parsley
2 teaspoons cut chives	1 teaspoon Worcestershire sauce
½ clove garlic	2 tablespoons dill pickle slices
1 cup mayonnaise	¼ cup chili sauce

Put the green pepper, olives, chives, garlic, and mayonnaise in the container. Cover, and run until the olives are chopped and the ingredients are well blended. Use a rubber spatula to push the ingredients down to the processing blades whenever necessary. Add remaining ingredients and process until coarsely chopped. Chill before serving on lettuce wedges or vegetable combinations.

ABOUT 1½ CUPS

CLAM DIP

1 small can minced clams	¼ teaspoon salt
1 tablespoon clam juice	¼ teaspoon Worcestershire
1 carton cream-style cottage	sauce
cheese	6 drops Tabasco sauce
¼-inch slice onion	

Drain clams. Put 1 tablespoon of the clam juice in the glass container. Add the remaining ingredients. Cover, and at high speed mix until smooth. When necessary, push the ingredients down to the blades with a rubber spatula. Chill for several hours before serving with crackers or potato chips.   1½ CUPS

JIFFY PATE DE FOIE GRAS

¼ lb. liver sausage, cubed	1 thin slice lemon, peeled
1 tablespoon mayonnaise	¼ teaspoon salt

Put ingredients into the glass container. Cover, and run until smooth. It may be necessary to stop the appliance once or twice during the processing to push the ingredients down from sides of container with a rubber spatula. Serve on toast, crackers, or thin slices of party rye bread. Decorate with hard-cooked egg yolks.

ABOUT 1 CUP

SHRIMP DUNKING SAUCE

½ cup catsup	½ cup chili sauce
2 tablespoons pickle relish	2-4 drops Tabasco sauce
¾ teaspoon Worcestershire	½ thin-sliced lemon and rind
sauce	

Put all ingredients in container. Cover and mix until well blended and smooth.   ABOUT 1 CUP

REALLY COLD EGGNOG

2 eggs	½ teaspoon vanilla
2 tablespoons sugar or honey	Dash of salt
2 cups chilled milk	2 small ice cubes

Break the eggs into the glass container, add the sugar. Cover, and blend until lemon-colored and creamy. Add milk, vanilla, salt and ice cubes. Cover and run for 2 minutes until the ice is completely liquefied. Pour into glasses and top with nutmeg.   2 SERVINGS

APRICOT CREAM

½ pint whipping cream	½ cup liquid from apricots
1 No. 2½ can apricot halves, drained	½ cup powdered sugar

Whip the cream in the container at low speed. Empty into a bowl. Put the apricots, liquid, and sugar into the container and blend at low speed until smooth. Fold apricot mixture into whipped cream. Pour into a freezing tray and freeze until solid.

BRANDIED-PEACH MOUSSE

½ pint whipping cream	2 cups canned peaches, drained
½ cup syrup from peaches	⅓-½ cup peach brandy
⅓ cup sugar	⅛ teaspoon almond extract

Whip the cream in the blender at low speed. Empty into a bowl. Put fruit syrup, sugar, cut-up fruit, brandy and extract into the glass container. Cover and process at high speed until smooth. Carefully fold this mixture into the whipped cream. Freeze.   3 CUPS

And finally:

A marvelous and immediate dessert can be made in all kinds of flavor combinations starting with a base of vanilla ice cream. You must watch the blending very closely. When properly served, it will be the consistency of Zabaglione. Many a man has approved the flavors and has considered the consistency less cloying than ordinary ice cream.

BLENDER CREAMS

Start with a pint of firm vanilla ice cream in a cool blender glass. After your flavors have been added, blend at high speed about 10 seconds. It's a good idea to stop the blender after 6 seconds, give the cream a stir and check the consistency. Remember, cooked custard or Zabaglione thickness is perfect. Following are some delicious flavor mates:

1 ounce brandy and a sprinkle of cinnamon on top before serving.

1 ounce kirsch, ½ cup frozen or fresh strawberries.

1 small banana, ¼ cup chopped pecans.

1½ teaspoons instant coffee, ¼ cup chopped almonds.

1 ounce apricot brandy, ½ cup fresh or frozen peaches.

1 ounce Cointreau, 1 small seedless orange (diced), 2 tablespoons shredded coconut.

1 ounce Benedictine, 2 tablespoons grated bitter chocolate.

1 ounce maraschino, ½ cup pitted black cherries.

After a few bouts with the mighty blender, you will find it takes on the same fascination as the slot machine; you'll be anxious to push the lever and see what comes out. You might hit a jackpot of your own.   4 SERVINGS

SQUEEZE PLAY:

sandwiches

11

CHAPTER

What makes a good sandwich? The question is virtually unanswerable.

The packers of every type of food—and many with justification—allege that their product is fantastically delicious when placed between slices of bread. When I was a boy at my mother's knee and table, I was well aware that the string beans I did not eat at dinner would appear in another incarnation, fried and cold, in my lunch box as the main ingredient of a sandwich. Whether or not my mother was clever or economical or both (I suspect the latter) it made a great hot string-bean eater out of me. I never left a bean untouched at dinner.

A number of people in the West believe that mayonnaise, peanut butter, and catsup mix wondrously and they inevitably spread at least two and often all three thickly on any sandwich, whatever its other ingredients.

These gaucheries are balanced by the wonderful delicatessen restaurants in New York which are world famed for their tasty and imaginative sandwiches. The beloved Stage, for instance, suggests the following combinations, usually on fresh rye or large roll:

Three-decker sandwich with corned beef, tongue and Swiss
cheese, Russian dressing, cole slaw

Three-decker sandwich with sliced turkey, tongue, corned
beef, Russian dressing

Three-decker sandwich with chopped liver, corned beef,
tomatoes, Bermuda onion

Three-decker sandwich with tongue, hot pastrami and
chicken salami, Russian dressing

Three-decker sandwich with genuine lake sturgeon, Nova
Scotia salmon, lettuce, tomato, Bermuda onion

Reuben's, of course, is another renowned Manhattan spot where
sandwich making is an art. You can tell something about a celebrity's status by his appearance on a Reuben's menu, where sandwiches are named for people. My own favorites—gastronomically,
if not artistically—on that famous list, are:

Hildegarde: Tongue, Swiss cheese, tomato, Russian dressing, rye bread

Walter Winchell: Sturgeon, Swiss cheese, sliced dill pickle

Frank Sinatra: Cream cheese, Bar le Duc, tongue, sweet
pickle, whole-wheat bread

Luba Malina: Imported Beluga caviar and cream cheese,
rye or white toast

Judy Garland: Nova Scotia salmon and Swiss cheese

Mark Goodson-Bill Todman: Turkey, tongue, cranberry
sauce, broiled French toast, maple syrup

Dean Martin: Turkey, Holland ham, rye bread

Ed Sullivan: Chopped chicken liver, turkey, cole slaw, rye
toast

Betty Hutton: Chicken liver and corned beef, rye bread

Ginger Rogers Special: Nova Scotia salmon, cream cheese,
French-fried onions

Lillian Roth Special: Corned beef, melted Swiss cheese,
bacon

These are all great combinations. And, of course, any combination
is great if you like it. I enjoy, for instance, ham and cream cheese
on rye—an order which leaves waiters speechless, and sometimes

so rebellious at this gaffe in the tradition of American or Swiss cheese that they virtually refuse to put through the order, or at least do so with great reluctance and head-shaking. It sounds awful. But it's good: try it.

I also have found that using sweet whipped butter on toasted rye, whole wheat, raisin, or other nonwhite breads brings out their intrinsic flavoring much better and supplies a fresh taste of its own, marvelous in sandwiches.

In other words, you can do almost anything with a sandwich, but it's a good idea to play around until you've found out what you really like. There's lots of room for experiment.

With the whole kitchen to draw upon, and the mathematics of multiplication suggesting infinite possibilities in the idea of a sandwich, I'm going to settle here for certain specific recommendations that you might reach only after some years of experimentation. These will be in general just a step past looking into the icebox, or at the shelf of tinned goods, and placing what catches your eye between slabs. May a few of these turn out to be your favorite squeeze plays:

BY-THE-YARD SANDWICH

This one is for the gang.

Buy the longest loaf of French bread you can find. Slice the whole thing horizontally in thick slices. Don't slice all the way through, however; stop about ½ inch short of the bottom so the loaf will hold together.

Spread between each slice some good butter mixed with a little mustard and a bit of minced garlic clove or garlic powder (you want just a hint, not an eclipse of garlic).

Layer between each slice of bread a thin round of sweet onion and a slice of good cheese.

Put the loaf on a baking sheet and into a moderate oven for about fifteen minutes. The result should be like this: Hot bread, melted cheese, crisped onion, and crisp crust—ready for breaking according to appetite.

Here is another long sandwich utilizing French bread. This one is an open sandwich better known as:

WORKINGMAN'S SANDWICH

Slice lengthwise through the middle of a long loaf of French bread. Lay the two lengths on a bread board, white side up. It's a good idea to cut a thin slice off the crust side so that they will lie flat.

Spread the lengths with butter and overlay sections of any of the following: cold sliced turkey or chicken, salami, ham, cheese, cold roast beef, pastrami, tongue, veal, pork, or liverwurst. Not more than 3 different things on a single length of bread. A crock of mustard and one of Russian dressing, as well as a selection of pickles, complete this picture, plus a sharp knife or two so guests can carve out slices of their choice.

Here's an oversized sandwich cut on the round:

PINWHEEL SANDWICH (open-faced)

Buy a large round loaf of bread: pumpernickel, rye, or French. Stand the bread on its edge and, with a sharp knife, slice right through it so that you have 2 or 3 nice ½-inch-thick rounds. One round will serve 5 people, unless they are ravenous.

Following are three compatible food combinations:

1. Leave the crust on the bread. Spread the entire round with a generous layer of fresh cream cheese that has been worked a little until it is easy to lather on. Wash, dry, and trim short some fresh scallions. Place a circle of these right in the center of the bread, fanning out like a pinwheel. Make a second circle of smoked salmon on the outside of the scallions. The slices should be very thin and overlapping each other. On the very outside edge of the bread, press in as many capers as possible. Get out your pepper mill, and give the salmon a good sprinkle. Squeeze a little fresh lemon juice over the salmon. Cut the entire round into small, wedge-shaped pieces like a pie, but leave them in the circular form for eye appeal. (This combination is particularly good on pumpernickel bread.)

2. Leaving the crust on the bread, spread the round with softened butter, then mayonnaise. In the center of the bread, make two generous circles of shrimp. On the outside of the shrimp, make a circle of pitted black olives. Around the olives, a good thick circle of sliced hard-cooked eggs. On the outside edge of the bread, press in as much coarsely chopped watercress as possible. Cut the round of bread in small wedge-shaped pieces and leave in the form of a circle till serving time.

3. Spread the round of bread with softened butter and mayonnaise. Sprinkle over this mixture a little finely chopped fresh parsley and chives. Fill the center of the bread with sardines (the boneless and skinless type tinned in olive oil). Arrange the sardines from the center like the spokes on a wheel. Around these make a circle of very thin onion slices, overlapping each other (use the sweet Bermuda onions if you can get them). A circle of tomato slices is next (salt these a little, and sprinkle on a little fresh or dried basil). On the outside edge of the bread, press on as much finely chopped lettuce as possible. Cut into wedges, and serve in pinwheel form.

Note: The secret of success with these sandwiches is *freshness*. All of the ingredients can be prepared early, but the sandwiches should be assembled as close as possible to serving time. The bread can be sliced early and covered with a damp cloth to keep it from drying out.

HOT SANDWICHES

Franks . . . with a difference.

RED DEVIL FRANKS

1 cup finely chopped onion
2 cloves garlic, minced
¼ cup butter
½ teaspoon salt
⅛ teaspoon pepper
1½ tablespoons Worcestershire sauce

1½ tablespoons prepared mustard
1½ teaspoons sugar
½ cup chili sauce
1 lb. frankfurters

Cook onion and garlic in butter over low heat about 10 minutes or until onion is tender. Stir frequently so as not to burn. Add remaining ingredients, except frankfurters, and heat a few minutes. Split franks lengthwise, arrange split side up in shallow pan and spoon sauce over them. Heat under broiler until piping hot. Serve between thick toasted slices of French bread that have been cut at an angle. Spoon extra sauce over.

BEEFBURGERS . . . AU NATUREL

The subject of what makes for a good beefburger goes on and on ad infinitum, but the possessors of the most-educated palates will tell you there is only one secret: top-quality beef, fresh, not frozen, and ground as near as possible to the cooking time. Top quality does not necessarily mean you have to have top sirloin or filet ground up. It does mean the beef should be U.S. quality Prime or Choice. Many good butchers will tell you they grind up chuck or round for their own tables, as they prefer the more robust beef flavor. Personally, I have found I like a little of many different beef cuts ground together. Tidbits of chuck, sirloin, round, a little tenderloin tip. Butchers usually have a lot of these delectable tidbits around after a full day of carving, and are usually delighted to do a package grinding job for you.

After you have the best-quality beef, why goo it up? It is certainly not in need of bread crumbs, tomato pastes, blue cheeses or whiskey mixed in with the beef.

Broiled, grilled, or pan-fried—all are good. Try to take the meat out of the refrigerator early enough so that it reaches room temperature before cooking. This is out of consideration for those who like their meat rare, and at the same time heated through.

Burger rolls should be hot and toasted. Burgers are fine to serve (open) on toasted protein bread. You can afford to get fancy with

the sauces and accompaniments that go "over and with": Special
chili (home-made if you can get it); some special pickles like
cucumber or bread-and-butter pickles; Jewish dills; or sweet pickles
and hot relishes; Dijon or Düsseldorf mustard; Bermuda onion
rings and scallions. Well, you get the idea. And nobody, but nobody
is allergic.

HOT HAM AND CHEESE SANDWICHES (pan-fried)

Trim the crusts from very thin slices of good, fresh white bread.
The slices should be only about ⅛ inch thick. A favorite bakery, a
good sharp knife, and a light, sawing motion on the bread will
accomplish this.

Butter a slice of bread lightly. Then spread with a little mustard.
Lay on a slice of Swiss cheese, a slice of lean precooked ham, another slice of Swiss cheese, and the top piece of bread. Trim off any
bits of cheese or ham that dangle outside the bread. Tie each sandwich with a string so that it won't fall apart during the cooking.

Get out a heavy frying pan. Slowly melt a generous amount of
butter (allow about 1 tablespoon per sandwich—more, if you use
a large pan and butter is spread out). Sauté the sandwiches on both
sides till the bread is golden brown and the cheese is melted. Serve
very hot, and clip off the string first, please.

BOSTON SPECIAL

Just Boston brown bread, buttered, spread with a heap of good baked
beans and stacked in the oven till piping hot.

BROILED ENGLISH

Break English muffins carefully in half, toast the outsides under a
broiler. Spread untoasted tops with a little butter and thin over-
lapped tomato slices and onion rings, sprinkle grated Parmesan
cheese over the top and slip back under the broiler till piping hot.

BAKED SARDINE FILETS

12 two-inch strips toast	12 two-inch slices American
Mustard	cheese
1 can sardine filets	1 lemon, cut

Make toast fresh and while hot spread with mustard and lay
sardine filet on each strip and cover with cheese slice. Place in hot
oven or under broiler until cheese melts (about 5 minutes).

SMALL-SCALE SANDWICHES
(Naturals with a bowl of soup or a cocktail)

Assuming you have a grill, a fireplace, or a hibachi that lends itself to do-it-yourself cookery, the best thing to have about the house is:

STEAK TIDBITS

A bowl of them, bite-size, to be speared by your guests on long skewers and cooked to their order over hot coals. A toaster should be plugged in close by, with a toast master always at attendance with hot bread slices to be cut into 4 squares and handed out as holders for the sizzling tidbits.

CHUNK LOBSTER SANDWICHES

White bread, decrusted and sliced ½ inch thick, then each slice cut into 4 squares. On each square place a chunk of cold boiled lobster. Cover with another square and refrigerate till serving time. Add nothing else. They are delicious just like this.

The fastest technique for making tidbit sandwiches is: Use fairly thin fresh bread; decrust it. Make a regular sandwich (not too thick for these tidbits), then cut across twice to make 4 squares. Put a damp cloth over the top of the sandwiches to keep them from drying out till serving time, and if they are made very early, they will have to be refrigerated.

Here are a few good flavor combinations:

White meat of chicken on salty rye bread that has been spread with butter and mayonnaise and lightly salted. (The salty rye will probably need only 1 cutting as the slices are small.)

A spread of crushed walnut meats, finely chopped prosciutto (Italian ham), and Philadelphia cream cheese. Blend together and spread on thin white bread.

Finely chopped hard-cooked eggs and fresh chicken livers. Blend together with salt and a little mayonnaise, and spread on thin rye bread.

Watercress . . . that's all—washed, dried, and crisped. Stack between buttered slices of thin white bread.

Smoked whitefish or trout, deboned and placed between slices of thin buttered rye bread.

Fresh, chopped hard-cooked eggs blended with mayonnaise and salt. Spread on thin whole-wheat bread. Put a layer of sliced stuffed green olives over the egg mixture before putting on top layer of bread.

White-meat tuna fish, mixed with finely chopped celery, a little onion juice, salt, a squeeze of lemon, and mayonnaise. Blend and spread on thin white bread.

Swiss cheese and cooked ham—a layer of each, a spread of butter and mustard on thin rye bread.

Fresh shrimp salad—put together with chopped shrimp, ⅓ as much celery as shrimp (also finely chopped), lemon juice, salt, chopped capers, blended with mayonnaise.

FOREIGN FLAVORED SANDWICHES

Then there are sandwiches with a foreign flavor. In this instance *Smörrebröd,* those sumptuous open sandwiches which the Danes serve on a large platter as an after-dinner treat, a midday meal, or an afternoon snack. Ice-cold Akvavit and beer are drunk with the sandwiches.

Here are some of the combinations:

On pumpernickel: Butter, a layer of watercress, a slice of Swiss cheese over the cress, and the middle of the cheese is heaped up with shrimp . . . a thin strip of jellied consommé on each side.

On rye: A slice of ham, a mound of liver pâté piled in the center of the ham slice, decorated with thin slices of dill pickle on either side, thin strips of pimiento over the top . . . plus a few of the tiny white cocktail onions and a sprinkle of chopped watercress.

On rye: A mound of fresh hard-cooked egg salad, over a layer of crisp cucumber slices; topping the whole thing, a high mound of plump red caviar running like a ribbon over the center of the egg mound.

On rye: Butter and a mound of raw, freshly ground beef. (This is the Danish Steak Tartar sandwich.) In the center of the mound of beef, place a raw egg encased in half an eggshell. Encircling the beef, a little ring of chopped onions, one of capers, and one of rolled anchovies.

On pumpernickel: Butter, slices of hard-cooked eggs topped with slices of pickled herring and pimiento strips.

On rye: A layer of seasoned cottage cheese. Skinless and boneless sardines arranged pinwheel fashion over the cheese. Thin slices of crisp radish placed between the sardines, and a twisted piece of thin lemon topping the whole thing.

On rye: Danish ham, thinly sliced. Top this with a large spoonful of cold scrambled eggs. Garnish with some asparagus tips and a sprinkling of chives.

On pumpernickel: A generous slice of corned beef. Topping it, a well-seasoned mound of crisp cole slaw. Over the slaw, a sprinkling of chives and finely chopped red radishes.

GULLETS AND SKILLETS:
potables before edibles

It would not be fair to write a book about cooking and eating without even so much as a final whisper about drinking.

A long apprenticeship in studying the thoughts of men in the presence of liquor leads me to believe that you can make yourself quite a bit of money betting your male guests—all of whom consider themselves, naturally, as authorities on liquor, an assumption usually based on consumption—that they can't name a dozen cocktails within a minute. Most of them will bog down after four or five. Furthermore, not one man out of a hundred can make more than three cocktails even passably well. Therefore, this chapter, concluding a book that I hope you will cleave to in your entertaining, assures you of being that 100-to-1 shot in the eyes of your proud girl by being prepared for practically any drink one of your guests might request.

Another bit of pertinent parlor badinage that might involve your more self-confident guests is the nomenclature of the sizes of champagne bottles. It is a golden list, and filled with the diapason boom of glorious poetry:

Split	6 ounces
Pint	12 ounces
Quart	26 ounces
Magnum	2 quarts
Jeroboam	4 quarts
Rehoboam	6 quarts
Methuselah	8 quarts
Salmanazar	12 quarts
Balthazar	16 quarts
Nebuchadnezzar	20 quarts

Splits and magnums and nebuchadnezzars your guests may be able to name, but the others not quite so facilely, and after the magnum size of two quarts, the fluid contents probably not at all. It's an interesting list to memorize, and not a bad sequence for a civilized gent to know.

A word about champagnes, gentlemen?

Our domestic champagnes are delicious, they are a triumph of our vintners, they are a good buy—but they are not yet in a class with the French champagnes and possibly never will be. Nature has blessed the Gaul with soil and temperature conditions that are well-nigh unequaled elsewhere in the world. And the rest of the French triumph in "bottling stars" has been due to the art buried deep in the heart of every citizen of Champagne and in the very air he breathes.

So, do you, for those great and intimate moments, serve imported champagne because the occasion demands the best. There is no need to go into vintage charts here—an honest supplier will advise you of the good years and the best brands.

Not to say that our domestic champagnes do not offer their own delights. But it just isn't fair to compare them with the champs. By all means, if your party is large, and your purse somewhat more moderate, serve domestic champagne. If you are mixing sizable amounts of punch (and there are a few good recipes in the pages to follow) and champagne is an ingredient, once again use the domestic, since the subtleties of vintage wine would be lost in the mixture of ingredients. There's a perceptible difference in flavor between the New York State champagnes and those produced elsewhere in this country (the New York champagne has a "foxy" flavor that is quite characteristic, since the wine is made of indigenous grapes and those elsewhere from imported vines), and it would be well to discover how your own preference runs.

At any rate, imported or home produced, champagne is always worth its price. And that being fairly high by comparison, you must needs treat it gently and with respect.

Here are a few reminders in handling champagne:

Until ready to chill before serving, keep champagne bottles lying on their sides. It is important to keep the cork moist to preserve the sparkle of the wine.

Before serving, champagne should be chilled to about 45°. This can be done by placing the champagne in the refrigerator for 2 or 3 hours, or placing it in a cooler with chopped ice for 20 to 30 minutes. Avoid overchilling, as this impairs the delicate bouquet.

Champagne should always be served in a clear glass. The saucer-shaped champagne glass is the most commonly used, though there are many acceptable styles. Do not fill glass to rim, but serve about ¾ full and refill frequently so champagne always stays chilled. A quart bottle holds 26 ounces, which is equivalent to 6 glasses.

Many occasions, such as weddings, anniversaries, birthdays would be incomplete without the extra festivity of champagne. It is also the ideal wine to serve throughout a meal, as champagne is suitable with every course, and there are many people who prefer it to cocktails as an apéritif.

The actual act of pouring champagne can be an indication of your poise or ignorance as a host. Here is a procedure guaranteed to keep you from spraying your guests, popping your mother-in-law in the eye with the cork, and wasting about three dollars' worth of the precious stuff on the rug:

First cut the protective foil around the bottle neck below the cap. Remove the top of lead cap at perforation, then the wire hood—actually a single piece of wire.

Next grasp the mushroom top of the champagne cork firmly, holding thumb over the top (if you're right-handed, the left thumb will be over cork). Hold lower part of bottle in one hand.

Now turn the bottle slowly in one direction, keeping it at an angle (angle helps to prevent spurting). Twist the bottle, not the cork: that's the expert's secret. Let the internal pressure push out the cork with that welcome "pop."

One section of the husky champagne cork has a paraffined outer layer, put there so the cork can be eased out.

Keep uncorked bottle at an angle for a few seconds to prevent excess frothing. Pour a bit of wine into your glass as host, taste it, then proceed to the right around the table—ladies first, of course, then men. Finally, fill your own glass.

Reminder: To prevent dripping, turn bottle slowly to the right as you raise it from the glass. Do not fill to the brim.

How Much Champagne? One quart bottle champagne yields about 8 servings in a punch cup or glass (3 fluid ounces). Therefore: One case of twelve quart bottles will yield about 100 glasses of champagne.

Wine as a subject can be so infinitely detailed and so difficult to state definitively, except in the context of thousands of pages of disclaimers and addenda, that I am going to risk the lurking dangers of oversimplification merely by suggesting that you follow the old rule of white wine with fowl and red wine with meat. Actually, many connoisseurs dispute even this well-founded idea. But I find some truth in it: a redolent red wine may overpower the flavor of your bird, whereas the more passive white wine combines happily with it. Similarly, a good red roast may subdue your white wine almost completely, but a red fights back with its own bouquet and urgency.

In this department, I think that American vintners fare better by comparison with the imports. The French are still the masters, and Spain, Germany, Italy, and Portugal have their traditional favorites, but we are coming along handily. Generally speaking, the Eastern white wines are the most successful, and the Western reds lead in their category, but here again you'll want to make your way by personal tasting adventures. It is probably still true that a good French champagne is better than the best domestic brand; but it is equally true that the best American wines are superior to vin ordinaire. So there you are.

This being a cookbook, temptation to have an entire section devoted to wine cookery was stoutly resisted in favor of the use of wine in certain recipes as they fell in with our "occasional" scheme of arranging your course au chef. And then there is the devastating remark by my friend Paul Gallico that "The only difference between cooking with wine and not cooking with wine is that you pour some wine in."

That's true. But in the same logique, it tastes great. So why not try it—at least in small experiments as you gradually devise your own variations on the recipe theme? Wine is a blender of flavors. It accents the savoriness of the food and lends both aroma and smoothness.

You follow the same familiar rule, actually. White wines are generally used in cooking chicken or fish (wine reduces much of the odor of fish cooking), red table wines in meat dishes, sherry in soup, and dessert wines in fruit. But these rules are also made to be broken—chicken in red wine is a classic dish, for example.

Other "easy-to-do" cooking ideas are using a half cup of red wine to replace some of the water in a stew or pot roast, adding a tablespoon of sherry to each serving of cream soup as it comes off the stove, including a tablespoon or two of either red or white table wine in French dressing, and pouring port over fresh sugared strawberries.

And here's a bit of a chart to help you along in your wine experiments. Give this idea a chance, sir: we are not for overcoming the natural flavors of beast or bird or vegetable at every opportunity, as we have proved, but there are moments when that touch of the grape is just what the Medoc-tor ordered.

Alors:

FOOD	AMOUNT	
SOUPS		
Cream soups	1 tsp. per serving	Sherry or white wine
Meat and vegetable soups	1 tsp. per serving	Sherry or red wine
SAUCES		
Cream sauce and variations	1 tbsp. per cup	Sherry or white wine
Brown sauce and variations	1 tbsp. per cup	Sherry or red wine
Tomato sauce	1 tbsp. per cup	Sherry or red wine
Cheese sauce	1 tbsp. per cup	Sherry
Dessert sauces	1 tbsp. per cup	Port, Muscatel, or sweet wine

FOOD	AMOUNT	
MEATS		
Pot roast—beef	¼ cup per lb.	Red wine
Pot roast—lamb and veal	¼ cup per lb.	Red or white wine
Gravy for roasts	2 tbsps. per cup	Red wine or sherry
Stew—beef	¼ cup per lb.	Red wine
Stew—lamb and veal	¼ cup per lb.	White wine
Ham, baked whole	2 cups (for basting)	Port, Muscatel or sweet vermouth
Liver, braised	¼ cup per lb.	Rhine wine
Kidneys, braised	¼ cup per lb.	Sherry
Tongue, boiled	½ cup per lb.	Red wine
FISH		
Broiled, baked or poached	½ cup per lb.	White wine
POULTRY & GAME		
Chicken, broiled or sautéed	¼ cup per lb.	White wine
Gravy for roast or fried chicken and turkey	2 tbsps. per cup	Red or white wine
Chicken, fricassee	¼ cup per lb.	White wine
Duck, roast—wild or tame	¼ cup per lb.	Red wine
Venison, roast, pot roast, or stew	¼ cup per lb.	Red or white wine
FRUIT		
Cups and compotes	1 tbsp. per serving	Any sweet wine

I am not generally in accord with the use of beer in cooking, except for certain tried-and-tested recipes such as Welsh Rabbit, where it truly belongs. There are those who claim that the beer lends food a fine, forthright odor as it cooks: to my dainty nostrils, it is about as forthright as the shrinking room in a woolen mill where the strands are giving up their olfactory all. I prefer my malt best when it's hopping cool and foamy.

But now to our actual drink recipes. Here are, in a sense, all the mixtures you really will need to know under normal social circumstances, with a fillip or two tossed in to give a touch of joie de vivre to your touch as a barkeep. So, skoal, prosit, à votre santé, salud, kanpai, proost, and vzhwru nohama!

By far the most popular drink among men, other than the downing of whiskey in straight or straightened form, is the martini.

This calls for a bit of a digression, because with barely a side glance at the innumerable recipes purveyed for the preparation of this famous drink, no one seems to agree at all on what is precisely right.

There is a growing trend *away* from, I am glad to say, the very, very, very dry martini. I am glad because it is largely the herd of status seekers which has reduced the noble martini to its present burlesque version—the naked martini—which is just gin on the rocks and no vermouth at all.

Formerly, in a more elegant era than our own, the martini was served with more vermouth in it, and straight gin was encountered only in the dreams of charwomen and in the depictions of Cruikshank and Hogarth.

Vermouth is the great civilizer of gin.

The martini as a drink is one of the most subtle and sophisticated concoctions ever devised. Gin itself is a compound of pure grain alcohol, water, and the flavor of juniper berries, cassia bark, coriander seed, angelica root, anise seed, sweet and bitter orange peel, bitter almonds, fennel, orris root, and other inspirational herbs. This permits infinite variation on the part of the distiller. But think what dry vermouth can add to it: itself derived from a white wine base, boosted with shots of grape brandy, and then made fragrant with varying amounts of leaves of peppermint, plants of yarrow, bark of wormwood, roots of valerian and gentian, buds and fruits of poplar, cardamon, and currant, flower of camomile, lungwort, juniper berries, and other secret ingredients which every distiller shuffles around with some or all of the above until he finds his family formula. A naked martini, indeed!—you're missing half of the essences of this fragrant world.

So use vermouth.

Mix it four to one, gin and dry vermouth.

Use too much ice, until it smokes as you stir.

Flavor it with a quick twist of lemon, touching the rind to the rim of the glass with a circular motion, but never dropping it into the drink.

Old-time martini drinkers still enjoy an olive in the drink. And, if you use neither lemon nor olive, but drop a pearl onion in it, it becomes a Gibson.

You may also enjoy rinsing the glass with a few drops of Pernod, before pouring your martini, to lend a whiff of its characteristic bouquet and flavor to the drink. Blends beautifully, too.

Or you may wish to sample my own invention, the vartini, which is 2 parts gin, 2 parts vodka, and 1 part dry vermouth. This softens the flavor of the drink (not too bad an idea if you're going to hit quite a number of them, in which the taste as much as the alcohol may potentially be your undoing in case of overindulgence) and diminishes in no way its authority.

For the regular vodka martini, of course, simply substitute vodka for the gin.

Make sure your glasses are extra cold before serving. Serve martinis directly after mixing. Never serve "leavings" that have lingered in the ice, losing their strength. If any remains in your shaker, pour it off, and add it to the next batch you mix. (This applies to all cocktails mixed in a shaker.)

And now for some of the other cocktails which seem to involve people less emotionally in the process of preparation:

Old-fashioned: Shake 2 or 3 dashes of Angostura bitters, then a splash of club soda or seltzer, onto a lump of sugar. Muddle, add 2 cubes of ice, a twist of lemon peel, and a cherry, if desired. Pour in $1\frac{1}{2}$ oz. of your favorite whiskey, or Scotch (which is whisky). A few drops of Meyer's rum, floated on top, is a nice touch. If you're using Scotch, try (1) a twist of orange rind instead of lemon or (2) a splash of Curaçao, or (3) use orange bitters. Stir well and serve.

Rob Roy: Dash of Angostura bitters, 1½ oz. Scotch, ¾ oz. vermouth. Put ingredients in a mixing glass filled with cracked ice, stir until thoroughly mixed, strain and serve. The dry Rob Roy uses French vermouth. The "perfect" Rob Roy (my recommendation) uses ⅜ oz. French and ⅜ oz. Italian vermouth.

Manhattan Cocktail: 3 parts rye or bourbon whiskey, 1 part vermouth, usually French for dryness. Stir with ice cubes, strain. Serve with maraschino cherry.

Dry Manhattan: 3 parts rye or bourbon whiskey, 1 part extra-dry vermouth, 1 part sweet vermouth. Stir with ice cubes, strain. Serve with maraschino cherry.

Whiskey Sour: ½ jigger lemon or lime juice, 1 teaspoon powdered sugar, 1 jigger favorite whiskey. Shake with cracked ice and strain into sour glass.

Hot Toddy: Place the following in an old-fashioned glass: ½ lump sugar, 1 slice lemon, 3 whole cloves, 1 jigger favorite whiskey. Put spoon in glass and fill with hot water.

Sazerac Cocktail: Pour the following over ice into old-fashioned glass: ½ lump sugar, dash orange bitters, dash Angostura bitters, 2 oz. bourbon, 2 dashes absinthe or Pernod. Garnish with sprig of mint. This is a New Orleans favorite; there are many variants of it.

Tom Collins: Dissolve 1 teaspoon fine granulated sugar, with enough water to dissolve, in glass. Add juice of 1 lemon or less, according to taste, and 2 oz. gin. Add lumps of ice, stir vigorously. Fill with carbonated water, chilled; stir slightly. The addition of a spiral peel of lemon, or a little grated yellow zest of lemon adds to the appearance and the taste.

The Grasshopper: 1 part crème de menthe, 1 part crème de cacao, 1 part fresh cream. Shake with fine ice and pour out, ice and all, into a cocktail glass.

Cuba Libre: 2 oz. rum, juice of ½ lime, a good cola to fill. Stir with chipped ice.

Side Car: 3 parts cognac, ½ part lemon juice, ½ part Curaçao. Shake with plenty of ice.

Scotch Mist: Fill an old-fashioned glass with finely shaved ice.

Pour 1½ oz. Scotch over ice. Add a twist of lemon or orange peel.

Mint Julep: Place leaves from 2 sprigs mint in a mixing glass along with 1 teaspoon fine granulated sugar and 1 tablespoon bourbon. Macerate with muddler until mint flavor is released from leaves. Add 3 oz. bourbon and half-fill glass with finely cracked ice. Blend ingredients in the glass, working a bar spoon up and down in mixture until outside of glass begins to frost. Fill remainder of glass with finely shaved cracked ice. Again work bar spoon up and down in mixture, topping glass with two sprigs of fresh mint. Do not touch glass with warm hands. Place in icebox until ready to serve.

Stinger: ½ jigger brandy, ½ jigger white crème de menthe. Shake with cracked ice until shaker frosts. Strain.

Planter's Punch: Juice of 1 lime, 1 teaspoon sugar, 1 jigger Jamaica rum, 2 dashes Curaçao. Shake well with ice, strain into collins glass filled with shaved ice. Garnish with fruit, flick a few dashes Meyer's Rum on top, and serve with straws.

Irish Coffee: Into prewarmed 7-oz. goblet, put jigger Irish whiskey and 1 teaspoon sugar. Add 4 oz. hot black coffee, stir. Float chilled whipped cream on top.

Vermouth Cassis: 3 oz. dry vermouth, ½ oz. crème de cassis. Serve in 8-oz. highball glass with cubes of ice. Fill with carbonated water and stir slightly.

Tom & Jerry: Beat yolk and white of 1 egg separately. After each has been well beaten, mix them together in an 8-oz. goblet or china mug with 1 tablespoon sugar. Then add ¾ oz. Jamaica rum and ¾ oz. cognac and fill the glass with piping-hot milk or water. Stir well. Grate nutmeg on top and serve.

Orange Blossom: 1 jigger gin, 1 teaspoon sugar, juice of ¼ orange. Shake well with ice, strain into cocktail glass.

Pink Lady: Juice of ½ lemon, white of an egg, 2 dashes grenadine, 3 parts gin, 1 part applejack. Shake well with ice, strain into cocktail glass.

Bronx Cocktail: 2 parts gin, 1 part dry vermouth, 1 part sweet vermouth. Stir with ice cubes. Add ½ slice orange to chilled cocktail glass. Strain and pour.

Ward 8: Juice of 1 lemon, ½ jigger grenadine, 1 jigger whiskey, shake well with cracked ice. Strain into 8-oz. glass. Decorate with slice of orange and maraschino cherry.

Hot Buttered Rum: 1 teaspoon maple sugar (maple syrup or brown sugar may also be used), 1 butter ball about the size of a marble, 1 pinch powdered cinnamon, 2 cloves, slice of lemon, 1½ oz. Jamaica rum. Mix ingredients in mug or glass and fill with boiling water. Serve immediately. Hot cider may be substituted for hot water.

French 75: Juice of 1 lemon, 1 teaspoon sugar, 2 oz. cognac (or gin, if preferred). Shake with cubed or cracked ice and pour into an 8-oz. highball glass. Fill with iced champagne and stir slightly.

Alexander: 1 oz. cognac, ¾ oz. sweet cream, ¾ oz. crème de cacao. Shake vigorously with cracked ice and strain into a cocktail glass.

Atholl Brose: Mix 1 tablespoon of honey and 1 tablespoon fine oatmeal in 2 oz. cold water. Add 2 oz. Scotch, stir, bottle, and keep overnight.

Milk Punch: 1 teaspoon sugar, ½ pint milk, 1 jigger of either cognac, rum, or whiskey. Shake well with ice, strain into 12-oz. collins glass, sprinkle with nutmeg.

Gin Rickey: Squeeze ½ lime over ice in highball glass. Add 1 jigger gin. Fill with soda. Add squeezed lime.

A punch bowl is often a good idea if you plan to entertain a number of guests and don't want to hire a bartender for the occasion, or be one yourself. For such a plan, hearken:

Champagne Cup: ½ pineapple cut in slices, 6 slices cucumber rind, 1 box strawberries, 4 oz. Curaçao, 1 quart bottle club soda or seltzer, 1 bottle champagne. Stir slowly in punch bowl with block of ice.   SERVES 12

Glögg: Into a large casserole put 2 oz. Angostura aromatic bitters, ¾ cup granulated sugar, 1 pint claret, 1 pint sherry, ½ pint brandy. Place over fire until piping hot. Put 1 large raisin and 1 unsalted almond in an old-fashioned glass and fill glass ¾ full (a spoon in the glass before pouring in the hot liquid prevents the glass from cracking).   SERVES 15

Traditional Eggnog: Beat the yolks of a dozen eggs, then add 2 cups sugar. Add a fifth of your favorite whiskey, and about ⅓ of that amount of rum. A few ounces of brandy, besides, if you're feeling frisky. Stir thoroughly as you add a pint of whipped cream and a pint of milk. Just before serving, beat the whites of the eggs and add to the mixture. Add a generous sprinkling of nutmeg on top, when mixture is in punch bowl. Serve in punch cups with ladle. (This recipe serves 20 to 25 cups. Reduce or increase proportionately for your party's requirements.)

Wedding Punch:

3 ripe fresh peaches, unpeeled   2 bottles champagne
1 bottle Sauterne   Fresh strawberries
1 teaspoon Angostura bitters

Rub peaches well with damp cloth, then pierce deeply and thoroughly with tines of fork; place in bottom of punch bowl. Put ice block in punch bowl on peaches. Combine Sauterne and bitters; pour into punch bowl and add champagne. Garnish punch and individual servings with fresh, unhulled strawberries.

ABOUT 25 SERVINGS

Champagne Bowl:

6 quart bottles champagne   3 pkgs. frozen sliced peaches
6 oz. cognac   1 lemon cut in lengthwise slices

Defrost peaches in a small bowl, add lemon, and allow to stand from 1 to 2 hours. When ready to serve, place large lump of ice in punch bowl, remove lemon slices and pour peaches, including their juice, into bowl over ice, add chilled champagne and cognac. Serve with one slice of peach in appropriate punch or Delmonico glass. Smaller or larger quantities in same proportions.

Alternate recipe: This punch is equally good using Dole frozen fresh pineapple chunks, except add juice of one lemon to each package of pineapple, but do not use lemon slices. Garnish either recipe with a few fresh strawberries if desired.

And there's my own favorite of all, *Fish House Punch,* the favorite toasting potable in Philadelphia when Washington's officers were on the town.

Dissolve 2 lbs. sugar, plus 1 pint lemon juice, 1 quart Jamaica rum, quart of brandy, pint of peach brandy. Add another quart of sparkling water (or champagne) and stir. Put a large lump of ice in the bowl and stir gently. Let it brew for a while.

SERVES ABOUT 12

And now, what with it?

I am of the opinion that a tray of assorted cheeses, with a mountain of crackers nearby, is an adequate masculine offering as an
hors d'oeuvre. Add caviar, if desired (and well heeled). Or get
the local caterer to make you up a few trays of goodies.

If you are really bent on making a few tidbits of your own, however, here is a line-up of tasty jobs that are not too complicated
to ready.

Cheese Wine Cubes: Cut Münster or Cheddar cheese into ¾-inch
cubes. Cover with Burgundy or port wine. Let stand 24 hours or
longer in refrigerator. Drain and spear with toothpicks to serve.

Caviar: Finely chop green onions (scallions), including part of
tops, mix with caviar, cream cheese, sour cream, add seasonings to
taste. Spread on crackers.

Raw Vegetables: Place your favorite raw vegetables on platter.
Dip in mix made of cream cheese, mayonnaise, mustard, salt, and
a dash of curry powder.

Caviar Tabs: Spread caviar on buttered crackers or squares of
pumpernickel bread. Top with pearl onion or minced green onion.

Cheese Spread: Grate 1 pound Cheddar cheese. Add salt, dry
mustard, chopped parsley, and a small chopped onion. Blend in 2
tablespoons soft butter, add dash of Tabasco and Worcestershire,
1 tablespoon tomato catsup and jigger of brandy. Blend until
smooth and creamy. Form into ball and roll in parsley. Serve on
platter with crackers and pumpernickel.

Olive Gizmos: Cut large stuffed green olives in halves crosswise.
With a butter spreader or knife tip carefully put about 1 teaspoon
pimiento cheese spread on cut side of stem half of olive. Stick a
toothpick through the stem end and up through cheese. Then put
other half of olive on it, and press together slightly.

New Orleans Topping: Combine 2 cups minced cooked or
canned shrimp, 1 cup chopped cucumber, 2 teaspoons minced
onion, 1 cup mayonnaise, 1 teaspoon sherry. Mix well.

Crabmeat Topping: Combine 2 cups chopped cooked or canned
crabmeat, 1 chopped hard-cooked egg, ½ cup mayonnaise, 1 teaspoon sherry and ¼ cup minced sweet pickle. Mix well.

Hot Sardine Canapés: Mix cream cheese with half as much butter
and add a few drops onion juice. Cut bread to fit sardine—use

canapé spread for base. Pour 2 or 3 drops catsup and splash of lime juice over sardines. Place under fire in oven for a few minutes. Serve hot.

FOOD FOR LARGE GROUPS

Bowls of shelled hard-boiled eggs, salt, pepper.
Bowls of fresh nuts.
Bowls of pitted olives.
Tray of fresh smoked salmon. Place beside it: capers, a large pepper mill, whipped butter, lemon wedges, thin-sliced pumpernickel.
Slices of Smithfield ham, smoked turkey, assorted breads.
Sour cream and chives for potato chip dip.
Cream cheese and fresh herb spread. Swedish crackers.

AFTER-COCKTAIL-PARTY SOUP

Short-cut onion:

1 can Hormel's onion soup	2 cans Campbell's consommé

Serve in oversize coffee cups with a sprinkling of Parmesan cheese and French bread.

Black bean soup:

2 cans Campbell's black bean soup	1 tablespoon sherry for each cup
1 can Campbell's consommé	A little water if too thick

Serve piping hot with slice of thin lemon on top, bowls of sieved egg whites and yolks on the side (hard-boiled of course).

Baked Corned Beef: Good prepared ahead for large groups: beef can be boiled 24 hours to 2 days before, allowed to cool in its own broth, and refrigerated till ready to bake.

Boneless beef	4 stalks celery and leaves
4 carrots	10 peppercorns
1 large onion	

Cover with cold water, bring to boil, then pour off all water. Repeat. Refill pot with hot water and return to stove.

Add vegetables, simmer slowly, allowing 1 hour per pound. Cool and refrigerate.

Remove from refrigerator an hour before party, place meat in buttered casserole, fat side up. Spread with 4 tablespoons dark brown sugar, a few cassia buds, 8 tablespoons sherry. Heat in 300° F. oven 1–2 hours, depending on size of beef.

Serve with mustard, green salad, bread, and coffee.

To make mustard:

¼ lb. Colman's dry mustard	1 teaspoon salt
2 tablespoons flour	Tarragon vinegar
2 tablespoons sugar	Olive oil

Mix dry ingredients, add water to thin paste. Cook in double boiler till thickened. Remove and thin down with equal parts tarragon vinegar and olive oil. Keep refrigerated in covered jar.

ENVOI

When all is said and done, and the dishes are washed and the silver put away, and That Man in the kitchen has scored another triumph, promise yourself a reward.

Mix it before you go to bed, put it in the refrigerator in a mighty cold spot, and drink it—if possible—just before noon tomorrow morning. This is a gesture of independence against the silly tradition that liquor is bad for you at 11:30 A.M. and wonderful at 12:30. The "sun over the yardarm" theory went out with the advent of planes that can fly you from one time zone to another in a matter of hours. And furthermore, in some of the most civilized countries in the world, including and stressing the Scandinavian, a shot of schnapps or Akvavit upon rising is considered excellent for a man's innards—it clears his arteries, wakens his taste buds, arouses his gastric juices, and brings warm comfort to the heart and mind.

I am not advocating a course of regular morning drinking. But I am thinking of your morning after your dinner party, or supper, or midnight gathering, and your need for one delightful extension of those pleasant moments, drunk thoughtfully, and if possible under the shade of a tree with some music and a light breeze playing nearby.

Make it a Bloody Mary (or Red Snapper, as they call it in the

St. Regis Men's Bar) and here is one way which a train of experiment suggests is the most rewarding:

BLOODY MARY

1 jigger vodka, with a splash extra

2 jiggers tomato juice

½ jigger lemon juice (or lime juice, as some prefer)

Dash Worcestershire sauce

Sprinkle of salt and black pepper to taste

Sprinkle of celery salt

¼ teaspoon horseradish

About ¼ white of egg, for smoothness

If you propose to down this drink immediately after combining the ingredients, shake with lots of ice for somewhat longer than the usual time, or put in your blender and give it a whirl.

If, however, you are storing overnight in the refrigerator, allowing the contents to marry, mix in a regular shaker, but omit the horseradish and white of egg, which would settle out overnight. Put them in the drink on the A.M. and mix without adding ice. No dilution. Big effect.

Good morning, Sweet Prince.

INDEX